BLOODY BURIAL AT SEA

The cooler sat ominously on the deck of *The Summer Wind*. 60 or 70 miles off the coast the Loran navigator said the depth of the ocean was 198 feet. Neither Tom Capano nor his youngest brother Gerry spoke as they picked up the cooler and wrapped it in a chain and locked it. They lifted it up and over the stern.

The cooler bobbed gently in the ocean. The weight of the chain had not been enough to make it sink. Gerry shook his head while his brother looked horrified. Gerry got out the 12-gauge, stainless-steel Mossberg shotgun he kept on board for shooting big sharks. Inserting a 1-ounce deer slug in the gun, he fired at the cooler. The slug struck it on the lower left-hand side and he saw something red pour out. But the cooler did not sink.

''You're on your own, brother,'' Gerry said and walked to the bow.

Hidden from view, Tom opened the cooler, removed the young woman's body inside and tossed it overboard to a watery grave.

THE CASE THAT SHOCKED THE NATION!

ABOVE THE LAW

Brian J. Karem

P

Pinnacle Books
Kensington Publishing Corp.

http://www.pinnaclebooks.com

For Pam, Zachary, Brennan and Wyatt with love

PINNACLE BOOKS are published by

Kensington Publishing Corp.
850 Third Avenue
New York, NY 10022

Pinnacle and the P logo Reg. U.S. Pat. & TM Off.

First Printing: September, 1999
10 9 8 7 6 5 4 3 2

Printed in the United States of America

Acknowledgments

It would be impossible, as the actor said at the Oscars, to thank everyone who helped in the process of putting this book together. But some definitely deserve mention.

First of all, the regular group of reporters who covered the trial on a daily basis: George Anastasia, Marisol Bello, Todd Spangler, Dave Madden, Sharon Mittelman, and Robert Dvorchak, just to name a few. It was a pleasure, considering the nature of the story we were covering, to get to know and work with a group of reporters whose professionalism and demeanor were without peer.

The two courtroom artists, Susan Schary and William Ternay, provided valuable insight and information. When the rest of the reporters could not see Capano, they always could. Their sense of humor and Bill's cartoons were also greatly appreciated.

Kathi Carlozzi, the "door warden," was an invaluable resource—as were the people in the court reporter's office.

Thanks should also go to Judge Lee for taking the time to walk and talk with me on several occasions—even if he is a Duke fan and I'm a Kentucky fan, he's okay.

Also all of the lawyers in the case were a pleasure to deal with—all dedicated to defending or prosecuting the case, but they still could step back enough to offer valuable insight and a keen sense of humor.

Kay Capano and her remarkable daughters were a pleasure to deal with and helped immensely, as well.

Kevin Freel and the gang at O'Friel's provided friendship, insight, and a good ale on the many days during the trial when a good ale helped us all keep our sanity.

Steve Romey and his fabulous Slim Jims made my writing

task go easier, and Kurt Schmidt and his new deck helped me work off my frustrations when writing became a chore.

Finally I wish to thank the Faheys. They provided insight and information, but more importantly, I believe it was their demeanor that made everything go as smoothly as it did for all of the reporters during the trial.

A joke, even if it be a lame one, is nowhere so keenly relished or quickly applauded as in a murder trial.
—Mark Twain, *The Gilded Age,* Ch. 54 (1873, written with Charles Dudley Warner)

Chapter 1
The Summer Wind

Friday, June 28, 1996. 5:45 A.M.

It was a cool, clear morning in Wilmington, Delaware. Sandy-haired Gerard Capano finished getting ready for work and walked outside his home. On his mind were the duties he would assign to the hired workers of his landscaping business and how much work his crew could get done that day.

He was surprised when he walked out the front of his house and saw his older brother, Tom Capano, sitting in a black Jeep Grand Cherokee reading the sports page of the local newspaper. Gerry's older brother, a wealthy attorney, father of four daughters and social scion in Wilmington, rarely visited him at dawn, so Gerry immediately thought something was wrong.

Gerry approached his older brother's car from the passenger side. Tom rolled down the window and Gerry leaned inside.

"Did you do it?" Gerry asked.

The older Capano nodded in agreement.

"Can you help me?" Tom asked.

"No. I don't want to get involved."

But Tom told Gerry he had nowhere else to go, no one else to whom he could turn—and after all, it was one brother asking another brother for a favor—and hadn't Tom done plenty for Gerry his entire life? The older brother, after all, had a simple request; he wanted to borrow Gerry's twenty-five-foot fishing boat. He couldn't understand why Gerry didn't want to have anything to do with it.

"I have a great life and I don't want to ruin my life. Look, Tom, I have a beautiful home and a beautiful wife and kids. I don't want to ruin my life. I'm sorry," Gerry said.

That seemed to upset the older brother. "He wanted to take the boat out himself. I knew he couldn't," Gerry later said. The boat, *The Summer Wind*, named for a Frank Sinatra song of lost love, was among Gerry's favorite possessions. His brother, Tom, did not know how to pilot the boat, and it seemed improbable, Gerry remembered, that he could not convince his brother not to take it out to sea. His older brother had said, " 'Don't leave me flat. Don't leave me hanging. I need you, bro,' and that was it," Gerry said.

Gerry was in.

Gerry watched his brother drive away from his house before he got into his own car and drove to work. Giving one man a ride and setting up the chores of the other laborers for their day of landscape work, Gerry quickly got the essentials done before he drove over to his brother's house.

The house Tom lived in was on Grant Avenue, an enclave for the rich and powerful in Wilmington. Across the street was Congressman Mike Castle's house.

Gerry drove around the back of the house, parked, and walked in through the open garage. He saw Tom had exchanged his Jeep for his ex-wife's Chevy Suburban. The dark-blue car was backed up to the garage. Inside, Gerry saw a new, white, 162-

quart Igloo cooler with a lock and chain wrapped around it. Next to it he saw a rolled-up rug.

Tom came walking out to him, sporting a T-shirt and a pair of shorts.

"Let's get the cooler in your pickup," the elder Capano said.

Gerry balked. He insisted his brother remove the chain and lock from the cooler so it wouldn't rock, then grabbed the handles of the cooler and hoisted it into the blue Suburban. Gerry heard noises from the cooler. "It sounded like ice was inside the cooler," he later said. The older brother also wanted to take the rug, but Gerry didn't want to do that, either. The cooler might look natural on his fishing boat, but a rug? If caught, how could he explain taking a rug with him to go fishing?

Gerry got back into his pickup, drove to a nearby grocery store, and waited. His brother visited an ATM and arrived in the Suburban shortly afterward. Then at Tom's request, Gerry got in and rode with his brother to Gerry's seaside home in Stone Harbor, New Jersey. They exchanged few words during the drive. At one point Gerry looked over and noticed that his older brother seemed extremely agitated. This was not the calm, cool, rational Tom Capano that had helped Gerry during Gerry's rough-and-tumble childhood. What had happened?

"I'm scared, Tom. This isn't right," was the only thing Gerry could think to say as the Capano brothers drove to Stone Harbor.

"Don't worry," Tom Capano said soothingly. "I won't let anything happen to you. Everything will be fine."

"If somebody was threatening to hurt your kids . . . ," Tom began. Gerry nodded.

Later that morning Tom backed up into the driveway at Gerry's Stone Harbor house and they both went inside, leaving the cooler and its ghoulish contents sitting inside the Suburban. Tom made a phone call, and Gerry decided to get a couple of fishing rods and put them in the boat so it would look like the two brothers were going to go fishing. With the rods in hand, Gerry made the walk out to his boat during that crisp June morning alone. Tom appeared shortly afterward. Gerry deposited the fishing poles and together they both hoisted the cooler onto the boat. Gerry then scrambled on board with Tom, fired up the twin outboard engines, and piloted his boat a short way over to a Texaco next to the Stone Harbor bridge. The gas station had been there for years, but seemed to change its name yearly. Tom handed the woman attendant approximately $150 for the gas.

For two and a half hours, under calm morning seas and a clear sky, Gerry, the experienced sea captain, tried to put his worries out of his mind as he headed due east and out to sea. Tom rested against a post, and seemingly calm told Gerry once again that he wouldn't let his little brother get hurt. "This is crazy," was the only thing Gerry could think to say.

When they had sailed sixty or seventy miles out, Gerry turned off the engine and looked around. His Loran navigator said the depth of the ocean was 198 feet. Nearly a quarter of a mile away he could see a small boat sporting a dive flag. Meanwhile, inside *The Summer Wind*, the cooler sat ominously near the starboard stern. Neither man spoke as they eyed the cooler and then silently picked it up, rewrapped it in the chain and lock, and then lifted it up and over the stern.

If the chain, the lock, and the weight were supposed to make the Igloo coffin sink, the men were sadly mistaken. The cooler sat bobbing gently in the ocean, clean and glistening-white in the early-afternoon sun.

Gerry shook his head with trepidation while his brother looked horrified. Then Gerry had an idea. He kept a 12-gauge, stainless-steel Mossberg shotgun on board for shooting big sharks. He knew the divers about a quarter of a mile away wouldn't think anything of it. Shark hunters often end up shooting the big ones. Gerry inserted a 1-ounce deer slug in the shotgun, aimed at the cooler, and fired. The slug struck the cooler on the lower left-hand side, and Gerry saw something red like blood pour out. But the cooler still did not sink. Sickened, Gerry put the shotgun down and fired up the boat's engines again.

Slowly he idled his way over to the cooler. The two brothers wrestled with ropes and grappled with the cooler, finally reeling it in. Gerry quietly walked over, picked up the two anchors he kept on board, and unceremoniously deposited them on the deck with a loud clank next to Tom Capano.

"You're on your own, brother," Gerry said.

He then walked forward towards the bow and purposely avoided looking back at his brother, Tom, who was engaged in the ghastly activity of opening the cooler and removing its contents. He heard Tom wrestle with what Gerry thought was a body, and then heard Tom vomit and wretch.

"This ain't right. This is wrong," Gerry stammered. He was near tears, but Tom kept working with the body. Gerry still didn't look, but said he could hear everything going on. It was apparent that his brother was taking the body out of the cooler, wrapping it in chains and the anchors and tossing it overboard.

"This is wrong. This is wrong," Gerry continued to yell from the bow.

Finally, when he thought he heard the body being tossed into the sea, he questioned Tom like a little boy. "Are you done yet? Are you done?"

"Yes," Tom finally answered, and Gerry turned around in time to watch a pale foot sink into the abyss. The cooler, now empty, but with blood still staining its insides, bobbed in the calm sea. The anchors and chain and the body were now gone. Gerry watched as Tom threw the keys to the lock into the water. They both grabbed the cooler, and Gerry removed the lid with a screwdriver and tossed it into the sea. The two brothers then hoisted the cooler into the ocean, as well.

It was a long, quiet boat ride back to Stone Harbor on calm, early-summer seas—and an otherwise beautiful afternoon. "This was wrong." The words echoed inside Gerry's head. He stole a look at Tom, who appeared outwardly calm.

"Don't worry," Tom told him. "I'll take care of you. Nothing will happen to you, I promise."

Gerry wasn't so sure.

Saturday, June 29, 1996. Midmorning.

Kathy Fahey-Hosey, a beautiful, Irish blonde, was wondering why she hadn't heard from her sister, Anne Marie Fahey, for the last two days. The two had gone shopping on Wednesday, and they usually spoke every day. It wasn't like Annie to stay out of touch. She was the scheduling secretary for Delaware Governor Thomas Carper, and for professional reasons she always seemed to be within earshot. The two Fahey sisters were very loving and close. Annie doted on her nephews and nieces, and Kathy enjoyed having a close and caring friend like her sister Annie around.

It wasn't just her family who enjoyed Annie's company, either. Her wit, her charm, and her outgoing personality endeared her to all who knew her. Kevin Freel, the owner of "O'Friel's," a popular local Irish pub, said she's the kind of girl "who just walks into a place and lights it up. She slaps you on the back and laughs. She's like everybody's favorite little sister."

But Annie wasn't around that weekend, and Kathy was worried.

Saturday, June 29, 1996. 9 P.M.

Kathy received a call from Annie's boyfriend, Michael Scanlan. He also hadn't heard from Annie in about two days. Then Robert Fahey, one of Annie's older siblings, called. Annie and Michael were supposed to show up for dinner. They hadn't. All three—Kathy, Robert, and Scanlan—decided the best thing to do was to go over to Annie's duplex near Brandywine Park and see if everything was all right.

The moment she stepped inside, Kathy later said she knew something was wrong. "Things didn't look right." There was a bag of groceries scattered on the counter. A dress had been left out. The bed was unmade and the closet was open with shoe boxes pulled out and left on the floor. Otherwise the one-room duplex was immaculate. On the face of it, there didn't seem to be much amiss. But for Annie, a compulsive neat freak, it seemed oddly out of character. Kathy called the Wilmington police. When they told her it would be awhile before they could send a car by, she called Ed Freel, the governor's chief of staff. Members of the governor's security detail arrived shortly thereafter.

Robert remembered writing checks to a therapist Anne Marie had been seeing. Could there be something going on he didn't know about? Could Annie have just bugged-out to get some time alone away from the pressures of her job? He picked up the phone and called Dr. Michelle Sullivan. Robert Fahey later said that without betraying her doctor/patient privilege, Sullivan had asked a simple question: "Can you think of anyone who would want to abduct your sister?"

"She knew," Robert Fahey says. "She knew."

At nearly the same time, while Kathy waited for the police to arrive at her sister's apartment, she found Annie's wallet, which contained her credit cards and cash. Kathy thought her sister couldn't have gone far without her money and credit cards. Where could she be? Then Kathy found Annie's diary.

Inside were details about a clandestine affair Annie was having with a man she referred to as "Tomas"(Thomas in Spanish).

Tomas could have meant Tom Carper, the current governor.

That would be a horrendous bombshell, devastating to the entire state, as well as to Annie and her family, if it were true. But the last page of the diary told of an even darker secret. Tomas stood for Thomas Capano—head of one of the wealthiest, most powerful political families in the state of Delaware. Some had called the Capanos the "Kennedys" of Delaware.

Kathy shook her head as she read the diary. What happened to her sister, Anne Marie?

Chapter 2

"A place to be somebody"

The sign greeting visitors as they pull off of Interstate-95 is succinct enough: "Wilmington, a place to be somebody." It turned out to be just that for Louis Capano. A first-generation immigrant from Italy, with a tenth-grade education, Louis was a hardworking, honest carpenter's assistant when Marguerite, his future wife, met him. "He was handsome and friendly and very nice," she says. "He was the kindest man I ever met."

Born in Calabria, Italy, in 1923, Louis Capano, Sr., came with his parents to Delaware when he was just seven. In the early 1940s he met Marguerite, who was the daughter of a stone mason from Wilmington's Little Italy neighborhood. Kindness and honesty served Louis well throughout his life. He could make deals worth hundreds of thousands of dollars on a handshake. Those he conducted business with said he never went back on his word. Capano valued his reputation so much that he put it before the bottom line, a former associate said.

In the beginning he was a carpenter's apprentice. But in the late 1940s he teamed up with Emilio Capaldi, a Wilmington builder, to form Consolidated Construction Co., which did store and office renovations. By 1958 they dissolved their partnership but remained close friends. Louis Capano, Sr., then formed Louis Capano & Sons Inc.—the firm that exists today.

"He could drive a hard bargain," says Don, an old-time Wilmington resident who used to sell paint to Capano. "But he was an honest and kind man. You won't find a person in town who'll say anything against him. He was a hard worker and a good man."

His specialty was custom homes in expensive Wilmington developments, but home building is cyclical. Sometimes he had a hard time making his loan payments. "He never played games," former Bank of Delaware Chairman Jeremiah P. Shea told a local reporter. "If he were having troubles, he told you. That was a nice thing for a banker, since so many of the builders tried to hide things and hope they'd go away."

With the sweat of his brow Capano raised his business to be worth more than $1.2 million, and his assets included an apartment complex, a hotel in New Jersey, several housing developments, investment funds, and a piece of a coal mine in Pennsylvania. But he never seemed to forget his roots. When poorer families couldn't afford to pay him, he let the debts slide. When someone ran across hard times, he made it his business to help them out.

In 1970 he put it all on the line. He was forty-seven years old and looking for a way to avoid the pitfalls of the cyclical building trade. He wanted to diversify. He got it in his head to build and own Cavalier Country Club apartments. The project was designed to create a steady revenue stream. It was the largest venture for anybody in Delaware at that time, Capaldi said of the 900-unit project. It was make-or-break time for Capano. He was stretched so thin he had to take out a loan from friends to make his first loan payment to the bank. The Capanos struggled, and as Louis, Jr., later said, "scraped" for every dime, but the family, sons included, made it work. It eventually became another success in a long line of successes for Capano.

He often told friends his success began when he married Marguerite, known as "Marge" to her friends. It was cemented, those same friends add, when Capano began raising a family. Marian, the oldest, adored her father. "He was my best friend growing up," she says.

Next, in 1949, came Thomas. He was, according to his father, "the pearl" of the family. As the years came and went, Louis, Sr., counted on Tom to do the right thing. He never failed him. "I love all my children very much," an aging Louis Capano later told Don. "They all have a special place in my heart. But I see Tom doing the right thing. He helps out those that need it. He's never forgotten the family roots."

"Tom was the Golden Boy," his sister, Marian, later testified. "My mother [and father] loved their children equally, but there's one that's always easiest to love, and that was Tommy."

Two years after Tom, came the affable Louis, Jr., who always looked up to Tom. While Louis would eventually turn his father's empire into a much larger fortune and increase the value of the family name, and could walk into any room full of strangers and turn them into friends, it was Tom who Louis could not stop admiring. "He was always right there with the right advice," Louis, Jr., testified. "I remember one time I wanted to conduct a business deal, and Tommy told me not to. He said it wasn't ethical. And I listened."

A year after Louis, came Joseph, who would also follow his father into the construction business. Joey, who could be laid-back, also had a bit of a mean streak in him. Kevin Fahey remembers a time when Joey handed a kid an M80, which almost blew off the kid's fingers in school. The boy took months to heal, but Joey's mother bailed him out and he was back in school with just a slap on the wrist.

Eleven years later, Marguerite had her last child: Gerard.

Gerry, as he came to be known by almost everyone, was both gregarious and fun-loving. By the time he came along, the family was also immensely wealthy. Those who know Gerry say his father, drained by heart disease by the time Gerry grew out of adolescence and into puberty, could not keep the firm hand on Gerry he had employed on his other headstrong sons. Gerry grew up spoiled and wild.

But Marge says as the others grew up, there was discipline in the home. "We were strict, but not overly so," she later said in court.

The house was also filled with the warmth and love of a close-knit Italian family. "I remember Christmas," Marian said. "It was the best time of the year. My father would be so happy, and there would be so many cousins around. It was a time of immense joy."

Louis, Sr., the stern, but loving patriarch of the Capano clan, also apparently found immense joy in his children—not only instilling the virtues of discipline and hard work into them, but sending them to expensive and exclusive Catholic schools. Tom went to St. Edmond's Academy for elementary school and Archmere Academy high school. While at Archmere, Capano excelled in sports, serving as a tackle and captain of the football team. He was also president of the student council.

"Tom was the perfect brother," Louis, Jr., says. "He was an 'A' student and was always there when I needed him. Tom was my role model ever since I can remember. I remember when I would get in trouble with my parents, Tom would help out. He'd tell my parents to 'lighten up' on me. He was always there." The outgoing, smart, and socially inclined Tom Capano grew up with a love of Motown music and a desire to please his parents. When Joey and Louis, Jr., would fight, it was inevitably their older brother who broke them up and made peace. When his mother needed a chore done, Tom would invariably volunteer to do it. He doted on his mother, and she on him.

One of the proudest days in his life was when he went off to Boston College. His father, always admiring of those who obtained an education, practically beamed the day Tom left. The day Tom graduated law school, his father cried.

In between those two times Capano's life changed dramatically. He went to school a cocksure son of a construction magnate, a big fish in the small pond of an exclusive prep school, where he had bathed for his entire life in all the privilege money can buy.

At college he jumped into a larger pond and found he was not the cock of the walk he had been in high school. There were others with as much money; others of privilege; others who were as smart as he. But his cocksure attitude remained and he flourished in college. And it was there in 1968 that he met his future wife, Kay Ryan. A pretty, petite girl with dark, intense eyes, Kay was as attracted to Capano as he was to her. "It was my freshman year at Boston College," Kay, a Connecticut native, says. "I was sure I was going to go off to college and have great fun and date lots of boys, and then I met Tom."

Introduced by a mutual friend, Kay met Capano for the first time at a college dining hall. "He was witty and charming," she says of him. "He would strut around and he looked very handsome." Kay remembers how sure of himself he was, seemingly different from other boys his age. That attracted her to him, as did his looks—dark-skinned, dark-haired, and with soulful eyes. He listened, and actually seemed to care. "But, my father never liked him. He never liked him," she said.

Nonetheless, in 1972, despite her father's initial disapproval, Kay and Tom Capano married on June 19. Right away she got swallowed into the extended and huge Capano family. "In a way it really was like being married to the mob," she says. "It's just a very close family and very overpowering." Kay didn't seem to mind. She even adopted her new husband's father, Louis, as a surrogate for her own. "He was the sweetest, kindest man I ever met," she says. "He never had an unkind word, never raised his voice."

In the beginning, Kay says she and Capano were a very happy couple. Working as a nurse, she paid room and board as he went to law school. "The family money was always there and his father always helped us out, but we both wanted to stand on our own," she said. When he graduated and went back to Wilmington, his wealth and his father's good name enabled the pair to socialize with the cream of Wilmington society. Governors, congressmen, other legislators, and lawyers were eventually among those with whom the couple would mix.

Some of their closest friends came to be Dave Williams and his wife, Debby.

"We ran in marathons together. She helped plan a birthday party for me. We were very close," Kay says. "There was harmless flirtation going on between all of us as couples, but I never thought anything of it. It didn't seem serious." But what became serious was Capano's eye for women outside of his marriage. By the mid 1970s, after having been married a little more than four years, Tom was already looking elsewhere for sexual fulfillment.

Linda Marandola later testified that she met Capano in 1976 when she was working at a Wilmington law firm and he was with the State Attorney General's Office. At a 1977 bachelorette party for a close friend, Marandola and Capano met again. They flirted. They smiled. They engaged in heavy sexual petting and they sneaked out to a car and had sex. "I'm engaged," Linda said as she put up a cursory defense to the stray sexual encounter. But, that did not deter Capano.

With his pretty, petite wife sitting at home unaware of the sexual predator arising in her husband, Tom Capano began calling Marandola, sometimes several times a day. He couldn't stop. "I want this to continue," he told her in no uncertain terms on the phone. She did not. "I feel guilty about this," she told him. Still, the calls did not stop. Capano propositioned her. She refused. He called. She avoided him. Later conversations between Tom and a friend were taped as legal steps were considered against Capano. His friend urged him to give up on Marandola. He said he couldn't. It was that simple. Finally, in October 1978, at her own bachelorette party, Marandola met Capano again. This time she didn't say no.

Again they went out to a car and had sex.

"It was just one of those things," she later said under cross-examination by Capano attorney Eugene ("Gene") Maurer. "He always told me he had to have me . . . he just loved me." A few days later at Marandola's own wedding reception, Capano showed up with his wife, Kay. Ever the observer, Capano watched until he got a chance to dance with Marandola. Then he had a surprise for her.

"I love you," she claims he said. "I don't want you to be married."

Marandola stared wide-eyed at him.

After her honeymoon Marandola and her husband rented a unit at the Cavalier Apartments outside of Wilmington—the very same complex Tom's father, Louis, Sr., had poured his heart and soul into to secure his family's fortune. It was then the Capano pressure took a turn. If he had been obsessive and relentless before, Marandola says after her marriage, Tom Capano began to stalk her. Capano continued to call her and pursue her even when she said no. He told Marandola each of them should divorce their spouse. She asked him to stop calling. He didn't.

"He bugged me about leaving Lenny [her husband]," she testified. "He said he'd divorce Kay." Then, shortly after Thomas and Kay Capano had their first child, Christy, Capano told Linda Marandola that he wished she could have been the mother of his children—not Kay.

By then, Marandola had more than enough. She finally told Capano to never call her again. She didn't want to see him anymore. But Capano told her Wilmington was "his town" and he was determined that his will should prevail. After a weekend trip with her husband to the New Jersey shore, she got Capano's answer to her refusals: An eviction notice was stuck to the door of her apartment. It simply said Marandola and her husband hadn't lived up to the terms of their lease.

To get away, she and her husband moved to New Jersey. Still Capano's calls continued and he even threatened to tell her husband about their sexual escapades. Marandola then received strange calls from an older man, Joseph Riley, who threatened to tell her husband about Capano's tryst with her unless she paid him money. Court documents show that Riley was working with Capano to intimidate Marandola. Those same documents also show that Riley wrote that Capano asked him to have someone run over Marandola with a car or break her legs. But that didn't happen.

By January 1981, Marandola was off the hook.

Why? Perhaps, as attorneys later speculated, it was the taped messages. Perhaps some of the older Wilmington attorneys that the strange incident had been reported to talked Capano down out of his tree. But, as others speculated, perhaps it was because Capano had already found another woman he could intimidate, a woman he would eventually harass for the next seventeen years, a woman who would allow Capano to run every facet of her life until it appeared she would have no life left at all.

That woman was Kay's good friend Deborah Williams.

Debby Williams met Capano about the same time he met Marandola in 1977. Her husband Dave worked with Capano in the same law office, but the pair did not get together when they initially met. According to Capano, "She wasn't the prettiest one in our group."

A small, petite blonde who stands about five foot three inches tall, Debby Williams has the build of a swimmer. Thick-necked and muscular, she has blond hair that complements a ruddy complexion.

In the waning moments of 1980, Capano and Williams trembled with mutual desire and looked eagerly to a shared future of a clandestine affair. On that New Year's Eve as they eagerly anticipated the arrival of 1981, Debby Williams remembered, clearly, Capano pulling her into a bathroom during the New Year's Eve party and telling her that he loved her. "I was flattered, but married," she later testified. They were in the bathroom, according to Debby's testimony, for nearly fifteen minutes. "We were all really flirtatious as couples," she sighed.

Where was Kay? Newly pregnant, she stayed at home that night, she says, because her doctor told her she was threatening to miscarry the baby.

A few months later Capano asked Debby Williams to help put together a surprise birthday party for his wife, Kay, who would be 31 on April 24, 1981. What would be more natural than Debby, one of her best friends, planning her birthday party? Williams readily agreed to help out. Just prior to that party, Williams visited her husband at work. After she met with Dave she walked down the hall to Capano's office. She opened the door and let herself in. Capano, although he would later say he was initially surprised to see her, didn't appear to mind it at all. They closed the door to his office and Capano picked Debby up and put her on his desk.

"He got me on his desk and was hugging me and kissing me," she said. "I enjoyed it. It made me feel good. But I stopped it because I was afraid someone would walk in."

Although they stopped that day, there would be other days to explore their desires for one another. But it would have to fit in Capano's busy schedule. During this same time, as Capano fondled Williams, he was busy harassing Linda Marandola, prosecuters later said, while working his way up through a law firm, and juggling a marriage to his faithful, and pregnant, wife, Kay, for whom he was planning a surprise birthday party with his new love interest, Deborah Williams!

Finally, on Memorial Day 1981, at the same time he considered finding someone to run down Marandola with a car, Capano consummated his new relationship.

As she recounted later from the witness stand, Debby Williams rode her moped over to Capano's house that weekend. He was alone and cutting the grass. She pulled the moped around in back. After brief salutations they went inside and made love on the floor of his den.

By the fall of 1981 a pattern had developed. Williams would skip her night class at the University of Delaware and she would meet Capano at the Motel 6 in the shadows of the Delaware Memorial Bridge. This pattern would remain relatively unbroken until Capano went to prison November 12, 1997. "I was fully in love with him," Capano's mistress testified. "He cared for me. He listened to me. He enjoyed my company. He made me feel good about myself. I really did want to spend all my time with him. I became satisfied with less and learned to live with that because he made me feel so good." Her desire for Capano eventually led her to leave her husband in October 1983 and to take back her own name. She became known as Deborah A. MacIntyre. After she left her husband she also became known as Tom Capano's steady Wednesday-night girl. "And sometimes Thursday, too," she said in court.

Kay Capano never caught on. Or, perhaps as she herself says, she didn't want to. "I was in what I thought was a loving relationship with someone else. I wanted to be trusted and I wanted to trust Tom." After all, in many respects Capano had been there for her, and she has never discounted the role Capano played in raising her four children. "He was a very good father to the girls," she says. "I did a lot of it, but Tom did his fair share. He always made time for his girls."

Apparently, as the prosecutors said in court, he made time for others, as well.

Kay says her mother-in-law, Marguerite, tried to let her know she thought Capano was having an affair with MacIntyre. "She told me they were fooling around, but I didn't believe her," Kay later said. Someone else also thought Tom Capano and Deborah were having an affair—Capano's oldest daughter, Christy, a second-semester premed freshman at New York University. Dark-haired and pretty, as all Capano's daughters are, Christy took a 3.8 grade point average with her into college. Her friends describe her as outgoing and smart. They also say she is not easily intimidated nor easily fooled—not even by her father.

"I was about six years old and I heard the doorbell ring," she says. "I always liked to answer the door, so I ran downstairs to answer the door. But my dad got there before me and I saw him open the door and Debby was there and she jumped into his arms and just started kissing him real passionately." Christy says she later told her mother, and then confronted her father at the dinner table about the kiss, but he denied it.

That incident aside, Christy says she led a very happy childhood and received more affection than she can remember from her father. "He was a very caring father and very protective—overprotective," she says. All four of the girls would eventually come to say the same thing. Christy, born August 6, 1980; Katie, born February 1, 1982; Jenny, born November 15, 1983; and Alex, born August 12, 1985—all came to see their father as a loving, caring, and giving human being who cared about their welfare above all else.

But Christy, who had seen her father with Deborah MacIntyre, also picked up other signals that all wasn't right in the Capano home. "My mom and dad were never very affectionate to one another," she said. "They would never fight in front of us, but I could always tell my mother was very unhappy."

Meanwhile, in the professional world of Delaware, Capano was making a name for himself that would do his family proud. His father, who had often referred to him as the "pearl" of the family, was almost misty, family members say, when he referred to his son Tom. By the time his father died, many considered Thomas J. Capano as the moral center and backbone of the Capano family. When Louis, Sr., died suddenly of a heart attack, it was Tom Capano who gave the eulogy. "There are two types of people in the world—givers and takers," he told his family. "Dad was a giver." The family openly wept.

That was in February 1980. From then on, Capano assumed the mantle of family patriarch. He was best man at his brother Louie's wedding. He helped guide Gerry through a rambunctious adolescence. "He was the man. He was the man," Gerry said on the stand. Capano, who had worked as a public defender and deputy attorney general, joined the firm of Morris James, Hitchens & Williams, handling commercial real estate deals and personal injury cases. He played rugby with Mayor Daniel S. Frawley, and in 1984 left his law firm to serve as Wilmington city solicitor. He managed the city government both in fact and in title. Police, fire, and legal officials all reported directly to him.

Capano then broadened his reach, dabbling in politics and playing an integral role in getting Frawley reelected as mayor. He was a full-fledged power broker in Wilmington, and by the later 1980s in a virtual sense, he owned Wilmington. He even proved to have cross-party appeal. In 1990 then-governor Michael N. Castle, a Republican, hired Capano, a Democrat, to be his legal counsel. "He did the job very well," Castle, now the state's lone congressman, told a local reporter. Two years later, though, Capano left government to join the Wilmington office of Saul, Ewing, Remick & Saul, a prominent Philadelphia law firm. Before long, he was the managing partner in the Wilmington office.

By the early 1990s Capano's steady rise had brought him to dizzying heights. While his brothers had gotten into legal troubles, some of them highly publicized, he had not. In fact, when the brothers got into trouble, they turned to their brother Tom as they had once turned to their father and mother. When Louie got into a knock-down-drag-out fight with his brother-in-law

Lee Ramunno, Marian [Lee's wife and Louie's sister] first tried to call her brother Tom to settle things down. When Joey got into trouble for allegedly molesting a twenty-seven-year-old woman he had an affair with, it was his brother Tom who helped bargain the charges down to misdemeanors. When Gerry got into trouble with drugs, it was brother Tom he turned to for help.

Tom Capano stayed clean and enhanced and soared with his father's good reputation. He was the "good brother," the "white knight" of the family who upheld his father's strongest convictions. He was actively involved in helping troubled teens at working-class St. Anthony's Catholic church. He gave time and money to help those less fortunate than himself. At the same time his wealth enabled him to join the prestigious Wilmington Country Club.

He was the prince of Wilmington. "His athletic, angular build and neatly trimmed, gray-flecked beard gave him a distinguished air. Possessed of a keen mind and engaging manner, he was both respected and admired," said the *Wilmington News Journal*.

The dark episode with Linda Marandola was behind him. He had four daughters and, if not an affectionate relationship with his wife, at least a respectful one, which flourished. There was a mistress on the side taking care of his other emotional and sexual needs, so by 1993 Tom Capano was riding high on the crest of a wave of his father's and his own making.

Then, in 1993, he met Anne Marie Fahey. He was immediately infatuated with her.

At first it wasn't a mutual affection. But that would change.

It was the beginning of the end for both of them.

Chapter 3

"Whatever you do, take care of Annie."

If Tom Capano grew up with the best tiny Wilmington had to offer, then Anne Marie Fahey grew up a far cry from the privileged life Capano's parents afforded him.

Born the youngest of six children, Annie was just nine years old when her mother died of lung cancer. Her brothers and sisters say they had a typical suburban upbringing, but in her early childhood, Annie seemed to get the worst of everything. The family wasn't rich and Annie typically got secondhand clothing and hand-me-downs.

She was, however, a happy child, and her mother smiled favorably upon her. Outgoing and able to make everyone laugh, Annie brought a lot of joy into her ailing mother's life—even as her mother was succumbing to cancer. Mark Fahey, for one, remembers the day his mother died from lung cancer. She had walked into the bathroom, collapsed, and was taken back to bed. "Whatever you do, take care of Annie," Mark remembers his mother saying. "She's the love of my life."

Her mother's death put a load of stress on the Irish-Catholic family. Kevin, the oldest, Mark, Robert, Kathy, Brian, and Annie all had to find ways to cope with such a tragic loss. For the older Faheys it was something they could at least understand. Kevin and Mark were old enough to have lasting memories of their mother. For Annie, though, it was different. She told friends years later that her mother's loss haunted her. That, along with a strained relationship with her father and a deteriorating economic condition at home, caused Annie a lot of pain.

Her father took the loss of his wife exceptionally hard and slid into years of alcoholism. Annie detailed some of the pain this brought to her in her diary. On March 24, 1994, she writes about her father: "Today is the day my father died! How sad. My dad was a bad father, but he was the only father I ever had, so therefore I loved him. I do not think that he conscienciously (sic) meant to be a bad father . . . He really made my life very sad and lonely. I will never forget the pain he caused me. He forced me to lie to protect my identity."

Stories about Annie fighting with her father became commonplace. Sick with alcoholism, Annie's father let the bills go unpaid, and on at least one occasion Annie had to wait until she got to school in order to get a hot shower because the electricity in her home had been turned off. On more than one occasion she stayed at the home of a friend in order to get a decent night's sleep.

Through it all she kept her sense of humor, grace, and charm.

"She was everybody's best kid sister," family friend Kevin Freel later said. "You'd just hear that laugh and know, 'Hey, Annie's here.' "

Freel got to know all of the Faheys very well. The owner of "O'Friel's Irish Pub," Kevin Freel hired almost all of the Faheys at one point or another to work for him. Mark Fahey was the first bartender he ever hired at his Irish pub. "He was the best day-bartender I ever had," Freel says. "He had a great sense of humor and could talk to people, and he could work the room.''

One day Mark was working behind the bar when a nervous young man approached him.

''What's wrong?'' Mark asked the young man.

''I have a job interview and I'm real nervous about it,'' the young man confided.

Mark assured him everything would be okay and offered to buy him a beer after the job interview was over. The young man returned and Mark kept his word.

The young man also got the job—and the girl. The girl was Kathy Fahey, a waitress at O'Friel's pub, and Mark's younger sister. The young man was Patrick Hosey.

The early 1980s was a busy time for the Faheys at O'Friel's. Mark worked downstairs as a bartender, and tall, stoic Robert worked upstairs. The eldest sibling, Kevin, occasionally worked the bar, as well. Kathy was a waitress. O'Friel's became the center of the Faheys' universe, and only Annie never worked at the Irish pub, at either its original location or the more tony location on Delaware Avenue.

Annie never worked at O'Friel's because of her age. As the youngest of the Fahey children, she was too young to work in a bar. But even as a child she spent time there. ''I remember her as a child,'' family friend and former O'Friel's waitress Terri Donegan-Arson said. ''She would occasionally come in— always full of smiles. They were the greatest family. Just the greatest family.''

Everyone who knew them said the same thing. Despite the turmoil in their lives, the Faheys were close, friendly, and outgoing. Among the six siblings, though, Annie stood out with her smile and warmth.

During the last half of the 1980s that familial sense of closeness also included Annie's father. He had beaten his alcohol demons and came to spend time with his sons and daughters. A reconciliation had occurred.

Freel remembers the times when the elder Fahey would come to the bar and talk with his son Mark, just sipping coffee and talking with his son. "I remember Mr. Fahey well," Freel says. "He used to come into the pub and sit down at the bar and drink coffee all day long. He had a beaten look about him, just like the world had beat him down." By 1986 he had recovered enough to be employed and his future was looking brighter. "Toward the end he was acting as an agent for artists," Kevin Fahey said. "He would put together deals for people who tried to sell things to the Franklin Mint." The success was short-lived, however. In March 1987 Annie's father succumbed to leukemia.

Losing her mother at nine and then her father at twenty-one had an indelible and lasting impact on Annie. She became clinically depressed and at times thought about suicide. She began seeing therapists, sometimes with her brother Robert picking up the tab. But little seemed to help. Annie thought of herself as ugly and became so anal-retentive she would sometimes put mints on her pillows and became known in a half-joking way as "Anal Annie."

She was never satisfied with her looks. She thought her breasts were too big and her legs too thick. She occasionally resorted to starvation diets and tossed down laxatives to help lose weight. She stood five feet ten inches and weighed anywhere from 125 to 137 lbs. In her diary she often detailed her battles with her weight. "I am starving myself as well as avoiding situations where food is involved. I now think of food as poisonous," she wrote March 2, 1994. Subsequently she was diagnosed with anorexia nervosa and bulimia.

Annie's diary documents a great deal of frustration with her father and other family members. The pain Annie felt from her childhood remained her entire life. Getting through her pain and conquering her internal demons were long-standing themes throughout her most personal correspondence. She detailed countless sessions with therapists, a prescription of Prozac, which left her with dizzying headaches, countless attempts to lose weight, and numerous remembrances of tragedies both fresh and old in her life.

In addition to her pain, Annie also detailed her growing infatuation with a secret lover, whom at first she even chose "to leave anonymous" in her diary. On the night of her twenty-eighth birthday, January 27, 1994, she claimed she fell in love with her mystery man, a man "who makes her heart smile." Later in her diary she referred to him as "Tomas." She had become fluent in Spanish and perhaps was being coy with herself in this reference to her new love. She also admitted the pair had problems because her lover had a wife and four daughters.

By the end of March 1994 she chronicled in her diary how her new love wanted to put her up alone in her own apartment. She was wavering because of his wife and children and lamented that she would be a "silent, secret girlfriend. Oh my God." But her infatuation, indeed her growing dependence on her new lover, is apparent throughout her diary. She wrote she was enchanted by him and her thoughts devoted to him. She struggled to realize that her relationship would never "be anything other than a secret," and yet she fantasized a life with him all the time. "He is very gentle, intelligent, handsome and very interesting. Why does he have to be married?"

By the end of April 1994, though, it seems it was over as quickly as it started. "He told me I need to find a man without children who has a lot of time for me, because I am very special and deserve much more," she wrote. She confided that she had dreams about making love to him and living with him—"but it will never happen." Just two days later, as if caught on a yo-yo, Annie is back in the good graces of her lover. All morning she wondered if he would call and when he did he told her that he loved her and they could still see each other. Obviously in control of the relationship, her new lover had also brought Annie to an important realization—"I also feel that my world is so out of control, and the only thing I can control is my food intake.''

Tortured by her weight, overburdened with her past, seeking help through therapy, Annie was—as is documented in her diary—extremely vulnerable. While she saw her new lover as a way to happiness, she was also upset with the secret nature of the relationship—not even her family knew of it—and she was obviously upset with the duality of the relationship. She fantasized about a life with her lover, Tomas, and at the same time struggled with the realization that she would never have it.

By the middle of July 1994 her interest in her friend Tomas seems to have waned. But her self-doubts remained, and by the summer of 1994 Annie's self-portrait had little resemblance to the witty, friendly, outgoing woman her friends and family knew. Kevin Freel said Annie often reminded him of Elle MacPherson. Kim Horstmann, another close friend, said when she was with Annie she (Kim) felt witty, beautiful, and smart. But Annie didn't see herself that way at all. ''. . . I am so paranoid that I am not pretty, smart, fun, exciting enough . . . ,'' she wrote.

Her self-doubts and her empty searching seems to have led her to the very pit of despair, and yet at this time she took off for Ireland and an extended visit. Page after page of her diary is devoted to describing the fun she experienced in Ireland. From this visit she later contemplated a career in international relations, perhaps overseas. The entries in her diary about her experiences in Ireland show her to be at ease and enjoying herself without fear of it falling apart, perhaps for the first time in her life. While she took a good deal of her time to complain about a stinky hostel and the fact that she was traveling with someone she considered a ''tightwad,'' the feeling of euphoria spread across her diary. When she met cousins in her ancestral home of Kilmecrennan, she started out nervous, but after just a few minutes: "I felt totally at home as if I had known these people my whole life."

Unfortunately, the euphoria of these pages did not last. By February 25, 1995—the next entry in Annie's diary—she was back in Delaware, and a cloak of unhappiness once again seemed to cover her life. She wrote of the tragic news of the death of a close friend who was killed by a drunk driver and then segued back into writing about her friend/boyfriend Tomas.

She was apparently deeply and intensely involved with him again, although for some ten months there had been no mention of him in her diary. She wrote of encountering him at a bar party with his wife and sadly ignoring him because he seemed to be upset that she was there along with his wife. She felt sorry for Tomas and wrote that she never wanted to hurt him or make him feel in any way uncomfortable. Never once considering her own comfort, she again lamented how Tomas would never be hers and how she's madly in love with him.

By the end of February her love for Tomas and their secret relationship brought Annie undeniable and unprecedented pain. She prayed to Jesus and struggled to understand how she allowed herself to fall in love with a married man. Then she rationalized it because Tomas was a kind, caring, responsive love and had a beautiful heart, although he was sometimes abusive and nasty with her on the phone. He had threatened to leave her before and she wanted to know what was wrong with her. "God, please help me!" she wrote. To a friend that night, Annie confided that she was losing her lover and couldn't understand why.

In a passage of such importance—Annie probably never fully understood—she wrote that Tomas, ". . . asked me how I would like to spend my last day on earth, I told him by playing hookie from work making marinara sauce together making love while it was cooking, drinking red wine, eating bread and watching all the movies we have talked about watching together. He said he did not believe anything I just said."

She could not hide the anguish she felt as she poured her heart out to her lover, only to have him throw it back in her face.

Searching for someone she could share her feelings with, Annie finally turned to her friend Kim Horstmann, who she believed would listen to her without judging her. Annie poured out her dark secret to Horstmann.

More than a year elapsed between her diary entries. Finally, on Sunday, April 7, 1996, just a little more than ten weeks before her death, Annie wrote of an epiphany and finally gave the full name of her lover in her diary:

"I finally have brought closure to Tom Capano. What a controlling, manipulative, insecure, jealous maniac . . . It hurts me when I think about that year. For one whole year, I allowed someone to take control of every decision in my life."

Therapy, her close relationship with her older brother Robert, and a new boyfriend, Michael Scanlan, "the first normal relationship I've ever had," she wrote, had brought her to realize she'd wasted her time with Capano.

When Kathy Fahey-Hosey found Annie's diary in her bedroom on June 29, 1996, she immediately suspected that Tom Capano had done something to her little sister. Bob Donovan, the big, heavyset detective who would be the point man on the investigation for the next seventeen months, was close behind her. He said it didn't take him long to figure out that when Annie showed up missing, Tom Capano had something to do with it.

Chapter 4
A Pivotal Weekend

Fifteen minutes after midnight on Sunday, June 30, 1996, Kathy Fahey-Hosey told Wilmington Police corporal Paul McDannell that her sister Anne Marie Fahey was missing. From the beginning it was no ordinary missing-persons report. Annie, being the governor's scheduling secretary, was a high-profile member of the Wilmington community.

She was also well-known outside of Wilmington. Her engaging manner and ability to make others laugh won her many friends in the governor's office. Her attention to detail and ability to make things work won her professional admiration. She spoke often with White House officials when she set up meetings between her boss and President Clinton. "She was an absolute joy to work with. Very easygoing and very professional," one White House insider said, while those who worked with and knew Annie said during the spring of 1996 they had never seen her happier. Many of those friends attributed her happiness to her new boyfriend, Mike Scanlan.

Scanlan and Fahey had been introduced by Governor Carper.

The governor apparently took delight in playing matchmaker and had a special spot in his heart for Annie. She had begun working with him in 1991 when he was a congressman in Washington, D.C., and he made sure that when he went back to run the state of Delaware he took Annie with him. Office workers say he seemed to be protective of the dark-haired, beautiful Fahey—almost like a father.

When Annie turned up missing, the governor, her family, and Scanlan all began a vigil, hoping for the best and expecting the worst.

Robert Fahey, who called Michelle Sullivan, his younger sister's therapist, was shocked that Sullivan immediately seemed to suspect that someone had kidnapped his sister. Why? Sullivan met with Annie seventeen times from February 28, 1996, until Annie disappeared. She last saw Annie on June 25, and based on her testimony in court, Sullivan also had reason to suspect that Tom Capano was somehow involved.

At 3 A.M. on June 30, according to Detective Bob Donovan's subsequent affidavit, a friend of Annie's who'd accompanied Kathy to Annie's house found a letter written to Annie from Tom Capano. The diary, with its reference to Capano as a manipulative control freak, had also been found. Detective Donovan said within five minutes a next-door neighbor was interviewed who claimed he saw Annie leaving with Tom Capano in a black "Bronco" type of vehicle several times during the last two weeks. Annie's downstairs neighbor, Connie Blake, later told investigators someone walked into Annie's apartment about thirty minutes after Annie and Capano left Ristorante di Panorama. She testified she heard only one set of footsteps and no conversation.

That was enough for Donovan who along with three other officers decided to drive over to Tom Capano's home on Grant Avenue. Capano had been living there for several months since his split with his wife, Kay. He rented the huge brick home and gave his four daughters plenty of room to live there when they visited. Just before 3:40 A.M. the detectives arrived at Capano's home. Capano answered the door in a housecoat and spoke with Donovan and the other officers. Wilmington Police sergeant Elmer Harris was the first to speak.

"Do you have any idea why the police might want to speak with you?" he asked.

"Yes. Kim Horstmann called me earlier and told me Anne Marie has been missing since Thursday," he replied.

Capano said he did have dinner with Annie earlier in the week, but was unsure as to whether it had been on Wednesday night or Thursday. "I think it was Thursday," he said after thinking about it. Suddenly, with much greater clarity, he remembered picking her up around 6:30 P.M. that night in his black Jeep Grand Cherokee and driving her to dinner at the Ristorante di Panorama in Philadelphia. Capano went into detail about what they had for dinner and that Anne Marie was wearing a light-colored floral-pattern dress. He used a credit card to pay for the dinner and he had her sign for the check because he had trouble calculating the tip.

After dinner Capano said the two drove straight back to Wilmington, about a thirty-minute trip, and then stopped at his house on Grant Avenue just long enough to pick up a bag of groceries, which included rice, bananas, spinach, strawberries, and soup. He'd bought her an outfit at Talbots department store and that ended up in the Jeep, too.

From Capano's home he said they then drove directly to her apartment, about a three- to five-minute trip and then they went inside. He said he put the groceries on the kitchen counter and placed the spinach and strawberries in the refrigerator. He gave her the gift, which he said she opened but did not take it all the way out of the box. Capano said he also checked Annie's air conditioner and used the bathroom, but he claimed he was only at the apartment for a few minutes before leaving at 10 P.M. He said he then stopped at a nearby Getty Station to buy some cigarettes. Capano also said he knew Fahey planned to take Friday off and that he hadn't seen nor heard from her since 10 P.M. on Thursday, June 27.

"She's airheaded," he volunteered to Donovan, and "very unpredictable." According to Capano, Annie also recently had a huge fight with her sister, Kathy, because Kathy, "puts her down." Oh, yeah, and Anne Marie was unhappy at work, Capano added.

"How recently, if ever, did you all have sexual intercourse?" Officer Mark Daniels asked him.

"About six months ago," came the reply.

Capano added that he'd given her gifts of art and money and other assorted things, and she had spoken of suicide a lot in the past because of her depression, anxiety, and anorexia. In fact, he added the medicine she'd been taking made her sick and she woke up in the middle of the night unable to get back to sleep. Capano even offered that he thought Anne Marie was going to the New Jersey seashore for the weekend until Kim Horstmann had called him sometime after midnight.

"Do these circumstances seem suspicious to you?" one of the officers asked.

"I guess she went off somewhere without telling someone. She'll probably show up for work on Monday," he replied.

"Is Anne Marie in your house right now, sir?" Officer Daniels asked.

"No. I don't know where she is," Capano answered.

It took the officers approximately thirty minutes to finish questioning Capano. At the end Daniels told him, "If she doesn't show up in the morning, we'll be back."

At that point Anne Marie entered the files as a missing person. Shortly thereafter, Capano called an old friend of his, Charles Oberly III, a former Delaware attorney general and onetime senate candidate, and asked Oberly to be his attorney.

The police were openly suspicious of Capano's story, but Donovan said until they began checking out the facts they didn't have anything on which to base their suspicions. One of the easiest and first things to check out was the Getty Gas Station. Later that morning one of the officers checked it out and found that the gas station had closed at 9:30 P.M. on Thursday, June 27. No one could've bought cigarettes there at 10 P.M. as Capano claimed, and the clerk who worked that Thursday night did not remember Capano ever showing up to buy cigarettes.

"I won't say that I knew that night that she was killed and Tom Capano did it," Donovan later told *Time* magazine, "but I didn't think things were right."

Donovan kept digging. In addition to a telephone call to Deborah MacIntyre, detectives were concerned about another telephone call placed to Keith Brady, in the Delaware Attorney General's Office. Brady, a longtime friend of Capano's, was also prosecutor Ferris Wharton's boss. He later admitted he spoke with Capano on June 28, 1996, and quickly excused himself from the Capano case.

By early-Sunday afternoon Donovan decided to go back to talk to Capano. He met up with Capano on Sunday afternoon around 2:30 P.M. Police had tried to reach Capano on the phone several times and had been unsuccessful in doing so. But they had tailed him and watched him leaving his wife's house. They confronted him there and followed him back to his house, where he agreed to a search. Although the police didn't have permission to search any drawers or closets, they noted that the house was "spotless" with "nothing out of place." One officer later even described the house as charming. The same could not be said of Capano. While polite the night before, he was now visibly agitated and quite put out. Capano later told a jury he was upset because he felt the police were pressuring him and not allowing him his right to privacy.

With an unsuccessful search behind them, and a belligerent Capano in front of them, Donovan walked away from Capano—convinced more than ever that something had gone horribly wrong and Capano was somehow behind it. That instinct would lead Donovan to invest the next seventeen months of his life in the subsequent investigation. "I knew early on something was up. I knew he had money and power, but I didn't know just what we would have to do to get an arrest," he later said.

Ferris Wharton, the man initially assigned as the prosecutor on the case, also proved to be up to the task. Wharton, described as a "grizzled veteran" in the local Wilmington newspaper, is a forty-six-year-old prosecutor who spent eighteen years in the Delaware Attorney General's Office. He won convictions against several high-profile murder defendants in Delaware including Christie Shipley, who shot and dismembered her husband, and Joyce Lynch, who shot a couple on Christmas Eve 1987 in order to steal their newborn. Wharton is also known as extremely competitive. He works out at the downtown YMCA almost religiously, starred in basketball and soccer in high school, and still likes to play both. If one were to ask around the courthouse, the term most often used to describe Wharton is "tenacious." The second most frequently heard term about him is "affable." But his kindness and affability do not translate to those he's prosecuting. Initially he said there was little for him to do in the Capano case. There was even some doubt that it would ever get to trial.

Detective Bob Donovan continued his dogged pursuit of the truth and did his best to bring Capano to justice. He gained valuable insight into Capano and Fahey by talking with the one person Annie had trusted to confide in about her relationship with Capano: Kim Horstmann. She was the first to tell Donovan that Fahey and Capano had been having an affair for about two years, but at the end of the summer in 1995 Annie had tried to break it off. Horstmann told Donovan Annie's attempt to break up with Capano didn't work. "He was obsessed with her," she told Donovan. Capano became enraged and went over to Annie's apartment and took back a television, some dresses, and other presents he'd given her. Horstmann remembered, too, what Fahey told her Capano had said at the time,

"No man is going to watch the TV that I gave you or see you in the dresses I gave you."

After he spent his rage, Horstmann said, Capano returned the gifts, and that eventually Annie and Capano had reached a stalemate—or agreed to be friends. At least Annie thought so, but Horstmann told Donovan that on at least two occasions she'd gone out to eat with Capano and he'd confessed his love for Annie and couldn't understand why she would or could be in love with her new boyfriend Mike Scanlan. Horstmann concluded her interview by saying from what she observed personally and what Annie had told her, Capano was "a control freak."

A picture was beginning to emerge of Annie's last months, and Donovan was getting the impression as he investigated the case that it wasn't a pretty one. Donovan and others who eventually came to work on the Capano case came to see Annie as a tragic figure. They described her as good-hearted, sincere, and vivacious—but at the same time a woman consumed with doubt who became involved with a married man. When she came to her senses and broke it off she began dating Scanlan, a devout Catholic who took her to see the Pope on one of their first dates. Annie didn't know if she was good enough for her new boyfriend, and at the same time, prosecutors said, Capano couldn't leave her alone. If he couldn't have her, then no one could. That was the working thesis for the prosecution once they zeroed in on Capano.

But Donovan, like most professional and intelligent investigators, could not develop tunnel vision. He had to check out other leads. The boyfriend, Mike Scanlan, could he have something to do with Annie's disappearance? Donovan checked. Could anyone else have been involved? What happened to Anne Marie? Donovan had no idea what actually happened to her, but thought early on that she wasn't going to come back. And the other leads? They always seemed to lead back to Capano. He was, after all, the last one to see her. He had an ongoing and—by the evidence Donovan had found at this point—an obviously strained relationship at times with Anne Marie. He was, according to those Donovan interviewed, a control freak. Donovan knew he was rich and powerful. All of those clues led him to believe his best suspect was Tom Capano.

On Tuesday, July 2, 1996, he got further confirmation. Prompted by the missing-persons report, Lisa D'Amico, who cut Annie's hair, called and spoke to Officer Daniels. She volunteered that Annie had told her in May that she was very excited about her new relationship with Michael Scanlan.

"Tom Capano is crazy," she also told Lisa. She was afraid of him, too. By May, Annie felt comfortable enough in her new relationship with Scanlan that she was talking to others about her problems with Capano. Annie told her hairdresser that she and Capano got into heated arguments all the time, and that Capano was always trying to give her unwanted gifts.

More importantly, Annie said Capano had been stalking her, waiting outside her apartment and watching her. She wouldn't let him in, and one time that caused Capano to go "crazy" and grab her. "You've ruined my life," Capano reportedly told Annie. "I left my wife for you and now you're rejecting me."

Another woman who knew what lurked behind the facade was Capano's estranged wife, Kay.

Just prior to the Fourth of July weekend of 1996 Capano called his wife, Kay. She hadn't spoken to Capano since he'd arrived at her home unexpectedly earlier in the week to borrow her Chevrolet Suburban.

"He came to the house," Kay recalls, "and then we sat on the back deck. He asked me if I'd heard the news that a young woman was missing."

Kay had. "Do you know her, Tom?" she asked. "After all," she later recalled, "he was involved in government and knew most of the key people in the state."

Yes, he confessed to Kay, he not only knew Annie, but he

was the last one to see her alive and there was going to be a big article in the paper about it during the coming weekend—and Capano was going to be named as the key suspect.

"You bastard," Kay said. "That's why you borrowed my car the other day—to dump the body."

"Kay, that's exactly why we aren't married anymore," Capano told her calmly.

By now, Capano wasn't cooperating with authorities at all. As he later testified, he felt extremely put out by the investigation and felt that the police were out to get him. He was upset with his estranged wife and wanted to get his family away from Wilmington for the long Fourth of July weekend while his "White Knight" reputation in town was slowly sullied.

He took the family to Stone Harbor, New Jersey, where his brothers and mother had homes. It was the perfect getaway, or so he thought. He hadn't counted on Charles Freel. Freel, or Bud, to almost everyone who knows him, is a large-framed man who has little to do with the media, little room for nonsense, and is known by his friends as a man "who wouldn't say shit if he were standing in a vat of it up to his armpits." Not that he is an obsequious man. He is a member of the Wilmington City Council, and state director of the Office of External Affairs. He is simply a man who won't comment about his own discomforts, but is a "straight arrow," his friends say, who doesn't suffer fools gladly. He is also the brother of Ed Freel, at the time Governor Carper's chief of staff, and the brother of Kevin Freel, who owns O'Friel's Irish Pub, gathering place for the Faheys and their friends.

In another twist that shows how close everything and everyone in Wilmington is linked, Bud testified he had been a friend of Tom Capano's for nearly twenty years and once dated Kathy Fahey. He found out Annie was missing on June 30, and at a legislative session the following day found out Capano was the last to see Annie alive.

Not satisfied with the progress the police were making, Freel tried on the afternoon of July 1, 1996, to telephone Capano at his Grant Avenue home. He finally reached Capano that evening.

"You're going to hear a lot of shit. Ignore it," Capano warned his old friend. "I'm going to need your support."

On the morning of July 3, Bud saw the Fahey family at Annie's apartment. They all told him that Capano had been less than forthcoming with the authorities, and they were now concerned for Annie's life. Kathy was even more forthcoming. To a local television crew from Philadelphia, she said, "I think Tom Capano has done something to my sister."

Apparently, Bud Freel had his concerns, as well, and vowed to talk to Capano. Without an invitation he drove up to Capano's Stone Harbor summer residence determined to find out what was going on. Freel walked through the back screen door, unannounced, in Stone Harbor and asked one of Capano's daughters where her father was. As Freel recalled on the witness stand, he walked into Capano's den at Stone Harbor and saw him on the phone, "Calmly smoking a cigarette. He had his legs crossed."

Capano was surprised to see his old friend. "What the hell are you doing here?" he silently mouthed to Freel as he spoke on the phone.

And when he hung up, Freel put it to him. "I asked him if he had any information on the whereabouts of Anne Marie. He said no and I tried to convince him to go and talk to the police, but Capano said he already had talked to them twice." Capano wasn't done explaining, though. "He spent a lot of time saying how good he'd been to Anne Marie and how they'd broke up and they were still friends. He said all the police were interested in were dirty details like sex and he wasn't going to violate Anne Marie's trust. He went on and on and talked about how good he'd been to Annie," Bud Freel testified.

The next day, on the Fourth of July, hundreds of local Wilmington residents turned out en masse to search Brandywine

Park near Annie's home. Meanwhile, as the big search commenced, Capano called his old friend Bud and asked Bud if he had been "wearing a wire." This got Bud upset. "I did a lot of shouting and cussing and told him he was hurting himself, his wife, and family, and if he didn't get his butt back to Wilmington it was going to get worse." Bud Freel had never worn a wire. He said he was acting as a friend for the Faheys and, although Capano would later deny it, Bud said he was also acting as a friend to Capano.

Later, on July 8 Capano felt compelled to call Freel at home to finish up their previous conversation. "He went into a tirade that the police wanted to use him as a scapegoat," Bud said. "I said, 'Tom, you just don't get it. You might know something and you don't even know that it could help them out.' "

Members of Capano's family were also concerned about Tom Capano's behavior and what, if anything, he had to do with Annie's disappearance. Capano's brother-in-law Lee Ramunno confronted him that weekend at Stone Harbor. As Ramunno later testified, Capano told him he couldn't come forward because he was protecting someone. That's all Capano was willing to say.

Also during that pivotal weekend, according to local newspaper accounts, Governor Carper spoke to his friend President Bill Clinton. When Carper mentioned his scheduling secretary was missing, Clinton offered to do anything for him to help, if he could. Two friends talking on the phone. Two powerful friends. Capano later claimed it was the seeds of a conspiracy being sown to bring him down. It was the first time on record the federal government was mentioned as being connected with the story.

Finally, in what Robert Fahey and many others, including the prosecutors, called "divine intervention," the one clue that would ultimately be Capano's undoing was found that Fourth of July weekend.

Kenneth Chubb, a retired prison maintenance worker, with

a summer home in Bay City, Delaware, said he was fishing about eight to ten miles off the coast of Delaware near Indian River that weekend. He was fifty miles due west from where Capano and his brother had dumped Annie's body the previous weekend.

It was a bright, sunny day, and Chubb said his son saw a pristine, white cooler off in the distance, bobbing in the water. "It looked like a brand-new cooler," Chubb said. So, his son pulled it into their boat. "It was missing its lid and a hinge, and it had two bullet holes in it. I said, 'Why would anybody shoot a cooler?' "

Chubb looked at the cooler and thought about fixing it up. It had a sort of pinkish stain inside, "but that wasn't unusual for a fish cooler, because, you know, fish bleed," he said.

Chubb got some epoxy and fixed the holes and bought a new lid and kept the cooler as his own.

Chapter 5
The Search

The Saturday following the Fourth of July in 1996, Colm Connolly ran into his boss, U.S. attorney Greg Sleet, at a local grocery store. Connolly, the young, aggressive assistant U.S. attorney, had only a passing interest in the Anne Marie Fahey missing-persons case. He'd read about it in the local paper, but hadn't given it much thought.

But the morning paper had mentioned the Carper/Clinton connection.

"It was news to us," Connolly said. "And as the U.S. attorney, Greg Sleet was the chief law-enforcement officer for all federal jurisdictions in Delaware, and it was news to him, too." The morning paper had mentioned Clinton offering help, but Sleet said he'd received no telephone calls requesting it, and Connolly said he certainly hadn't, but having the federal government involved in the search for Annie didn't seem like a bad idea at that. Was there a federal angle to play in the Anne Marie Fahey case? "That weekend Greg and I discussed the article, and on Monday the FBI called the Wilmington

Police to see if they could offer any assistance that would be helpful," Connolly said.

On July 8 the FBI called Sleet and told him that the Wilmington Police could indeed use some help. But was there a way for the federal government to get involved? Had any federal laws been broken?

"We knew that Anne Marie Fahey had last been seen alive in Philadelphia, and we knew about the tumultuous relationship between her and Capano," Connolly said, "but did he kidnap her? We decided there were enough questions and possibilities to get involved."

Connolly and FBI Agent Eric Alpert began by looking at some financial records of Capano's, Scanlan's, and lots of other people. "At that point in time we weren't just targeting Capano," Connolly said. "Despite what Mr. Capano later claimed."

While Connolly began his long, arduous task of investigating Annie's disappearance, on July 9, 1996, Capano, responding to the increasing public pressure for him to come forward and speak, finally decided to do so—but not to the police. He wanted to issue a press release.

"The disappearance of Anne Marie Fahey remains as much a mystery to me as it does to her family and friends," began the press release. "I can only say I share the gut-wrenching emotions of Anne Marie's family and pray for her safe return." Since, as he later testified in court, he'd dumped Annie's dead body at sea, it is unclear—said Connolly—short of a miracle how Capano expected Annie to have a "safe return." But, as prosecutors would later take great pains to point out, Capano's duplicity did not end in the first sentence of his press release.

Capano outlined how he had dinner with Annie and pointed out that she "had some problems," but added that he was at a "complete loss to explain what caused her disappearance." Capano also said he found out about Annie's disappearance and stated, contrary to what police were claiming, that he was

and would "continue to fully cooperate with investigators."
As much as anyone else, Capano said in the press release that
he wanted to know Anne Marie's whereabouts.

He knew as he wrote the press release that Annie was tied
to two anchors and a lock and chain, and was resting at the
bottom of the Atlantic Ocean in about 198 feet of water some
seventy miles off the coast of southern New Jersey. That did
not stop Capano from thanking his friends for encouragement
and concluding his press release by saying he would not be
granting any interviews, nor would he make further statements—although he did ask for all concerned to pray for Anne
Marie's safe return.

J. Brian Murphy, a longtime political lobbyist, pollster, and
former Wilmington commerce chief, helped Capano draft the
press release. He wanted to do it because he said Capano
was a "distraught friend," and Murphy wanted to help him
"counter a tide of negative publicity," he later testified. Murphy
had worked for Capano and they had played on the Wilmington
Rugby Club together. He said he first heard of Annie's disappearance while vacationing in South Carolina, and when he
returned to Wilmington on July 7, he looked up his old friend
Capano because he was puzzled that Capano wasn't proclaiming his innocence publicly.

Together they talked about putting together the press release
and then did so. But, Murphy said, before it could be released,
Capano's attorneys decided against it.

It sat for months unread until Capano's trial.

Also on July 9, Capano tried to call Robert Fahey. The
recording and transcript of that phone call were later entered
in court as evidence.

The call came to Robert shortly after noon.

"Uh, Robert, I don't know what to say. Um, uh, I really, I
really do want to talk to you," Capano said toward the beginning of the tape.

"And, um, I'd like to see you face-to-face, if you're willing to do that. Um, I have some things I want to show you. I have some things I want to tell you. I care for Anne Marie a great deal, Robert . . . I guess apparently from what Buddy's (Freel) telling me that hasn't come through, and I, I don't understand that . . . I know I'm babbling because I'm out of my freakin' mind with, um, with everything . . . there's one thing I want you to know. I talked to the police twice. I've told the police that I will talk to them as many times as they want. But I am not gonna talk about ancient history . . . Anne Marie's got a right to privacy and I have a right to privacy and I am not gonna tell them of things we did a year ago . . . or all this incredible personal stuff they want to know from me . . . I will talk to them about last Thursday night. I will talk to them about anything but I am not gonna talk about ancient history. And I just am not budging from that . . . I wanted to come see you all, at that apartment, but I know that Kathleen would just, frankly gouge my eyes out. Oh, shit, I'll stop. Please call me, Robert.''

Neither the police nor Robert Fahey could ever figure out what Capano meant by ''ancient history.'' Fahey just wanted to know what happened to his sister—and at the time Capano left the recording she'd only been missing for a week—hardly ancient history, Robert Fahey pointed out. Donovan, the Wilmington Police detective, believed Capano was making reference to his sexual relationship with Annie, but again Donovan wasn't as concerned about that as much as Capano seemed to be. ''We pretty much just wanted to know where Anne Marie Fahey was,'' Donovan said. ''And Mr. Capano did everything he could to keep us from finding out.''

That is not, however, Capano's story. From the beginning he tried to stress how often he cooperated with the authorities. He maintained up to and during his trial that he had done as much as he could to cooperate with Connolly, Donovan, and the rest of the prosecutorial team. Capano's one caveat was that he did not want to put his children under any stress. He also claimed the federal government never treated him fairly. Capano said, for example, he knew as early as July 11 the federal government was involved and there was a vendetta against him. Consequently, he didn't want to talk to the federal government.

"I believe that was the one thing he never really counted on," said Kevin Freel. "We all heard that Capano was saying this whole thing would blow over in a couple of months—and if it had been kept at the state level it might have. But he never really counted on the federal government getting involved. He certainly never counted on Colm Connolly or Ferris Wharton."

In retrospect, Freel also said, it was easy to see that one of the other things Capano never counted on was the vigilance with which the Faheys would pursue the case. Robert, Brian, and Kathy would make up the nucleus of the Faheys' vocal dogged determination to find out what happened to their sister, but older brothers Mark and Kevin were also there, making their presence known in the media and to Capano himself. "All we wanted, all along, was just to find out the truth," Robert Fahey said on numerous occasions.

That was the tenor of a letter the Faheys drafted to Capano, in response to Capano's lack of enthusiastic cooperation with the police. The letter was sent to Capano privately on July 24, and was later entered as evidence and widely reported in the local newspapers.

"We are writing to request your assistance in locating our sister, Anne Marie Fahey," the letter began. It then went on to recount that four weeks had passed since she was last seen alive and it was Capano with whom she was last seen. The Faheys urged Capano to come forward with whatever information he had on Annie's disappearance, and they also urged him to think of his own family. "Do what your father Louis would expect of one of his sons—come forward and share all you know about Anne Marie's disappearance . . . Imagine, if you will, that this case involved one of your four daughters, not our sister. We know you would expect the last person to be seen with your children to come forward and be helpful." The letter ends with a plea for Capano to do the right thing and come forward. "We are talking about someone's life, please help us **today**." It is signed: "The Fahey Family."

Capano never replied, and by July 24 he had much bigger problems—the federal government. What had started as a casual conversation between Connolly and his boss at a grocery store on July 6, had mushroomed two weeks later into a full-throttle investigation.

By July 18 Connolly said he had enough information that he could do something with the case, but the problem would be one of jurisdictional politics. Did Detective Bob Donovan want to hold onto the case and keep it at the state level and run the show himself, or would he give up being the quarterback to play on a much larger team—the federal government's?

"We brought Bob in and told him he had to choose," Connolly said. "We had a meeting with Donovan and his two superiors and told them that if they signed on with us they couldn't even talk to their state prosecutors about what we were doing. They agreed to do that. So then we formally at that point launched the federal investigation."

Eight days later on July 26 Donovan and Connolly met again at Connolly's Wilmington office. In a spacious conference room they spread out all the information they had up to that point. It amounted to a lot of paper, including bills, receipts, and telephone logs, but nothing seemed overly alarming. Then Connolly noticed Capano's Visa bill. "I saw an entry for 'Wall Paper Warehouse' and thought, why is a guy spending $300 for wallpaper when he lives in a rental house?" Connolly said. "And we thought that was odd, so I went over to the phone and got the number for Wall Paper Warehouse and when I called the number the voice on the other line said 'Air Base Carpets.' " It turned out that Air Base Carpets also did business as Wall Paper Warehouse. "As soon as I heard that, I told Bob and we both said, 'My God, he rolled her up in a carpet.' "

Connolly marked that incident down as the first turning point in the investigation. That night he interviewed Capano's maid, Ruth Boylan. She told Connolly that when she last cleaned the house on July 22 she noticed that a love seat and a carpet in Capano's Grant Avenue home that were in good condition had recently been replaced.

Michelle Sullivan, Annie's therapist, told the FBI on July 29 that she last saw Fahey on June 26—the day before she disappeared. Annie was frightened of Capano, according to Sullivan, and doubted that she would have gone to his home willingly. She speculated that Fahey would only have gone to dinner with Capano in order to break off the relationship. That supported earlier information Donovan had retrieved from the Ristorante di Panorama in Philadelphia. Earlier in July the waitress who served Annie and Capano remembered the dinner the two had together. She said Annie (whom she identified from a photo) was wearing a light-colored dress with a floral pattern. Capano was wearing a dark sports coat and tie. Capano ordered everything that night, including drinks, appetizers, and the main course. Annie didn't say much and appeared "solemn" and had a "forced smile" whenever the waitress approached.

It was Annie's last meal.

Sullivan also said she had encouraged Annie to report Capano to the Attorney General's Office, but Annie didn't want to take that step—even though she was frightened of him.

At the same time the prosecution team was developing the information from Sullivan, they also discovered that on June 30 Capano used his credit card at a local drugstore near Annie's apartment. A manager there told the FBI that a man resembling Capano inquired about blood remover that day.

On July 29 Detective Donovan interviewed the hairdresser Lisa D'Amico a second time. She told him that Fahey told her she was afraid of Capano and that he was "very controlling" and dictated to Annie what she could and could not do. In May of that year Annie told D'Amico she'd gotten into an argument with Capano and that he had started "screaming and yelling at her" and called Fahey a "slut and bitch" and grabbed her around the throat. Fahey jumped out of the car and ran into her apartment.

During this period, Connolly learned Capano had borrowed his estranged wife's Chevy Suburban about the time Annie disappeared.

With all of this new information in hand, Assistant U.S. Attorney Connolly now had enough to get a search warrant for Tom Capano's home. But along with this new information Connolly also had a choice to make. "So, on July 30, I called Ferris (Wharton, the state prosecutor), and I asked him to come over here, and when he got here, for the first time I told him we had an investigation going," Connolly said. "We had enough evidence to get a search warrant, but we didn't just want to do that if the state wanted to take the case. So I asked Ferris if he wanted to take the case over, or we could continue our investigation. But I had to explain to him that if we did (continue the federal investigation) I couldn't share information with him under the federal rules." Wharton didn't hesitate. It wasn't a matter of jurisdictional pride with Wharton, a matter of getting a suspect to trial. Wharton admitted the state with its limited resources had not made anywhere near the progress Connolly had, so he, like Donovan before him, let Connolly run with the ball.

While this was going on, Donovan was still out gathering more evidence. On July 30 he spoke with Jill Morrison, another friend of Fahey's, who told the burly officer that Capano was possessive, "controlling, psychotic, and needs counseling."

At one point in time during the previous year, Morrison said, Capano locked Fahey in his car and then drove without her permission to his house. When he got there he drove into his garage, locked the garage doors, and refused to let Annie out of the garage until she "listened to what he had to say about her attempts to dissolve their relationship."

Morrison also told Donovan she was present at Annie's home in January when Annie was getting ready to go out with her boyfriend, Michael Scanlan. The event, which was to play an important role in the case, was the "Grand Gala," the pinnacle of social life for Wilmington's well-heeled. "It's like a senior prom for adults," was the way one Wilmington resident described it.

Each January, just prior to Annie's birthday, the annual event drew the small town's rich and famous together for dancing, charity, and socializing. It was Annie's dream to attend, and she was going with her new—and she hoped lasting—love, Michael Scanlan. But Morrison told Donovan that Capano wouldn't let her go. He threatened to get a date, attend the gala himself, be seen in front of Annie and her date, and make the event "miserable for her."

According to Morrison, someone called numerous times while Annie got ready to go to the Gala. Each time the person hung up. "It's Capano," Annie told Morrison. "I know it." Fearful that Capano was on a mobile phone and waiting outside her apartment for Scanlan to pick her up, Annie wasn't even sure if she wanted to go to the Gala.

"He won't leave me alone. He's stalking me," Annie told Morrison.

The day after Donovan interviewed Morrison, the federal government executed a search warrant on Tom Capano's home, and Capano's world came crashing in on him. It was the one thing he'd never counted on. It was the one thing he couldn't prepare for, and as he later testified in court, it angered him to no end. If everyone had just let him alone, Capano later told the court, things would never have gone as far as they did.

For eleven hours the federal government went through every conceivable nook, cranny, and crevice in Capano's home.

Agents also searched his car, as well as Kay Capano's Suburban. Officers seized hairs and fibers from Capano's Jeep and Kay Capano's vehicle, various stain removers in a laundry closet, including one labeled "milk and blood stain" remover. Agents also found in a briefcase several hard copies of numerous e-mail messages between Anne Marie Fahey and Tom Capano.

But the most promising evidence the investigators found appeared to be a few small stains on the woodwork of Capano's great room, a radiator in the great room, and a laundry closet door. Tests conducted in Capano's house that day showed the stains were blood. At that point it was unclear whose blood it was, but investigators sent the blood samples to Quantico, Virginia, to the immense FBI laboratory for further testing.

With the search warrant executed, and some successful results, it was time to take stock. The investigators had numerous statements about Capano's controlling and obsessive nature. They knew he was the last one to be seen with Annie. They now knew about Annie and Capano's longtime secret affair, and they knew Annie had tried to break it off with him. They also had bloodstains, bloodstain remover, a missing rug and love seat, but nowhere near enough evidence to arrest, let alone convict, Capano. They had run into a brick wall after their initial surge of good luck, and they were left facing a belligerent Tom Capano and a lot of unanswered questions.

Where was Annie? What happened that night in June after she and Capano went out to dinner? Those were the key questions that Connolly, Donovan, FBI Agent Eric Alpert, and the rest of the investigators (which would grow to include IRS investigators, as well as members of the Bureau of Alcohol, Tobacco, and Firearms) still needed to answer.

"We sat down and thought about it," Connolly said. "It only made sense that he couldn't dispose of the body himself—that he probably had help. It had to be a real close friend or a family member, who else could he trust? We figured it had to be a member of his family."

But getting to the family, and ultimately to Capano, would prove to take close to a year and a half and would ruffle feathers all across Wilmington. After all, during that early stage Capano was still highly regarded in Wilmington. He was "the good Capano," and as news leaked out about the investigation in dribs and drabs, disbelief set in. "He (Capano) fooled a lot of people for a long time," Bud Freel said one night while sitting at the bar in his brother Kevin's Irish pub.

"He was the go-to guy in the family," Kevin Freel said. "Any time there was a problem, it was Tom Capano who straightened it out. In the beginning we sat in the bar one night talking about it saying how unbelievable it was that he could be so controlling, and then somebody said, 'Yeah, he's acting just like a Capano.' " The disbelief, Capano's power, his charm, and his money brought a unique perspective and its own unique set of problems to the table—Connolly was forced to deal with all of it.

"We encountered, throughout, reluctance from prominent people in the community, especially lawyers to help us out," Connolly recalled. "They did not want to cooperate. There were people who just did not believe Tom Capano could be guilty of anything, and they thought we were intrusive and they just didn't want to cooperate with us. It was very frustrating and it was especially frustrating being a relatively young lawyer and seeing older members of the bar not being fully cooperative."

Connolly also had another problem to contend with, and this one was much more delicate—the Fahey family. "They really have a lot of class," Connolly said. "I was impressed with the way they handled themselves from the very beginning." They were equally impressed with Connolly, but in the beginning they were frustrated because Connolly couldn't tell them much.

"They told us early on that they don't like to lose," Kevin Fahey said. "And they told us they had a game plan. But they also told us they only had one shot and we had to be patient."

It wasn't easy sometimes, for any of them, especially Mark. He'd been living in Washington, D.C., at the time of Annie's disappearance and moved back home to Wilmington vowing to stay until the end to find out what had happened to his little sister. "It was frustrating. I tell you it was very frustrating. At times I wanted to go strangle Capano myself. I thought about my mom and what she said about Annie, it was just very hard," Mark said.

The Faheys' torment, which became very public at times, was the emotional side to the equation that Connolly, Wharton, Donovan, and all the others involved had to consider every time the investigation went forward, even though their main concern was how to bring down Capano and how to get his brothers to talk.

On July 8 Tom Capano agreed to consent to an interview with the state, but only if the investigators didn't ask him about his relationship with Anne Marie Fahey before June 27, 1996, nor any other relationships he may or may not have had, and any other aspect of his personal life. On July 16, 1996, Capano offered again to submit to an interview, but it was conditioned on the state not asking about any relationships he may or may not have had other than with Anne Marie, and again, of course, he didn't want to talk about any other aspect of his personal life.

In August 1996 Capano had his attorney, Charles Oberly, call Colm Connolly and tell Connolly that a person fitting the description of Anne Marie Fahey had been spotted in Newark International Airport in New Jersey. Oberly then requested that Connolly have federal agents investigate this matter.

Late in July the investigators found out from an informant that Gerry Capano, Capano's youngest brother, had recently sold a boat without an anchor on it. They also found out from Shaw Taylor, a project manager for Capano's younger brother Louis—a prominent Wilmington developer—that on July 1 Louis Capano had ordered the Dumpsters emptied of trash from a construction site in northeast Wilmington. Those two facts made Connolly and Donovan suspect that Capano had help from his brothers, and it alerted them to the possibilities that Annie had been killed and then dumped in either a landfill or at sea.

On August 5, 1996, Connolly sent Capano and his attorney Charles Oberly a letter naming Capano as the target of a federal investigation. A federal grand jury convened, and in late August, Connolly began applying pressure on Capano's family. His first target was someone he knew, from the man's past criminal record, could be broken: brother Louis Capano.

Chapter 6
The Sting

By August, Annie's disappearance and the story of the search to find her, and/or bring her killer to justice, had already mutated into a macabre story of sex, violence, and betrayal. Her pretty features, her easygoing air, indeed her very memory was in danger of being lost in the vortex the case had become.

Disclosures of a secret love affair with one of Wilmington's most powerful nouveaux riches; the conversation between Governor Carper, Annie's boss, and President Clinton; the high-profile raid on Capano's Grant Avenue address—all of these had turned up the pressure and the media scrutiny on the case to levels rarely seen in Wilmington.

In the month of August it looked like the case was going to take another turn. It would pit brother against brother.

When Louis Capano, Sr., died, he left Tom, Louis, Jr., and Joseph trustees of his estate and gave them power to invest the money, open new businesses, and continue current businesses as they deemed appropriate. They also had to pay their mother, sister, and youngest brother monthly stipends and give Gerard shares of the estate at age twenty-one and thirty-five.

Louis, Jr., actually took over the day-to-day operation of the family empire and soon made the Capanos even more wealthy. Louis, Jr., was a likable, tall, tanned fellow with a reputation of being a bit rough around the edges, but he was a "get the job done" kind of guy. He was also the kind of guy who had been in trouble with the law himself.

In 1988 he was granted immunity from state prosecutors and admitted to violating campaign contribution laws. He then cooperated with authorities in a successful prosecution of a top-ranking state transportation department official. A year later he had to help the FBI in a sting operation. That came after investigators learned he was being asked to pay a $100,000 bribe to a councilman for a zoning favor. The councilman was convicted of extortion after Louis wore a concealed microphone when he made a payoff to the councilman.

It was Tom Capano who used his legal and political connections to guide Louis through those turgid affairs. Now that the older brother was in trouble, Connolly thought he might be able to use Louis to get to Tom Capano, but he also knew the Capano family bonds were tight, and getting Louis to help him out would be much more difficult than getting him to turn on a councilman. Yet, Connolly said he remained confident that Louis not only knew something, but he also remained confident Louis Capano would eventually talk.

By age thirty-three Louis had bought a 332-acre former du Pont estate in Greenville. Business associates who watched and dealt with him claimed he had "the Midas Touch." Some said he did all the wrong things and they turned out all right. "You could dip him in shit and he'd come out smelling like roses," another associate said. But, there had been those payoffs and illegal campaign contributions.

There had also been the incident with Lee Ramunno, his brother-in-law. When Louis was just twenty-nine he got into a property and money dispute with Lee. Lee, an attorney himself, decided to sue Louis, Jr., and have his brother serve him at a local Wilmington restaurant where Louis was guest-bartending. When Louis found out, he was furious.

He left the restaurant, drove to Ramunno's house, and threw a wooden chair through a sliding glass door. When he began choking Ramunno, Marian, Capano's sister, called the cops— only after trying to get her brother Tom to do something about it. Connolly knew Louis could be volatile, and if the right buttons were pushed, he might budge. If his own survival were pitted against his older brother's, investigators felt confident Louis Capano would see the light.

"We decided to concentrate (on Louis) early on in the investigation based, in part, on what we heard about the trash Dumpsters," Colm Connolly later said.

When interviewed by investigators, Shaw Taylor, a Capano construction-site project manager, recounted the candid details of what occurred the day he was asked to dump the trash. July 1 was not the normal day to empty the bins and they were not full. Three times Taylor quizzed his boss, Louis, Jr., about the peculiar request. Finally Taylor was told to stop asking questions and empty the bins. But Taylor was extremely uncomfortable and felt Capano was putting him in the middle. He wanted to know why the Dumpsters were to be emptied.

"I'm not going to tell you and you should do what you were told to do. There's something in the trash bins that doesn't belong there," Louis finally offered.

Armed with this information police and FBI agents searched between August 12, 1996, and August 16, 1996, through trash and construction debris at two local landfills, where Louis Capano dumped his construction garbage. They found nothing.

On August 29 Louis got a taste of federal pressure—he was hauled in to testify before the federal grand jury. He was asked numerous questions about his business dealings, his relationship with his brothers and other relatives, and he was asked about

Annie. Louis denied any involvement in Annie's disappearance and also said his brother Tom had nothing to do with the disappearance. Federal investigators were not impressed with the testimony and because of information they already had, remained convinced Louis Capano had lied to them. Louis later admitted as much, but said at the time he thought his older brother Tom was innocent. He'd looked up to his big brother all his life. He'd trusted him. He'd believed him. And Tom Capano had told Louis Capano he wasn't guilty.

Tom Capano did tell Louis on June 30 to come to his house. When Louis got there, as he later testified, his older brother told him about his affair with Anne Marie Fahey.

Three nights earlier, Tom Capano said Fahey had slit her wrists while he was in the upstairs bathroom. Those wounds, Capano said, were minor but it would explain the blood found in Capano's Grant Avenue home. Tom Capano also told his brother Louis that he'd helped Anne Marie bandage the wounds, and Annie didn't need to go to a hospital. But, she had stained the sofa with blood, and Tom Capano said he and his little brother Gerard had taken the sofa to Louis's construction Dumpster. He also said a nightgown and other personal belongings of Annie's had been dumped there, too. Louis Capano said his older brother didn't appear concerned, but did tell Louis about meeting with police. Then Tom Capano asked Louis to have the Dumpsters emptied. Louis did it, but advised his older brother to get a lawyer.

Tom Capano then asked Louis for another favor. Would Louis say that Tom was visiting him on the morning after Fahey's disappearance if asked? Tom Capano had successfully explained the sofa removal, seemed to be telling the truth— and after all, could Louis Capano's older brother be capable of murder? Would he actually kill someone? Like everyone else who ever knew Tom, Louis Capano decided his brother could not actually kill someone. So, Louis lied to the grand jury.

But Colm Connolly had apparently anticipated that move. As he later said, he had multiple undercover investigators working on the case and they helped immensely to bring out the truth. What did these undercover operatives do? "Well, did you ever see the movie *The Sting?*" Connolly later asked. "The trick to a good con is not letting the mark know he's been conned—ever." Connolly would never say who the "marks" were, but said the federal government did apply a lot of pressure on both Louis and Gerard Capano.

By the time Louis appeared before the federal grand jury, Connolly had a good idea what really had happened. And when Louis's testimony didn't jibe with the known facts, Connolly knew he would have to bring Louis back before the grand jury again. It was all part of the pressure designed to get the truth from the Capano brothers.

The investigators continued on other fronts. On August 23 Tom Capano was forced to go to Riverside Hospital in Wilmington and give a blood and hair sample. Connolly was looking for a match with the blood found at Capano's rental home at the end of July during the government's search, but it wouldn't come from Capano.

During those hot days of August, Connolly found out that Anne Marie had given blood just a few weeks before her death. The blood bank had called and Detective Donovan and others had tracked the blood down—it was being shipped to Europe for use there. The blood was recovered and tested against the blood drops found at Capano's rented home. When the two samples matched, it turned out to be another big, early turning point in the case against Tom Capano.

"Once we knew it was Anne Marie's blood there, once we had that, I knew we were solidly on the right track," Connolly confided. "We were starting to build a case, point by point, that led to Tom Capano having killed Anne Marie Fahey."

Connolly remained confident, even though he knew he was many months, perhaps even years, away from bringing the case to trial. He never wavered. It was his first capital murder case, but he had several experienced investigators and lawyers to rely on. "I never felt overwhelmed, but I knew I had a lot of work ahead of me," he said. "At times it seemed harder than at other times, but we stuck it out."

At times it must have seemed difficult at best, like when confronting Louis Capano, Jr. He was adept at maneuvering himself around the gray areas of the law, and did so, in the beginning better than some thought he could. There was an IRS investigation into his finances, and an interview with his second wife. Louis had divorced his first wife and married professional golfer Lauri Merten. While he enjoyed being her caddy on the LPGA tour, he was also rumored to be stepping out on her.

In what even the defense attorneys came to say was one of those bizarre sideshows that seemed to pop up when it came to the Anne Marie Fahey/Tom Capano investigation, Lauri Merten would for a brief moment take a featured role in the Capano circus.

The federal government already knew of Louis's affair with a woman named Kristi Pepper from a previous well-reported investigation, and they came to find out that Lauri Merten had hired a private investigator to trail her husband because she suspected his infidelity. She'd even tape-recorded some conversations between Louis and others—including his brother Tom. Whatever Lauri found out, it had led her at one point to take her 7-iron out of her golf bag and use it with menacing pleasure on one of Louis's cars. However, when it came to the outside world, she remained solidly behind Louis. In December 1996 she refused to turn over the audiotapes she'd made of several conversations Louis had on the telephone. Some of those conversations were between Tom and Louis Capano.

Because of the possible windfall of evidence on those tapes, the actual murder case against Tom Capano took a backseat to Merten's tape issue. Finally the Third Circuit Court of Appeals ruled in April 1997 that Merten did not have to turn over the tapes because the people on the tapes did not know that they were being recorded—a violation of the Capanos' right to privacy.

The woman who had captured the U.S. Women's Open in 1993 was now back in the spotlight under media scrutiny, but it had little to do with her ability to sink a birdie. Merten, who was described in the *Arizona Republic* as being "vivacious and down to earth," now was accused of being an accessory to murder—by none other than Robert Fahey.

"We pled with her for months to come forward and tell us what she knew, but she completely blew us off," Robert Fahey told the *Republic*. Fahey agreed with Merten's attorney who said whatever was on her audiotapes was pure speculation, but Fahey wondered in public why Merten would fight so hard to keep them private if there was nothing on them about Annie's murder. "She hid what she knew, and that's why we feel she's an accessory (to murder)," Robert Fahey said.

Merten's involvement in the case was mentioned in *Golf World* magazine, and she herself wrote to the *Arizona Republic* in response to the things said against her. She maintained that she knew nothing about Annie's death and said, "I have the deepest sympathy for the Faheys in their loss, no matter what they believe. I also understand why they would lash out at anyone they believed was standing in the way of the investigation. But they are wrong about me."

Merten had been embarrassed to find that Louis, the man many credited with helping her win the Women's Open in 1993, was fooling around on her. This anger manifested itself in hiring investigators, tape-recording conversations, and going after a car with a set of golf clubs. However, Lauri Merten, as far as anyone ever determined, never had any idea what happened June 27, 1996, between Tom Capano and Anne Marie Fahey.

Connolly and the federal investigators thought Kristi Pepper might know something. They enlisted the help of Louis's twenty-seven-year-old mistress, Kristi Pepper, to see if Louis knew more than he was letting on. Pepper wore a wire and was taping Louis Capano for the FBI at the same time his wife was taping him to see if Louis Capano was cheating on her.

In some of the Pepper conversations Louis Capano pressured her to forget some of the things he had said about his brother Tom. That pressure eventually helped bring Louis to the prosecutor's table with the truth, after it became apparent Louis could be prosecuted for trying to coerce a federal witness.

But Louis's wife, as was later shown, had nothing to do with the Tom Capano investigation. She was among the first who was involved only peripherally in the case but came to suffer greatly. Her reputation was sullied in the press, she was degraded, and she was caused considerable pain. As Connolly later pointed out, it wouldn't be the last time someone close to Capano would suffer.

In fact, if Merten was among the first to have her name sullied, then Governor Tom Carper may have indeed been the very first. In the first days of the investigation it was bandied about, some say by Tom Capano, that Carper (who shares the same initials as Capano) was the man with whom Annie Marie was having a fling. While that got some local play in the press, and was even mentioned in a national magazine article, it was put down vehemently by Carper's own wife in a news conference in Wilmington.

It was, as investigators later said, just another red herring thrown up at them to shake them from the trail. As the end of 1996 rolled around, investigators were convinced they were on the right track. Bob Donovan, for one, said he always expected that he would eventually arrest Tom Capano. But Capano had other ideas. He once again tried to solicit public support for his cause.

Early in January 1997 the probable-cause affidavit had been unsealed revealing that the FBI suspected Capano killed Fahey in his home on June 27, 1996, and disposed of the evidence. On January 4 Tom Capano issued a press release through his attorney, Charles M. Oberly III, which sought to blunt the impact of the probable-cause affidavit. "I caution those who read reports of what is included in the affidavit to remember they are one-sided presentations made by investigating authorities, filled with unsubstantiated hearsay, and are rarely, if ever, denied by the issuing courts," Oberly wrote. He then compared Capano to security guard Richard Jewell, who had been blamed for the infamous Olympic bombing in Atlanta. He was similarly "publicly identified and stripped of all privacy before being exonerated as a suspect months later." Oberly maintained, in his press release that Capano had cooperated throughout the investigation with authorities, and he said the "unsubstantiated self-serving statements made by the FBI distort the relationship that existed between Tom and Anne Marie." To assist reporters who were interested in painting a "fairer picture," Oberly attached to his press release notes from Annie to Tom that showed how affectionate the two were to each other. In words that foreshadowed Capano's own testimony in court, Oberly went on to write that because of Capano's and Annie's "prominent positions" in the community the investigation had been fueled by "innuendo and rumor."

"As a result Tom has been subjected to unparalleled rumor and suspicion. Both his and his family's right to privacy has been totally destroyed by the FBI." The letter closed by saying Capano "is devastated by Anne Marie's disappearance and like everyone else hopes she will be found safe."

Colm Connolly had once played junior varsity soccer with Gerard Capano. They were not close friends, but Colm knew him prior to the investigation into Annie's disappearance. Their connection, as slight as it was, was indicative of the entire case and its interwoven complexities of who knew whom and for how long.

Bud Freel knew and was good friends with Tom Capano for twenty years. He'd also at one time dated Kathy Fahey-Hosey. His brother Ed Freel was at one point in time Governor Carper's chief of staff, and it was Ed whom Kathy Fahey-Hosey called after she called the Wilmington Police the day she discovered her sister was missing. The interrelationships were deeper than that. After Annie disappeared, Kevin Freel, brother to Ed and Bud, held a vigil at his pub. He had signs made up and posted them on the fence outside his pub. They said "Friends of Anne Marie." They hang outside his pub to this day. In fact, "O'Friel's" became the nerve center for the dissemination of information to friends and Fahey family members during the long, arduous investigation and court trial to follow. It was Kevin Freel, another well-known political operative in the state, who years earlier had told Tom Capano, "the good Capano," that if he wanted to run for office in Delaware he could get elected, "as long as he changed his name."

There was little that went on during the course of the investigation that needed much analysis when the investigators were trying to figure out how a suspect or a target might react to their inquisitions. Wilmington is so small, and the Capanos—through their wealth, power, and fame in the area—were already so well-known that it didn't take a tip-off for the investigators, who would all prove to be exceptionally resourceful and intelligent, to figure out how to play someone. That's not to say that there weren't some surprises. Despite the gossipy nature of Wilmington, and there would be ample evidence of that nature during the next eighteen months, there were some heady and surreal twists in the case. "In Wilmington everybody either knows everyone else or is fucking everyone else," one of the lawyers involved in the case said on the first day of the trial.

Still, the prosecutors had enough information on the main

characters in the case to easily decide how to play them in their investigation. Thus, they knew because of Gerard Capano's demeanor they could let him wait for a while before he was questioned. "We decided we would not bring in Joe or Gerry Capano until we were convinced they would tell the truth about whatever question we would put to them," Connolly said. "And people would ask, and did ask, for a year and a half, 'How come you're not talking to Gerry,' and so it had to be pretty obvious to Gerry and his lawyer and everyone else that there was a reason to that."

The reasons manifested themselves during 1997 and later during the trial. Gerry said the thoughts of what happened on that day in 1996 when he hoisted onto his boat and later threw out to sea the cooler/coffin that held Anne Marie's remains haunted him. "He was clearly having nightmares and was upset about it for a year and a half," Connolly said.

In early October 1997, Connolly decided Gerry Capano had waited long enough. Using confidential information, Connolly had enough to move on Gerry for something that had nothing to do with his brother Tom's activities, but Connolly remained convinced the info could be used as a bargaining chip to get Gerry to talk. Twenty-five federal agents, armed and ready, tore through the streets of Wilmington's upscale Brandywine Hundred. By 8:30 P.M. on October 8, they were in the front yard of Gerry's house. They burst in and immediately put Gerry on the floor with a gun to his head. They let his wife, Michelle, and children leave, and for the next eleven hours they searched Gerry's house as they had previously done Tom's. After probing every square inch of the house they found twenty-one firearms, two grams of cocaine, and a small quantity of marijuana. One of the guns was found openly stored in the closet of a room occupied by Gerry's son.

Gerry immediately went to his older brother Tom for help. The raid had come without a warning, and Tom had promised Gerry back on the day they dumped the body that no harm would come to him. But Tom Capano could offer Gerry no shoulder to lean on. He wasn't there for him as he had been Gerry's entire life. Tom Capano simply told his younger brother "to be a man."

A few days later Connolly executed a second search warrant. This one was on the home of Gerry's best friend, Edward Del Collo, a convicted felon. Ultimately, Connolly said, it would even be more important than the raid on Gerard Capano's home because Gerry had allegedly purchased one of the firearms found in Del Collo's home for him as a favor.

That gun turned out to be the one piece of evidence that would bring Gerry, ready to deal, to Colm Connolly. "When we raided Gerry's house the question under sentencing guidelines was whether or not all of those guns were simply for sporting and collection purposes. And they had to be for lawful sporting and hunting purposes. And he had an argument that he was a legitimate hunter and collector, and so we were ready for that argument," Connolly said. "But once we did the other search warrant we found a gun that Gerry had sold to a convicted felon—and that meant, absolutely, that Gerry was going to jail for three to five years. And he knew it and his lawyer knew it and there was no getting around it—and it would have been a very easy case to prove—and that's what made the difference."

A few days later a Delaware family-services official paid Gerry an official visit about the gun found in his son's closet. A child-neglect inquiry was opened to determine whether or not his two children, ages three and four, should be allowed to remain in a home containing accessible guns and drugs. The case went nowhere. It was closed on November 7, 1997, less than a month after the raid on Gerry's home. But the message got through to Gerard Capano.

Gerry had begged Tom for months, since Gerry found out that it was Anne Marie he'd helped dump at sea, for his brother to come forward. Tom had not. Louis, who'd already lied to the grand jury twice, and pressured a grand jury witness (Kristi

Pepper), had also begged Tom to come forward. He had not. Gerry and Louis wanted desperately to be able to help their brother, but it seemed Tom was unwilling to help out his siblings. With the raid on Gerry Capano's home, the raid on his friend's home, and the possibility of an ugly child-custody case, Gerard Capano knew he had to talk.

On November 8, 1997, Gerard Capano finally spoke. Along with attorney Dan Lyons, he walked into Colm Connolly's office and told everything to the federal government.

He was nervous, stumbling, and at times emotional. He admitted his own part in the scheme and told a story that had even the prosecutors in shock. In quiet and yet menacingly accurate detail, Gerard Capano outlined the specifics of June 28, 1996. He told the prosecutors he was scared when his brother Tom called him and was fearful that Tom Capano had killed an extortionist who was trying to harm Tom Capano's children.

During the confession Gerard Capano told investigators that months prior to Annie's disappearance, his brother Tom came to him and told him he was being harassed by extortionists. Gerard said his older brother asked him if he knew any "leg breakers" and also asked to borrow a gun. When pressed, Gerry Capano said his older brother told him of a man and a woman who were trying to extort money from him as early as February 1996. Gerry had even given Tom $8,000 to pay off the extortionists. At one point, he'd also given his older brother a big 10-millimeter Colt handgun. Protection, Tom had told him, in case any of the extortionists wanted to try and harm Tom's four girls. Gerry had recommended a shotgun, which doesn't really have to be aimed all that accurately, if Tom was serious about protecting himself. But Tom Capano opted for the Colt. Gerry had shrugged that off.

The day Tom Capano showed up on Gerry's driveway reading the newspaper, and Gerry asked Tom if he had done something, Gerard Capano said he thought his older brother had killed the extortionists. Gerry never tried to find out who was in the cooler, but came to believe a short time after he'd helped his brother that it was Annie and not an extortionist that they'd dumped at sea.

Gerry said he didn't want to have anything to do with helping his brother dispose of the cooler, but what could he do? Didn't family stick together? Isn't that what he'd been taught? Gerard Capano seemed to talk forever about the cooler, the lady to whom his brother had given money for gas, the trip to the ATM, the hinges on the cooler in incredible and, to the investigators, almost unbelievably frank detail. "When we first heard Gerry's story, we had no way of knowing what he was going to say. It was a fantastic story with all kinds of incredible details," Connolly said. "And it turned out to be all true."

Gerard Capano even supplied the prosecution with Tom Capano's alibi. On the drive back to Wilmington after dumping Annie at sea, the elder Capano told Gerard exactly what to say if the police ever questioned him. Gerry had written it down on a Post-it notepad and supplied the details to the prosecution.

It was the big break in the case against Tom Capano, and because Gerard Capano had provided so much rich detail, many aspects of his story could be corroborated.

On November 10 Louis Capano came in from the cold, too, and confessed everything he'd done in helping his older brother. His statement came just two days before he was supposed to appear before the grand jury for a third time. Louis told Connolly he saw a sofa in his trash bin on July 1, the day after his brother told him he had dumped things relating to the case there.

Louis Capano also said his older brother called him earlier, on June 30, and asked him to come over to his house. It was then Tom confessed his affair with Fahey and told Louis about the alleged wrist-slitting incident. He told Louis about Gerard's visit with him to the dump, and that he had dumped the gun, as well.

"He said he hoped they would find the gun because it hadn't been shot," Louis said. He hadn't come forward for so long because he thought that Tom was innocent. Then he told investigators that he knew about Gerard and Tom's boat trip. Gerry had told him months ago. Both of them had been working on getting their brother to come in, and that had been to no avail.

The day after Louis came in, November 11, Connolly went over the evidence. Donovan had tracked Capano's and Annie's activities during the last few months of her life. The facts had shown, according to several witness statements, that Capano was jealous of Annie's new romance. He'd threatened her, argued with her, and tried to control her. Gerry Capano and Louis Capano's testimony showed, Connolly would later argue, that Thomas J. Capano had exercised the ultimate control over Annie's life.

On November 11 Connolly was sure it was time to act. Tom Capano, now a public pariah in the city he once claimed to own, had lost his job. Unemployed but still affluent, he was living at his mother's home since the police had raided his Grant Avenue address.

Chapter 7

The Arrest

After hearing Gerry's story and the initial corroboration by his brother Louis, Connolly was convinced there was enough to bring in Tom Capano. Just two days after talking to Louis, Connolly brought in Bob Donovan, the lead investigator. Donovan, who'd put in some sixteen months going after Capano, could sense the excitement. He filled out a twenty-nine-page affidavit and signed it. It outlined the basis of charging Tom Capano with murdering Anne Marie Fahey.

Now all that was left was to bring in Tom Capano.

Tom awoke the morning of Wednesday, November 12, 1997, at his mother's house as he had almost every day since Annie's disappearance, and went about his daily routine.

Joe Hurley, a flamboyant and well-known local criminal attorney, who had been hired by Capano to lead his growing defense team, awoke that morning to the disturbing news that the federal government finally intended to arrest his client. Hurley, Charles Oberly, and a third attorney hired by Capano, Eugene Maurer—another well-known and affable local attorney—had been prepared for the government to arrest Capano, but none knew when it would fall. When they found out the federal government was ready, Hurley's only request was that he be allowed to bring Capano in himself. But after sixteen months of tortuous investigation and stonewalling by Capano, the FBI and Connolly were not obliged to let Hurley have his way.

They pulled Capano over on I-95 while he was driving to the airport with his brother Joseph and his brother's wife. He was quickly and quietly arrested for the murder of Anne Marie Fahey and then taken to Gander Hill prison. He put up no fight. In handcuffs he was led out before the television cameras as a prisoner for the first time. Instead of his ubiquitous suit and tie, he looked somber wearing a jogging suit.

Afterward Hurley met reporters outside the prison. At the time of the arrest Gerard Capano's confession became public knowledge, but Hurley was ready. He said Gerard Capano had made up the entire story about dumping a body at sea, and Tom Capano would plead not guilty. Hurley's client, facing a potential death penalty trial in the murder of Anne Marie Fahey, was in shock. He could not understand his brother's betrayal.

"How could he do this to me?" Capano asked Hurley.

Ferris Wharton, who'd taken a backseat for seventeen months while the federal government put together the case, was brought back. The federal government had made the case, but it would be up to the state to prosecute. The charges that were filed were state charges. Wharton would be the lead prosecutor, and Connolly would be brought in to assist him.

Wharton viewed the high drama of Capano's arrest with the disinterested eyes of a man who'd been out of the loop. Consequently, he watched everything closely. One of the things he remembers most was what happened when Hurley and Capano were brought into an interrogation room with himself, Connolly, and Donovan.

They played some of the audiotapes of Gerry's and Louis's

confessions. They also provided Hurley with a transcript of what the prosecution had recorded. "The room was absolutely silent," Wharton said. "It was just those tapes and nothing else. Then Joe (Hurley) pulled out this highlighter and he was marking through things that Gerry said on the tape. So now you just have those tapes, silence, and occasionally the squeaking coming from Joe Hurley's marker. It must've drove Capano nuts, because he finally reached over and grabbed Hurley's hand and said, 'Stop it.' Joe then put down his highlighter and got out a pen and kept marking through the transcript."

It was Wharton's first insight into what he called Capano's controlling and fastidious nature. Wharton eventually came to believe that "Tom Capano will be the first guy to be sentenced to death who will argue about what vein they're going to use when they give him the lethal injection."

Now that Capano was in custody, Connolly, Wharton, Donovan, and the rest of the prosecutorial team had loose ends to tie up. They interviewed everyone whom Gerard Capano said he and his older brother interacted with on the day they dumped Annie's body at sea. They got still pictures from the bank where Tom Capano had withdrawn money from an ATM that same morning. Donovan reinterviewed many of the witnesses and continued his hunt for others.

While on this search for additional evidence, Connolly and Donovan ran across a piece of paper that Capano had given to a member of his law firm. It amounted to a well-choreographed alibi in the form of a time line that gave a detailed account of Capano's activities on June 27, 1996. The alibi, which paralleled instructions Tom Capano gave to his younger brother Gerry, had some problems. Many of the things Capano claimed he did on that day prosecutors could already prove were lies. Some of the other activities were highly suspect. Prosecutors said it was a masterful weaving of fact and fiction. According to Capano's highly detailed one-page time line and its nine-page supporting document, Capano was very busy on June 27, 1996.

In his alibi Capano admits he met with his brother Gerry, saw his wife, Kay, ran on a nearby track, saw his longtime mistress Deborah MacIntyre, as well as Louis, and visited the automated money machine, where a picture of him had been taken. But he also claimed he met his sister, Marian, and his mother, and had lunch with Gerry and discussed a business deal—even looking at a piece of property together. Then by 5 P.M., according to his alibi, he did dump the love seat, then went to his wife's house for dinner. The time line dovetailed nicely with what Gerard Capano said his brother told him to say, and what Gerard put down on a Post-it note. Connolly and Donovan were even convinced some of it was the truth, because Capano could not explain away certain facts. However, their investigation had established that many of the things Capano claimed he did, he, in fact, did not do.

By now Connolly had a strong circumstantial case against Capano, but there was little direct evidence of the crime Capano was accused of committing. There was no murder weapon. Most of the forensic evidence at Capano's home, where he was suspected of killing Annie, had been sanitized or removed. The couch and the sofa were gone, and except for a few stray drops of Annie's blood, there was nothing to show a violent crime had occurred in Capano's great room. There wasn't even a body. Capano and his brother had gotten rid of that, too. It was a problem that would plague the prosecution for the duration of their investigation and the trial that followed it. There was a very real possibility, Connolly conceded, that Capano could beat the charges against him.

But there were things working in the prosecution's favor, as well. For perhaps the first time in his life, Capano could not completely control things. Capano, a man who thrived on interacting with people, was reduced to living in a small jail cell. Prison spokesman Anthony J. Farina said Capano was given a physical examination and had to speak with mental health counselors upon his arrival at Gander Hill. Afterward he was issued his prison whites (a white jumpsuit) and placed in protective custody.

Capano, the man who once claimed to a mistress that he owned Wilmington, a man who was used to dining in the finest restaurants and traveling the world at his leisure, was now confined to a 7-by-10-foot cell twenty-three hours a day. Once a day for an hour he got out for recreation. Farina said it wasn't punishment for Capano but a precaution to protect him from other inmates, like a man named "Squeaky" Saunders, whom Capano had put behind bars for murder. The psychological weight of Capano's imprisonment began working on him from his first day inside Gander Hill. But in the beginning, Charles Oberly, one of Capano's attorneys, said his client was just worried about his family. "His number one concern is his four daughters and the impact it's having on them and his mother," Oberly said. Louis Capano said the arrest would likely kill his mother. Tom, the good son, had dutifully taken care of her since his father's death. What would happen now?

In Wilmington, the news of Capano's arrest was met with a variety of emotions: relief, disbelief, and in some cases cautious euphoria. The Faheys, who'd suffered since Annie's disappearance, heaved a sigh of relief as they found themselves over one of their biggest hurdles.

"To say this has been an emotional day would be a gross understatement," said David Weiss, the family's attorney. "The family has run the gamut of emotions, from a sense of relief to absolute horror at learning what they learned today."

What they learned was the story, as of yet untold to the public in any great detail, of the day Annie died, and how Gerry and his brother Tom dumped the body at sea. "We really had faith all along that there would be an indictment," Annie's older brother Brian said. "But we really just took it on faith. We all took a sigh when he was finally arrested."

But the sigh gave way to shock as the grizzly details came out. The local newspaper described Kathy, who was expecting at the time, clasping her hands "beneath her pregnant belly," and wringing them silently as David Weiss talked about the details that came out about Annie's death. "We were shocked, no doubt," Robert Fahey said. "Colm Connolly said to have faith in him and we did, but we didn't find out anything, none of the details beforehand. It was hard."

Brian Fahey said he found out when he left work early on November 12 and met with his other brothers and sisters at their attorney's office. Just before Connolly went public, he briefed the family on what he could about their sister's murder.

Waiting to find out what had happened, Brian later said, was excruciating. On the stand he said he wondered openly what her last moments were like. "Was she afraid? Did she know what was going to happen to her?" He had felt, as his older brother Mark and indeed his whole family had, protective and responsible for their youngest sibling.

They'd spent the last seventeen months paying tribute to Annie: Kathy raising money for Annie's favorite charities— Creative Grandparenting and the Ministry of Caring. They held a private mass and dinner on the first anniversary of her disappearance. They had also dedicated a park bench to Annie in the park so close to her home where some 300 of her friends and neighbors had searched for her that Fourth of July weekend in 1996.

Through it all they'd struggled to make sure their sister would not be forgotten. Soon that would become even a more monumental task as the lurid details of Tom Capano's life became front-page news. But for the day of the arrest, there was, at least, some small amount of relief.

Kevin Freel had a private dinner and shared drinks with the Faheys that day on the second floor of his pub. With a mist in his eyes he remembered Capano's arrest and his own determination to see the case through. "I just wanted everybody involved brought to justice," he said as he shook his head. Then he turned and looked up. "The sad thing is that no one covering this trial, not one reporter, will ever know the person that brought us here. No offense, but I wish I'd never met any of you. You will never know what we lost when we lost Annie."

That sentiment was echoed in the Governor's office, where Annie worked. In the days after her disappearance her coworkers say they had been in a state of shock. "It was too quiet," one of Governor Carper's closest aides said. "We knew she wasn't coming back. But we watched the case closely, very closely, and there was a considerable amount of relief when Capano was arrested."

It was almost unbelievable in Wilmington social circles. Many of the power elite had come to believe that something had gone horribly wrong between Annie and Capano, many more believed he'd killed her. But few believed he would ever be arrested.

"He told a friend of mine that it would all blow over in a couple of months," Kevin Freel said. "And until the federal government got involved, I believed it, too. But it was a big relief when he got arrested. Just a big sigh."

On the Capano side of the family there was shock. They still did not know exactly what had happened, but Marguerite still believed in her son's innocence. "You write in that book that my son was a good son. He would never do those things they said he did."

Equally stunned was younger brother Louis whose testimony, in part, helped authorities to put Tom Capano behind bars. The day after Tom's arrest Louis released a statement through his lawyer, which was delivered to the media. In it Louis said he voluntarily contacted federal authorities and provided the information and cooperation that led to his brother's arrest. Louis also admitted to signing a plea agreement and pled guilty to a misdemeanor charge for harassing a grand jury witness. He also said he had no direct knowledge of Tom's actions on the night of the murder, and admitted he misled the authorities but did so because he thought Tom was innocent. After he found out otherwise (after Gerry told him about the boat trip), Louis said he then tried to persuade Tom to come forward.

"Saddened by the whole thing, Louis Capano in the past acted out of loyalty to his family, but more importantly he acts now out of concern for doing the right thing," the letter concluded.

But Louis wasn't around the day his brother was arrested. He was in Phoenix with his wife, pro-golfer Lauri Merten. She, too, released a statement: "I wish to say I support my husband at this difficult time for our family. At the same time, and as has been true throughout this ordeal, my prayers are also with the Faheys."

Gerard, who'd supplied the most damning evidence against his brother, had no comment. But he did help prosecutors further. He agreed to search with Coast Guard and Navy officials for Annie's remains. It meant a gruesome reliving of that nightmarish morning with his big brother Tom when they took *The Summer Wind* out to sea, but Gerard had to face it—he'd also made a deal with the prosecutor.

The U.S. Coast Guard loaned the search party a 180-foot cutter, and Navy divers searched the ocean floor in the commercial shipping lanes Gerard said he'd taken his boat more than a year previously. Officials began asking fishermen and owners of commercial trawlers if they had spotted Gerard Capano's boat on June 27, 1996, or if they noted anything unusual that day near 73.9 west longitude and 39.5 north latitude. But the search and the requests turned up nothing.

At this point Connolly had enough to arrest and charge Tom Capano with murder, but Capano's attorneys had good reason to be convinced there wasn't enough to convict. After all, there was no body. There was no case prior to this in Delaware history where a jury had convicted someone of murder without having a body.

Joe Hurley and Charles Oberly made sure that point was stressed in the newspapers. They also scoffed at the blood evidence found at Capano's home, as well as the fact that it had been made public at this point that Gerard Capano had recently sold a boat without an anchor. "We have the anchor and will be able to produce it at trial," Hurley said, adding that he had a registration record that would prove the anchor came from the boat.

As for the blood evidence, Oberly said it would not be unusual—without going into lurid details—for a woman with whom Capano had intimate relations to leave a tiny amount of blood in his home.

Hurley said all the circumstantial evidence couldn't prove Anne Marie was dead. "The young lady hasn't shown up, but that's a far cry from proving this guy did something," he told local reporters.

On November 13 that dynamic changed forever. Connolly remembers it well. He was at his office with FBI investigator Alpert and other members of the investigating team.

Alpert was sitting at his desk when the phone rang and he picked it up.

"I'll never forget that," Connolly recalls. "He was sitting at a desk and we were watching. And we heard him say 'bullet hole' and 'cooler.' We knew right away it was the cooler, and we had never made public in the arrest warrant about the cooler being shot. So we knew we had the cooler," Connolly said.

"It was heaven-sent," Robert Fahey later said. "I firmly believe Tom Capano never figured on the federal government getting involved in the case, and I firmly believe that he never counted on the cooler being found. It was as if it was put there by God."

But God didn't give the cooler to the prosecution. That came from a friend of Kenneth Chubb's, who upon watching the local television news thought the story Gerry Capano told the prosecution sounded eerily familiar. He called Chubb and told him Colm Connolly was looking for his cooler.

The next day Donovan went out to investigate and found the cooler sitting in a shed. The holes caused by the shotgun slug entering and exiting the cooler were filled with epoxy. There was a new lid on it and it looked like it had more wear on it than when Gerry Capano saw it last, but Donovan was convinced it was the crucial piece of direct evidence the prosecution had been waiting for.

The cooler was retrieved and taken in for study. A square was cut out of the cooler that contained the bullet holes. That portion of the cooler was tested and those tests showed traces of lead and some minute traces of a red fabric. The Faheys had said a red running outfit from her apartment was missing the night Annie disappeared. No traces of Annie's blood were found, but the cooler had been used extensively in the seventeen months since her disappearance, and no traces were expected to be found. As for the cooler itself, Chubb, when questioned by authorities, relayed the story he would later tell in court. He found the cooler floating in the ocean and wondered who would've shot up a perfectly good cooler. He decided he'd take it, repair it, and replace the lid. It was cheaper than buying a new one. The find was important to the prosecution, and devastating to Capano.

"I could argue all around this case," Capano attorney Joe Oteri later said. "But I just couldn't get around that cooler."

Gerry Capano had been proven right. He remembered details so vividly about the day he'd gone to sea with Tom that he even remembered the hinges that held on the cooler top were Phillips-head screws. He remembered distinctly taking them off so he could heave the cooler and the cooler top into the sea. Prosecutors corroborated that piece of testimony when they found the cooler, which had briefly served as Annie's coffin.

A day after the cooler was found, Delaware attorney general

M. Jane Brady officially assigned Wharton to the case and deputized Connolly to assist him.

The preliminary hearing was scheduled in municipal court on November 20. On December 22, the New Castle County grand jury indicted Tom Capano for murdering Anne Marie Fahey.

A day later, Judge William Swain Lee was assigned the case.

A down-to-earth sort with a wry sense of humor, Judge Lee has more than a passing resemblance to actor Orson Bean. Thin and with an aquiline nose, he has an infectious laugh and struggled hard during the course of the trial to keep things in control.

He has served on the superior court since 1986, following a decade as a family court judge. Before that, he was both a successful prosecutor and a politically connected private attorney.

He did not hail from Wilmington. He came from rural Sussex County, near the coast, and was reported to frequent a couple of nightspots near Rehoboth Beach, where his sense of humor and storytelling ability made him a local celebrity.

All who know him said he was just the type of "level head" that was needed in the Capano trial. He proved to be not only levelheaded, but exceedingly fair. Attorneys on both sides of the case commended him for the way he conducted himself during the Capano trial.

"This is a judge who lets you try your case," Joe Oteri later said. "This judge is very fair. I've worked with a lot of them and I can tell you, you won't find a fairer judge."

Lee was a privileged child, born on December 18, 1935, the son of a doctor. He grew up believing in the *Ozzie and Harriet* cliches of modern American life. "I hear people say Ozzie and Harriet weren't real," Lee told a local reporter. "I'm sorry, but it was real where I grew up."

He grew up in a town of fewer than 2,000 people, and he thought he got to know them all. He went to Duke University, where he got his bachelor of arts degree, then attended the University of Pennsylvania law school.

Lee said he learned about discipline when he joined the Marine Corps and found his education and pedigree meant nothing to those people who ruled over him in the Corps. "They didn't care who I was or how smart I was or how nice and friendly I was. I couldn't talk my way out of situations in the Corps. I either had to put up or shut up. I learned, though, that there was nothing I couldn't accomplish if I put my mind to it."

Lee is no stranger to controversy or big cases. As a prosecutor he tried one of the most infamous murder cases in Delaware history, where a black trash collector raped and killed a fifteen-year-old baby-sitter. The case became infamous in Delaware not only for its brutal nature, but because of its racial overtones.

A Republican, he was also at the center of a controversy involving former Governor Russell Peterson. Peterson was challenged by Attorney General David P. Buckson, one of Lee's distant cousins. Lee was his campaign manager and drew censure from his own party after he accused the governor of lying and cheating to get votes.

In 1977 he was tapped by Governor Sherman W. Tribbit, who defeated Peterson in the previous election, to serve on the family court as a judge. Lee proved he could get into controversy there, too, when he jailed an attorney for six hours—an attorney who attended the same church as Lee. The jailing, according to the incarcerated attorney, was unprecedented. In 1986 Capano's good friend, Governor Michael Castle, appointed Lee to the superior court, where he's been ever since.

When he was assigned the Capano case, he had no idea what he was in for. He did set up some ground rules early on to make sure things went smoothly.

"I decided to have morning meetings with the attorneys involved prior to court each day," he said. "There is a selfish reason for that, I keep myself informed and involved. But, more importantly in a case like this where a man's life is at stake, things can become very heated. I decided early on that we would try to forge a working relationship between the attorneys. They had to be adversaries in court, but I believe that can be done professionally and without animosity.''

For the most part it worked, attorneys on both sides said, unbelievably well. The atmosphere in court on many occasions got extremely heated and emotional. At times it was confrontational, but the lawyers never let the animosity get personal. They remained cordial to each other throughout a very long and difficult trial.

On January 8, 1998, Capano pled not guilty and asked for bail. Connolly and Wharton opposed it, and Lee said for the first time that it would appear that the state would seek the death penalty. This was because in the state of Delaware, the prosecution can only oppose bail if the prosecutor intends to seek the death penalty.

Charles Oberly was ready for that, however, and using an argument similar to one he'd made in another capital murder trial, tried to get Capano released on bail by conducting an end-run around the "proof positive hearing," the name given to bail hearings in Delaware. But the argument did not convince Judge Lee and he went ahead with the bail hearing.

Before that could come about, in early February, Connolly and Wharton continued to pursue the case. They still did not know for sure what had happened the night Annie died, and they said they probably never would. They wanted to interview again Deborah MacIntyre, one of Capano's other mistresses. Since finding out Capano had placed a call to her the day after Annie died, and since he also mentioned in his alibi seeing her the morning after Annie's death, the prosecutors had been extremely curious as to what knowledge MacIntyre had about Annie's disappearance and if MacIntyre had anything to do with it. But by the time the bail hearing rolled around in February,

Connolly and Wharton didn't feel comfortable yet with Mac-Intyre, and they didn't call her as a witness.

Capano was also interested in MacIntyre as a witness. He was convinced she could help him get bail. The quiet school administrator was a solid character witness, Capano and his attorneys said, but they didn't call her, either.

There were many others who did make it to the bail hearing. It began with Delaware State Police lieutenant Mark Daniels showing how determined Capano was to cast blame elsewhere. Capano apparently had kept in close contact with Kim Horstmann, Annie's close friend. On July 11 she met Capano to try and figure out what happened to Annie.

"He was saying there were all kinds of rumors about the governor, about Anne Marie having an affair with the governor when they worked in Washington. He didn't know if they were true," Daniels said on the stand, repeating Horstmann's testimony before a grand jury.

Horstmann also said Fahey told her she never had any extramarital affairs except with Tom Capano. Capano also mentioned to Horstmann there was a state trooper who had been harassing Annie and a neighbor. Capano said the trooper wanted to show Annie nude photos he'd taken of himself. Capano also mentioned a man who'd been a coworker of Annie's at T.G.I. Friday's restaurant whom he intimated may have caused harm to befall Annie.

Capano couldn't name those people, but he did predict three possible scenarios as to how Annie's disappearance would play itself out: Fahey would return home unharmed; her body would be found and evidence would point to the killer; or no body would be found and Carper would pressure police to make an arrest by Labor Day in 1996.

"I'm going to be the fall guy," Capano told her.

Other friends of Annie's painted Capano in front of the grand jury and during subsequent hearings as a controlling, jealous, obsessive man intent on using whatever means he could to keep Annie under his control. One friend even said Capano invented a story about his daughter having brain surgery to win Fahey's sympathy. When Daniels brought forth that testimony two of Capano's daughters sitting in court looked at each other and raised their eyebrows.

Annie was described as a Catholic woman wracked by guilt over her affair with a married man and fearful of Capano because he'd begun to terrorize her. Annie was mortified when Capano told her parish priest about their affair. "She couldn't go back to church, she was so embarrassed," Horstmann told the grand jury.

Capano's ability to embarrass and anger Annie and even her siblings was one of the surprises that seemed to be a theme during the bail hearing. Capano apparently told Horstmann that he cared for Annie more than her own brother. He said Annie had purchased two books about bulimia and given one to Capano and one to her brother Robert. Capano said he read his in one night, but Robert hadn't bothered to read it at all. That angered Robert, who was sitting in on the hearing. He shook his head angrily and later told reporters he had indeed read the book. But Capano saved his greatest venom for attacking the way Annie had been brought up.

"You're nothing but white (Irish) trash. You should be lucky I'm interested in you. I can give you anything you want," Capano apparently told Annie.

That testimony revealed a seldom-spoken, but certainly well-implied dynamic of the entire case. The Faheys were working-class Irish-Catholics. The Capanos were upper-class Italian-Catholics. Both communities are well-defined in Wilmington and have had conflicts in the past. The Capano case was about to acerbate an age-old cultural and ethnic division.

It began when Capano's comments about Annie were made public. It certainly didn't end there. The town became heavily divided. There were bars and restaurants where it was safe for Capano fans to attend and those that were safe only for those who sympathized with the Fahey family. Few local denizens braved both sides of that street. When they did, occasionally arguments and fisticuffs ensued.

On the second day of the bail hearing Louis Capano, Jr., took the stand and talked about how Tom told him he'd thrown a gun away within three days of Annie's disappearance.

The drama reached a fever pitch when Gerard Capano took the stand. Wearing a dark sports coat, bright tie, and light khaki slacks, Gerard walked into court with his attorney, Edmund D. Lyons, Jr., and took a seat on the witness chair.

For the first time the public heard of the events the morning after Annie's disappearance. Gerard Capano told about the cooler, the locks and chains, as well as the story about extortionists. Gerard captivated the courtroom with the bizarre details, which included Gerard offering his older brother a gun, Tom's concerns about his daughters, and the request by the elder Capano to find a "leg breaker" to take care of the extortionists. But the boat ride was the most compelling evidence the audience heard that day.

Gerry was scared he was going to ruin his life, but his big brother Tom reassured him everything was going to be okay. "Everything would be fine," Tom told him. Gerry Capano reiterated that pledge in a courtroom brimming with hostility against him, his older brother, and the entire Capano family.

Joe Hurley then tried to hammer Gerry on the cross-examination. Tom Capano sat ashen-faced and silent as the lawyer, whom he'd hired to defend him on murder, began attacking his own little brother. Hurley accused Gerry of lying, inventing stories, and being a hopeless drug addict.

"Everything would be fine," Tom had told him.

Where was protective Tom Capano now? Gerry's protective older brother was not around, and there was a real concern by the prosecution as to whether Gerard could handle Hurley's expert grilling. Gerry surprised a few as he readily admitted using and abusing drugs. He talked about many years of cocaine, alcohol, and marijuana abuse. He confessed that many times during the last two years after Annie's death he had self-medicated to reduce his pain. But to the prosecution's relief his credibility as a witness held up—at least the judge seemed to believe Gerry was telling the truth about the boat ride.

The prosecution went to great pains to show that Tom Capano had meticulously planned to kill Annie because their relationship had soured. They used Gerard and testimony about extortionists to show that.

The defense brought out testimony that Capano had planned to golf with fellow lawyers on June 28, 1996, the same day Gerard said he and his brother were at sea. Capano didn't make that outing, but at the very least the attorneys were trying to show that Capano had no plans for June 27 and 28 that included dumping bodies at sea.

The defense also tried to rebut the prosecution's claim that Gerard sold his boat without an anchor—even though the anchor was wrapped around Annie and sitting at the bottom of the Atlantic. Michael K. Caputo of Arundel testified he purchased the boat from Gerard Capano for $27,000 without the anchor because Gerard said he'd put that and other safety equipment in a new boat he'd purchased.

"Did you walk around the boat and look at it?" Charles Oberly asked.

Well, not exactly, but Caputo said Gerard told him it was a good ship and "he had it out sixty miles." Joe Hurley had promised to produce the anchor and a receipt to show it belonged to Gerry's boat. They never showed.

Joey Capano made his debut on his brother's behalf during the bail hearing. Joey told the court that Tom Capano bought the cooler for his brother Gerry as a present.

"Tom wanted to get Gerry something to thank him for all the effort he's put into taking Tom's children out during the summer months in Stone Harbor, jet-skiing, boating, and things of that nature—for both the '95 season and the upcoming (at that time) '96 season,'' Joey said.

Joey also said Tom bought the cooler in April or May of 1996, and it was upon Joey's suggestion that Tom did so. Joey said he thought it would go well with a new boat Gerry was thinking of buying.

It sounded innocent enough, but Detective Bob Donovan said, as he got on the witness stand, that Gerry told him he hadn't received any presents from Tom since he was a small child. Kay Capano told Detective Donovan that she was unaware of any presents given to Gerry during the last five years.

The spectacle of the bail hearing was unprecedented in Delaware, at least according to the judge. After Charles Oberly closed, Judge Lee felt compelled to speak.

"Thank you, Mr. Oberly. Quite frankly, in a proof positive hearing, I've never had such an extensive defense presentation. Therefore, I'm not exactly sure whether I ought to offer the state an opportunity to present rebuttal testimony or not."

"Well, Your Honor, we would like the opportunity to do so. I can promise it will be very, very brief,'' Colm Connolly said.

Judge Lee capitulated. Capano was denied bail. Later in the month Capano was also denied a new bail hearing.

The local media were predicting that it was all over for Capano, as were local attorneys. "The ship's going down,'' said Wilmington criminal lawyer Michael W. Modica.

It would be another eight months before Capano would have to go to trial. Judge Lee set the date for jury selection in early October. Tom Capano would have many months to cool his heels while both sides prepared for the main event.

At this point it seemed as if the Capano story might fade from the headlines for a while. But, once again, the strange case would get stranger. And it all began with a woman named Deborah MacIntyre.

Chapter 8

"Little Mac"—The Debby Factor

Deborah MacIntyre once dreamed of swimming the English Channel. Instead she got to swim through the deepest, darkest portions of the Tom Capano case for more than two years of her life. During this period she exposed the most intimate, and as many attorneys described it, sometimes disgusting details of her life in such a way that even veteran police and prosecutors were made to blush.

Much of it, prosecutors claimed, was of her own making. It took her months to come around to believing that Tom Capano was guilty of murder—and even then she seemed to hedge her bets. She only believed it for real after she found out Capano had plotted to have her home broken into and after a Gander Hill inmate told prosecutors that Capano asked him to kill both Gerry Capano and Deborah MacIntyre.

She was, as she later said publicly and privately, madly and deeply in love with Tom Capano. She had schemed with him for years, first behind the back of Tom's wife, Kay, and then later plotting to eventually marry him.

The lurid aspects of this quiet school administrator's life became public for the first time at Tom Capano's bail hearing. However, Detective Bob Donovan and prosecutors Colm Connolly and Ferris Wharton had known about her from the beginning of the case.

Telephone records showed that Capano placed a phone call to MacIntyre's home within two hours of the time police believe he killed Annie. At some point in time her involvement with Tom Capano, especially on the day Annie was murdered, was of extreme importance. What did MacIntyre know? When did MacIntyre know it? Did she herself have anything to do with Annie's death? What exactly was her involvement with Capano?

These were all questions Detective Donovan as well as Connolly and Wharton had to ponder as they prepared their case. But, there was something the general public would not come to know about until the bail hearing: MacIntyre bought the gun that killed Anne Marie Fahey.

That stunning announcement came before a packed courtroom. Neither the prosecution nor the defense would call MacIntyre as a witness at the bail hearing, but according to testimony by FBI Agent Eric Alpert, MacIntyre bought a .22-caliber Beretta pistol on May 15, 1996, just six short weeks before Annie died. At first MacIntyre lied about it, saying she'd bought it two years earlier and then threw it away in a trash can. Only Tom Capano, she said, knew she bought the gun.

MacIntyre, formerly Kay Capano's good friend, at first had lied to a grand jury and said she did not become romantically involved with Capano until late 1995. She'd then decided to come clean and told investigators all about the 1981 moped ride she took and the subsequent sex in Capano's den. Finally, the phone-call information came out. Tom Capano called MacIntyre within two hours of the time the prosecution was saying he'd killed Annie.

* * *

Deborah Ann MacIntyre, the second of four children, grew up in Wilmington's Highlands, a comfortable, upper-middle-class enclave. She was a protected child, she said. Her father, William R. MacIntyre, Jr., was general manager of Joseph Bancroft & Sons Co., a worldwide textile company with a mill on the Brandywine River. Her grandfather was the president. Her family was well-off and athletic. She herself was an athlete and enjoyed rooting for the Green Bay Packers. "My great uncle, Don (Miller), was one of the Four Horsemen," she said with a disarming and charming bit of pride. Her uncle Creighton Miller was also an All-American halfback at Notre Dame. "I just grew up cheering with my dad at football games. It was part of our family."

MacIntyre, known at Tatnall High School as "Little Mac" (where she eventually would become an administrator until dismissed during the Capano debacle), played field hockey and lacrosse, chaired the athletic committee, and wrote for the school newspaper. She swam for the country club to which her family belonged. Her high school yearbook stated she would be remembered for her parties, record collection, and sparkle. She loved driving around in her Fiat.

She married her high school sweetheart, David H. Williams, the quiet son of a prominent Wilmington attorney. Williams co-captained the football team. After they married, they briefly moved to Pennsylvania, but after Williams got his law degree they moved back to join his family law firm: Morris, James, Hitchens & Williams—where a young Tom Capano also worked.

Williams filed for divorce in 1984. MacIntyre did not contest it.

Instead, she bought a $255,000 old farmhouse just blocks away from Tom Capano's home.

By then, according to testimony later offered in court, she'd already been having an affair with Capano for close to four years.

Her testimony was eagerly sought by the investigators, and on numerous occasions Bob Donovan had interviewed her. As early as July 23, 1996, MacIntyre met with police investigators at Wilmington Police headquarters. She came with Adam Balick, an attorney handpicked to represent her by Tom Capano. MacIntyre told Donovan and the other investigators that Capano was just a "very good friend," whom she had known for twenty years. She said she talked with him every day and saw him once or twice a week. He had never talked about Anne Marie Fahey.

On that day police already knew MacIntyre had called Capano on June 27, 1996, around 10:30 P.M. They learned she'd left a message on his answering machine. Tom Capano, she claimed, had called her about an hour later and they talked for about five minutes—or rather argued. "It was a bad conversation," she told Donovan.

That didn't sit well with MacIntyre. "I had been under the control of my father when I was a little girl and then I got married to a controlling man and then I left him and went with Tom Capano and he was another controlling man. I was used to it," she later said.

She was used to it, and couldn't let it rest. She called Capano back shortly after midnight. When he did not pick up the phone she hung up without leaving a message. Shortly thereafter she received a return call from Capano, who apparently had used the *69-feature Bell Atlantic offers its customers.

He asked why she'd hung up on him and they eventually made up.

The next morning MacIntyre said she saw Tom on her way to work. Capano was walking at a track nearby. That was between 8 A.M. and 8:30 A.M. on June 28.

As for the call the police were aware of the morning Annie was dumped at sea, MacIntyre said she later heard from Capano around 10:30 A.M. when he called her at work and told her he was playing golf at the Wilmington Country Club with a friend, Dave McBride.

She also claimed to have talked to Capano around 5:30 that afternoon and spoke with him on the phone the following day. On Sunday, she told Donovan, Capano stopped by her house at 1 P.M. but didn't say anything about the investigation. He came by again after he took his children back to Kay's house and told MacIntyre that the cops had been to his house and searched it. Capano, she said, was extremely upset and said he was "being set up." MacIntyre didn't ask what he was being set up for, and Capano didn't tell her.

By her words she didn't find out until Tuesday, July 2, 1996. Capano called her at work that day around 3 P.M. and told her for the first time that he was the one that had been out to dinner with Anne Marie Fahey.

All very interesting testimony and certainly relevant—Donovan said those were some of his thoughts after that meeting. But soon investigators would find there were gaping holes and contradictions in MacIntyre's statements.

After she testified, and later admitted lying to the federal grand jury, Donovan felt compelled to go back to her. On February 4, 1997, he found that she had bought Capano some blood and stain remover—apparently right after Fahey's death. Why had she done this? MacIntyre said Tom "bleeds anally due to his colitis and gets blood on his boxer shorts as he bleeds from his anus."

How wonderful, the investigators thought. Rarely, they said, had they been treated to such graphic descriptions of a suspect's most intimate habits. Still, Donovan and Connolly weren't convinced MacIntyre was telling the truth.

Also in that February interview MacIntyre said she only started dating Capano in September 1995. Deputy Attorney General Keith Brady was, as MacIntyre implied on that day, a witness to the platonic nature of their relationship in the summer of 1995 as he was at her house during that time with Capano "to have a drink."

She then admitted that she had sex with Tom Capano on that day, not saying whether or not it was before or after Keith Brady showed up. But the point was she was caught in another lie. She then admitted to the investigators that she had sex with Capano at other times before September 1995. She also admitted that she and Capano liked to watch movies together, but at that time she only admitted to watching *Agony and the Ecstasy* and *Braveheart* with him.

Again, the investigators left that meeting not at all convinced MacIntyre had told them the whole truth. They'd caught her in a lie about her sexual relationship with Tom Capano and suspected she was lying about much more. By the end of February, though, 1998 investigators had put enough pressure on MacIntyre that they believed she was beginning to tell the truth about crucial elements to her story.

While in the past she'd said she bought a gun and then later threw it away, by February she came forward and said Capano had asked her to purchase a gun for him. This had only come after the ATF records had been retrieved and shown to her, along with the purchase receipt for the gun.

The Fahey family was encouraged by MacIntyre's testimony. Kathy told the press she found MacIntyre's previous story about throwing away a gun she'd bought hard to believe. She was also upset that it took MacIntyre some twenty months to come forward, but Kathy perceived MacIntyre's latest story as being a step in the right direction.

Charles Oberly, one of Capano's attorneys, wouldn't comment about MacIntyre's "latest version" of the truth until he reviewed it. Eugene Maurer, another attorney, was unimpressed with MacIntyre, to say the least. "She's changed her story before. Her credibility has to be suspect," he said.

Indeed her credibility was suspect. She later admitted to lying dozens of times. But her latest change of heart and change of story accompanied a change in attorneys. MacIntyre later confided that she was beginning to get scared in the early months of 1998. She wasn't entirely sure, anymore, that Tom Capano was innocent. She was even afraid she was somehow going to be drawn into the case. She dumped her attorney and found a new one, Tom Bergstrom.

This infuriated Tom Capano. He referred to Bergstrom on numerous occasions in court as "that loathsome attorney" and "the Malvern Malefactor" (Bergstrom's office and home is in Malvern, Pennsylvania), as well as numerous other condescending terms.

Capano was as angry as he ever had been to find out MacIntyre was leaving his sphere of control. For more than fifteen years Dave Williams had been divorced from Deborah MacIntyre. He never spoke publicly about why they divorced and certainly never appeared, after the divorce, to be friends with Tom Capano. It was he, the man MacIntyre had left to have a clandestine life with Capano, who recommended MacIntyre's new attorney. Coincidence or not, fifteen years after Capano took up with MacIntyre her former husband helped Tom Capano reap what he had sown.

Things were about to get a lot worse for Tom Capano. By the end of February, Deborah MacIntyre was no longer a Tom Capano confidante. She was a government witness and had signed an immunity deal.

On February 27, 1998, Colm Connolly's office drafted a letter to Tom Bergstrom that outlined the terms of the government's agreement with Deborah MacIntyre.

The first thing she had to state was that "she did not kill or conspire to kill or aid or abet the killing of Anne Marie Fahey. If that representation proved to be false, the government would not be bound by the terms of this Agreement." She also had to admit she made false statements to federal investigators, gave false testimony before the federal grand jury on September 10, 1996, made false statements on the ATF form she filled out when she purchased her handgun, and finally lied under oath on January 28, 1998, when interviewed under the edict of a Delaware attorney general's subpoena. There were numerous other stipulations, which included helping the federal government and being truthful.

The end result was that Deborah MacIntyre, for the first time since the early 1980s, was not under the influence of Tom Capano. This not only angered Capano when he found out, but would cause MacIntyre a load of trouble, as well.

She and Capano had been exchanging correspondence since he'd gone to jail. They continued to do so now, and every letter they wrote would come under the scrutiny of the federal government. They certainly showed, the attorneys argued, Capano and MacIntyre at their best and worst. She openly bad-mouthed Colm Connolly, as did Capano. Their sexual dialogue rivaled the worst steamy *Penthouse* "Letter to the Editor" the prosecution showed. And Capano could be seen in these letters, Connolly made a point of arguing during the trial, as both threatening and trying to manipulate his former mistress.

There were also the telephone calls. MacIntyre recorded a series of calls Capano made to her from his jail cell in early 1998. These would come back to haunt him when he least needed it.

Slightly more than a month after MacIntyre fell under the protective wing of the federal government, lead defense attorney Joe Hurley asked to leave the case. He promised to take his reasons for doing so "to my grave." The request came on April 6 and was announced in court shortly thereafter.

"Are you in agreement with this decision, Mr. Capano?" Judge Lee asked.

"Yes, I am, Your Honor. It is a mutual decision, an amicable decision," Capano answered.

Hurley told the press he was saddened to leave the case. "I

have a friend that I see—tears in his eyes—and he's walking out the door and I'm not there to help him. The last thing he said to me is 'Are we still friends?' and I said, 'Yes.' "

Hurley, Oberly, and Maurer were concerned at this point with Capano's physical condition, which seemed to be eroding. "Today I saw somebody who shuffled around like an eighty-year-old man. It seems like he's lost fifteen to twenty pounds," Hurley said. Hurley then requested, as he had shortly after Capano had been incarcerated, for his client to be released into the general population of the prison, but that request was denied.

Jailers still saw the wealthy, powerful Capano as a risk if he were turned loose in the general population of the prison. The risk the jailers believed was that someone would hurt, or possibly kill, Capano. Putting Capano in the general population, "may jeopardize not only Mr. Capano's personal safety, but that of the other inmates and our staff," Department of Correction spokesman Anthony J. Farina told local reporters.

As for not eating, Farina said Capano was fed the same meals as the other 1,900 inmates at Gander Hill, and if he didn't want to eat, that was his decision. "He is getting screwed, screwed, screwed by the adult-correctional system," Hurley said.

Hurley was still convinced even if he was gone that Gene Maurer and Charles Oberly could provide Capano with the defense he needed. Capano, though, began interviewing replacement possibilities almost immediately. Celebrity Miami attorney Roy Black and Edwin J. Jacobs of Atlantic City were interviewed, but didn't for a variety of reasons, sign on with the case.

Black recommended another attorney he said could help Capano immeasurably: famed Boston lawyer Joe Oteri. Oteri, a sixty-seven-year-old lawyer from the northeast had made his reputation defending drug dealers and some alleged mafia associates. He was also a former consultant for *Playboy* magazine's "Forum" section.

"The reputation on him is impeccable," Chris Napalitano,

a *Playboy* editor, later said. "Those who've dealt with him here at the company say he's a tough, aggressive lawyer with a great sense of humor." Oteri is all that and much more. Until the Capano case, he'd never had a single client given the death penalty.

The next twist in the Capano case came from inside Gander Hill prison from the lips of a convicted felon: Tito Rosa. After it became public knowledge that Deborah MacIntyre had decided to cooperate with the prosecution, Capano apparently not only got upset, he decided to get even—and while he was at it, he had a score to settle with his little brother, too. That, at least, is the story Wilfredo "Tito" Rosa, a cocaine dealer, told the prosecutors. Rosa said Capano offered him $100,000 to arrange the murder of both MacIntyre and Gerard Capano.

On June 8 Oteri signed on to the case. On June 9 Tom Bergstrom, MacIntyre's attorney, and Dan Lyons, Gerard Capano's attorney, let it be known about the alleged murder-for-hire plots.

"Welcome to the case, Joe," Fahey friend Kevin Freel remembers thinking. Almost immediately Oteri was successful in getting the Rosa revelations banned from evidence. It was a huge victory for the defense, but also a muted one. While the information couldn't be used as evidence in Capano's murder trial, the state was still free to file charges against Capano for conspiring to kill his brother and former mistress.

At about the same time as the Rosa revelations, investigators got another break in the case. Another inmate in Gander Hill prison came forward: Nick Perillo. A habitual offender and burglar, Perillo came forward and said that Tom Capano wanted to hire him to burglarize Deborah MacIntyre's home. He also brought more than just his word with him to prosecutors; he brought maps and instructions written in Tom Capano's hand.

* * *

Another milestone was reached in the case on June 18, 1998, when a Delaware chancery court judge declared Anne Marie Fahey dead. It was an emotional day for her family.

Kathy Fahey-Hosey recounted how she had kept going back to Annie's apartment daily for a month after Annie's disappearance, hoping her sister would show up.

"One of us was always planning to be there. We just wanted to be there in case she might call or come home," she later said.

Kathy paid Annie's bills and rent, and as her guardian took care of her bank account. Kathy finally closed Annie's account on August 8, 1996, and at the end of the month moved all of Annie's belongings to her house. In June 1998 it became official. Annie was dead.

The next week, on June 25, just two days shy of the second anniversary of Annie's disappearance, the Faheys filed suit against Capano for wrongful death. Also included in the suit were Capano's three brothers. They were charged with conspiring to hide the slaying.

Two days later, on June 27, 1998, investigators made one last attempt to find Annie's remains. The search took place southeast of Stone Harbor, New Jersey. Members of the search team used a miniature submarine and were optimistic because a previous ocean scan using high-tech equipment had spotted items along the ocean floor that were thought to be an anchor and a chain.

"We had high hopes. It was a grisly search, for sure," a member of the search team later said. "We hoped we could just give something to the Faheys to bury. Think of that—all that pain and not being able to at least bury a loved one. It affected us all."

An anchor and chain were found. But they were not the same anchor and chain Gerry Capano gave to Tom that morning in

June 1996. No other searches took place. Over the months, there were rumors of Annie's remains washing up along the shores of Delaware and New Jersey. Tests were performed on a piece of skull some boys found, but Annie has never been found.

The Faheys not only lost her, but the ability to bury her, forever.

On August 18, 1998, Judge Lee held a suppression hearing to find out if the telephone conversations between Deborah MacIntyre and Tom Capano could be admitted as evidence. It was a hearing Capano did not want to attend, and Judge Lee struggled to understand why. "Again, I have no desire to pry into any personal feelings you have, but I want to know why a lawyer would not want to be present at the time that his counsel is attempting to suppress statements made by him when his presence could be very helpful in supporting that application," Judge Lee said.

Capano took a breath. "Okay. I'll explain in a moment why I'm speaking in the manner I am. First of all, I am disturbed that I have to be here today. I represented through my very competent counsel my position . . . the principal witness today is someone that I have very deep feelings about, and it will cause me greater distress to be in such close proximity to her . . . I was under the likely mistaken impression that she also had some feelings towards me . . . that is probably an imaginary thought, as I've come to find out in the last few days, but nevertheless I am somebody who keeps my promises. . . ." He continued to ramble and then he said the words that would haunt him for a considerable time to come, "This may be the only time you hear me speak, so I am going to take advantage of the few moments I have."

Capano then went on to admonish the judge and the adult-corrections system in the state of Delaware and complain that he would be a wreck because he was in withdrawal as he hadn't had his prescription mood-altering medications. Judge Lee, feeling inclined to respond to Capano's admonishment, then spoke: " . . . I understand why you don't want to be here, and while I don't feel the need to respond to your comments, I will.

" . . . You're wrong to say I'm not sympathetic to your needs. I certainly have no reason to see you treated other than as a worthwhile human being who needs, for very practical reasons . . . needs to be in good health, needs to be able to assist counsel.

"But I'm also not going to treat you any differently than I would any other prisoner in your situation." At this early stage, and indeed throughout the trial, Judge Lee bent over backward to try and be fair to Tom Capano. On almost every occasion, as even his attorneys later admitted, Capano reacted by throwing it back in the judge's face.

On this day he took the judge's kind words and responded by saying, "Your Honor is sadly naive." The nine months Capano had spent in solitary confinement were not meant to protect him, he said, but to break him. "And it has worked, by the way," Capano added. Capano's solitary confinement did not end that day, nor throughout the trial.

But Capano's attorneys did get a break. None of the tapes of Capano and Deborah MacIntyre talking on the telephone, which the prosecution had worked so hard to obtain, could be used at trial, unless Capano took the stand in his own defense.

In August, Capano was charged with three counts of criminal solicitation for allegedly planning to burglarize MacIntyre's home, as well as planning to kill her and his brother.

The last member of the defense team, Jack O'Donnell, joined up. Jack, a college friend of both Kay Capano (now Kay Ryan since the divorce) and Tom Capano, only signed up with the Capano team after Kay asked him to help out.

With twenty years of experience, O'Donnell specializes in death penalty cases and intended to try his best to help out an old friend. He recalled the day he met Capano in prison for the first time. "I came in to see him at Gander Hill and he was all smiles and said, 'What the hell are you doing here?' I said, 'You called?' " It wasn't the best of places nor times for a reunion between two college buddies, but the stage was now set.

Chapter 9

Let The Games Begin

When Joe Oteri was a young attorney, a rather infamous incident occurred to him outside of the courthouse in Boston. He'd represented the wife of a cop in a divorce case and as he walked down the courthouse steps with his client, he came face-to-face with his own mortality. His client's ex-husband greeted the pair on the steps of the courthouse with his loaded service revolver. The first shot grazed Oteri's nose and nicked his face. "I put all my Marine training to use that day. I dropped, I rolled, and went for cover."

He ended up under a car, but not before a second shot broke his leg, and a third shot pierced his body but miraculously missed all of his vital organs. His client wasn't so lucky. Her husband's first shot caused a fatal wound. As the gunman marched toward Oteri to finish him off, he heard his wife moan and that saved Oteri's life. The man turned, put another slug into his dying wife, and then used the last bullet on himself. "I learned something that day," Oteri said. "Never walk out of the courtroom with your client."

He learned something else, too. During the Capano trial he was asked which was more painful, getting shot or working the Capano case. "Working this case," Oteri said without hesitation. "Getting shot was over a lot quicker."

Oteri knew from the beginning he was going to spend a lot of time in Wilmington. He rented an apartment not too far from where most of the events that brought Capano to trial took place and shared that apartment with the other out-of-town member of the defense team, Jack O'Donnell.

O'Donnell and Oteri—one Irish, one Italian—were all smiles during the early days of the trial. They would go to one of the many Italian restaurants in Wilmington for dinner. O'Donnell could occasionally be seen at a local pub socializing and laughing.

But Wilmington, being what it is—small—and O'Donnell being what he is, gregarious and outgoing, there were a few times when the combination caused him problems. He ran into Mark Fahey at least twice.

"I tried to avoid the Faheys whenever possible," O'Donnell said. "But I couldn't avoid Mark. He's as social as I am. Finally I had to talk to him and let him know it was just professional, and if it had been my sister I would be as upset as he was. I never bad-mouthed her and I tried to respect the Faheys."

Finally, one night after closing arguments in the guilt-phase of the trial, O'Donnell and Mark Fahey made their peace at a local bar. Sinatra's "Summer Wind" was playing on the juke box, and Mark, who had suffered through many indignities during the trial at the hands of the defendant, reached a truce with O'Donnell. "I can respect him," Fahey said. "Hell, if we met under other circumstances we could've been friends."

It was a healing that was rare during the trial that rubbed the small community of Wilmington raw. No one knew that better than Capano's two local attorneys, Charles Oberly and Eugene Maurer. Oberly had been friends with Kevin Freel for years—they had even worked on political campaigns together, but after the trial they would no longer be friends. Eugene Maurer fared a little better and took great strides to let everyone know what he was doing was just a job.

After Capano had been found guilty, Maurer even approached Brian Fahey outside the courtroom one day to let Brian know how he felt. Pain is something with which Maurer is acutely in tune.

Maurer is one of Delaware's top criminal attorneys with almost twenty-five years of experience. He played college basketball and is a testicular cancer survivor, having beaten the odds at a young age.

Charles Oberly, the first attorney Capano hired, also knows something about pain. His professional career reached several high-water marks, including serving time as the state's attorney general. He also has, his friends say, a keen and sharp wit. He is the father of a teenage daughter, who was good friends with Capano's daughters, and he cares for a wife who suffers from multiple sclerosis. The Capano trial would test Oberly severely as he tried to care for his ailing wife and at the same time defend Capano.

As the trial got under way, court watchers were particularly interested to see how this strange team of attorneys would pull together for Capano. Oteri, the over-the-top Boston shark, came into town teasingly upset that a local newspaper described his suit as being "off the rack."

"Let me tell you something, I haven't bought anything off the rack in years," he said. At sixty-seven he looked trim and fit, and he made sure people understood that he gave up physical fitness the day he left the Marine Corps. "I promised myself three things when I left the Corps. I swore I would never stand in line for chow again; I would never sleep outside in a tent, and I would never exercise again."

Oberly became the group's note-taker. He sat through most of the proceedings with more than twenty large, black bound binders fanned out in front of him, frequently and furiously scribbling notes. O'Donnell interviewed most of the prison witnesses in the trial and handled most of the questions with the federal investigators. He also delivered the closing arguments in the penalty phase. Maurer handled MacIntyre and a host of other witnesses and was the first to advance a new theory to the jury as to what happened the night Annie died. Oteri handled Gerry Capano, Tom Capano, and the opening and closing statements in the guilt phase.

They began their courtroom work for Capano on October 6 as jury selection began. A total of 1,500 New Castle County citizens had been summoned. Five hundred were to report on October 6, 500 would appear a week later, and then finally the final 500 were to appear on October 19.

The trial began on a cool, overcast day, the same day the House voted to study the possibility of impeaching President William Jefferson Clinton. The impeachment was an event that seemed to dominate the attention of the world except in Wilmington, Delaware. This was Tom Capano's world, and even mentioning the impeachment during the proceedings was only done in context with how it had something to do with Tom Capano. A taxing process had begun, and even before Judge Lee could actually begin the process of weeding out undesirable jurors, a young woman in tears bolted out of the courtroom and threw herself on the ground.

"I can't do this. I can't do this," she said in huge rasping sobs.

Kathi Carlozzi, who picked up the nickname of "door warden" and worked as the court administrator throughout the trial, seemed stunned, as did the bailiffs and the local police standing guard outside of the courtroom to provide security. The Capano case was affecting everyone.

Inside the courtroom Capano appeared sporting a pale pallor and a prison haircut. Judge Lee sat stoically and proper on his bench and began trying to select jurors. Before that could happen, the judge was once again reminded that Capano was being ill-treated in prison. This time Capano was upset about the lack of medication. He was being fed a psychotropic soup of Wellbutrin, Xanex, and Paxil and hadn't received these medications in a timely fashion. Judge Lee smiled and assured Capano he would look into the matter.

The jury pool had been given a lengthy list of possible witnesses. There were no surprises. Many of the names had already been mentioned in countless news articles and television pieces since Annie had disappeared. Potential jurors would also be questioned about the possible witnesses. If there was a close association between the two that could cause problems on a jury, it would be the basis for removing a potential juror from the pool.

Those questions did not bog down the process too much, but the ones about whether the potential jurors had seen any media coverage of Annie's disappearance, and if they had— did they form an opinion based on that coverage and what was that opinion—began to slow it down considerably.

Judge Lee hoped to get through eight jurors an hour. He wasn't getting half that many on the first day of jury selection. The interruptions concerning Capano's medical condition didn't help. "The board of corrections doesn't care about our client," Oberly told the judge.

"We hear that all the time," Dr. Keith Ivens told reporters outside the courtroom. He was called into court to explain why Capano hadn't received his medication and left wondering what it was he had to do differently. "We're not trying to single Mr. Capano out for any retribution," he told reporters outside. "We're trying to follow the letter of the law."

Capano's mood, either because of the medications, or the lack of them, shifted dramatically during the day—sometimes within the space of a few minutes. Late in the afternoon, around 3:30 P.M., Capano's attorneys were busy interviewing potential juror number seven. Capano, at that time, was enthusiastically involved in the process—offering notes and asking questions.

A few minutes later he was playing with a couple of stray breath mints.

The attorneys found their first juror a short time later. He was the eighth person interviewed. He was a man in his mid thirties with dark hair and glasses. He worked at night and said he was "caught by surprise" at being a juror. By Delaware law the first juror selected is also the foreman, so upon this juror's shoulders rested the responsibility of making sure the deliberations would proceed in a proper manner. Juror #1 seemed up to the job. He'd served as a jury foreman before.

The next potential juror was a woman who had a sister-in-law who worked for the government. She was dismissed, but apparently not without some concern from Capano himself, who despite his pledge in August that he would rarely be heard in chambers, spoke up and even admonished the judge when Judge Lee mistakenly said the potential juror's sister worked for the government. "Sister-in-law," Capano said in a stern voice.

The second juror, also a male, was found after interviewing eleven more potential jurors. Also a white male, he had a wife who worked. He, too, wore glasses and worked in an automotive warehouse. He was in his early thirties and had three children.

After the second juror was chosen, the court ripped through a whole stack of people who were dismissed—either they knew too much about the case and had already formed an opinion, or they found themselves not fitting the parameter of what either the prosecution or defense attorneys were looking for in a juror.

A good example of this occurred toward the end of the day. An older man was seated on the witness stand. Judge Lee asked him the predetermined questions he put to all of the potential jurors. "And have you come into contact or seen any information about this case in the media that would cause you to form an opinion?" Judge Lee asked.

"Yes, I have, Your Honor," came the forthright reply.

"And have you formed an opinion?"

"Yes, I have, Your Honor."

"And what is that opinion, sir?"

"I think Mr. Capano is guilty as sin and should confess right now and save the taxpayers a whole bunch of money and maybe save his own life."

The judge looked at the man coolly and said, "Thank you for your time, sir, you are dismissed."

After the man had left, the judge turned and with a small smile on his face said, "Would the defense like a moment to consider the gentleman's proposal?"

Everyone but Capano seemed to think it was funny.

On Tuesday the jury selection continued and again the day began with Capano upset with the correction department. That morning he refused to take his medication and later, as the attorneys on both sides of the case tried to ask questions of a potential juror, Capano interrupted and corrected the judge yet again—this time in a very authoritative and not so humble voice. Colm Connolly, the prosecutor, had by this time had enough and addressed Judge Lee about Capano's constant interruptions.

But the attorneys did get some work done. After going through some twenty potential jurors on the second day, they found their third juror, a blonde, white female in her late thirties.

On Wednesday, Capano showed up, unshaven since Monday, and refusing to wear his business suit. A potential juror got to see Capano handcuffed and led from court, and the defense noted this, but no one seemed to care much. Capano was losing friends in court fast.

"The Tom Capano I know could not have done this murder," a potential juror said moments later. "But I have to say watching the stuff in the press, it sure looks like he did it." That potential juror, too, was dismissed.

Capano was back after lunch and wanted to address the court. Despite his complaints about his medication making him lethargic and muddled, he seemed to have no problem walking to the podium and making himself heard in a cogent fashion.

"I am a marked man," Capano said, referring to the treatment he had allegedly received by his jailers—not the inmates themselves. "You can inflict death by a thousand tiny cuts." The prison management, Capano inferred, was out to get him.

Again he chastised Judge Lee, and talked about the abuse of his rights by his jailers. When Judge Lee said he was trying to understand, but was also concerned about the violations of human rights that occurred to the victim, Anne Marie Fahey, Capano did not hesitate to jump in. "Alleged victim, Your Honor, not victim," Capano said.

"He's a control freak and has dug himself a hole," Robert Fahey said later, after watching Capano's blowup in court.

Capano was upset with what he said was "harassment by my jailers," and preferred, he said, to spend his entire time in his cell at this point rather than get up and deal with the jailers every morning. "I'm safer in my cell," he told Judge Lee.

"I think this is ill advised," Lee said. "I'm sure you've discussed it with your attorneys ... "

"No, we haven't, Your Honor," Oteri chimed in.

"I'm not going to subject myself to degradation and humiliation," Capano jumped back in. "There's a strip search and then there's the extra-special search."

Capano left it to everyone's imagination as to what the "extra special" search was, but Lee had heard enough. He rolled his eyes and allowed the courtroom to be cleared so Capano's attorneys might have ten minutes with their client to talk him out of leaving the courtroom during jury selection.

"You're seeing a guy who's been brought up his entire life to believe what he thinks is more important than what anyone else thinks—lose it," Brian Fahey said outside of the courtroom.

Ten minutes later, Capano had backed down. It was going to become a familiar routine. As soon as court reconvened,

Capano was back passing notes and looking very much as if he were running the show. "In forty-two years I've never had a client overrule me before," Oteri said outside of the courtroom. "Mr. Capano is a first." Court again broke a few minutes later so Capano could receive the medication he complained earlier he wasn't getting. "Must be quite a sensation to be eating a bagel and have thirty people watching you," Judge Lee offered with a smile as Capano chased down his medication with a plain bagel.

By midmorning Capano's lawyers were openly fussing with each other, but Oteri later apologized for it and told reporters, "I went off half-cocked and acted like an asshole." O'Donnell openly agreed. "You're an asshole, all right," he said with a grin. "Why are you guys in the press always paying attention to him? He's not the only guy here."

The laughs and goodwill outside the courtroom did not translate inside the courtroom, where the defense was concerned that with all the pretrial publicity, Capano could not receive a fair trial nor find impartial jurors in Wilmington. That concern manifested itself in the explicit and specific questions the judge asked during voir dire. The defense was also concerned the publicity concerning Capano's extramarital activities with Annie and others would taint a jury. Potential jurors were often asked about their opinions toward adultery, and some of those questions caused Judge Lee some concern. "I don't want to get into a House impeachment hearing type of thing," he told the attorneys. Capano's own questions and comments regarding his captivity and the way he claimed to have been treated by the judge, the prosecution, and his jailers also slowed down the process. But after three weeks, a jury of twelve and eight alternates were seated so the trial could begin. Opening arguments were scheduled for October 26.

Chapter 10
A Horrible, Tragic Accident

For close to twenty-eight months, Tom Capano kept silent about what he knew about Anne Marie Fahey's last day on earth. He had spoken with police only twice and offered a couple of press releases and public statements from his attorneys—but that was it—other than to deny he had any idea as to what happened to Annie after they had dinner in Philadelphia.

The prosecution's investigation, through interviewing Annie's friends and acquaintances, had determined by the time the trial started that Capano had become obsessed with Annie. They had, through Gerard and Louis Capano, determined that Tom Capano had dumped Annie's body at sea. Through Deborah MacIntyre they had determined that Capano had purchased a gun and conspired to lie about it. They knew of the story of extortionists and they'd heard at least three different explanations as to how Annie's blood found its way onto the floor of the great room in Capano's house. Because of the discovery process Capano also knew everything the prosecution had. On October 26, 1998, the opening arguments began, and the jury got to see how all of the information the prosecution and defense had obtained would play itself out in court.

Ferris Wharton, in his "aw-shucks" disarming baritone, during a ninety-minute monologue, methodically laid out what prosecutors believed had occurred more than two years ago. He began by reading Anne Marie Fahey's last diary entry, and that set the stage for what Wharton and Connolly would seek to prove during the duration of the trial: Tom Capano was a "controlling, manipulative, insecure, jealous maniac" who came to the conclusion that if he couldn't have Anne Marie Fahey, then nobody could.

Two weeks after Annie wrote her revelations about Capano in her diary, Capano bought the cooler he would later use as a coffin, Wharton said. A month later, Capano had MacIntyre purchase the gun. Then on June 27, after the nervously solemn dinner at Ristorante di Panorama in Philadelphia, the prosecution claimed Capano executed his plan and his ex-mistress.

"Tom Capano had determined that if Anne Marie Fahey did not want to be with him, she would be with no one—forever," Wharton calmly declared.

The veteran prosecutor also went on to describe the grim sea burial, how Capano's brother Gerry said Tom told him he had nodded his head in the affirmative when asked if Tom had killed two extortionists who were allegedly threatening his family, how the morning after Annie's dinner with Capano he went to his ex-wife's home and uncharacteristically borrowed her Chevrolet Suburban and how he bought a carpet and stain remover just days after Annie disappeared. Wharton also conceded, in his opening statement, that Capano had been generous to Annie, once offering to buy her a Lexus, but his generosity was a way to manipulate her and that eventually she became repulsed by his actions, only trying to humor him by going out to dinner and exchanging friendly e-mails. But Capano, Wharton said, couldn't accept that.

"So he killed her," he said.

It was a very good outline of the state's case, but it did gloss over some very important facts: The state had no body, no way to prove Annie was dead. There appeared, according to the opening statement, that the state would have little direct evidence to support its claim of murder, and indeed Wharton didn't offer the jury any explanation as to what happened the night Annie died. As Wharton would later say, no one really knew what happened.

That situation is not an ideal way to endear oneself to a jury. Close to twenty-eight months after Annie disappeared, and after steadfast denials that he had any part in her death, Tom Capano, through his lead attorney Joe Oteri, made a complete about-face when Oteri gave his opening statement.

Anne Marie Fahey, Oteri claimed in a thirty-minute diatribe, had died in a horrible, "tragic accident." Only one other person besides Capano was still alive, Oteri told us, who knew what had happened that night. Yes, Oteri admitted, Capano dumped Annie at sea. Yes, it occurred exactly as Gerry Capano said it occurred—with a few notable exceptions. Yes, the Igloo fishing cooler the prosecution had in its possession was the cooler Capano used as Annie's coffin. Yes, "Tom Capano lied to everybody except one person who knows the horrible truth," Oteri claimed. Yes, Tom did all these things, Oteri said, but the one thing Tom did not do was kill Anne Marie Fahey.

"You are going to hear testimony that Capano did not murder her. She died as a result of an outrageous, horrible, tragic accident," Oteri said as he concluded his opening speech to the jury. While burying her at sea was a despicable act, he conceded, it wasn't necessarily the act of a murderer. Buying the cooler in itself didn't mean anything, either. If Tom Capano wanted to put Annie in a cooler, "he wouldn't buy it at a Wilmington store using a credit card," Oteri argued. "Tom Capano's a bright guy. That's insanity."

"Maybe he'd have better luck with arguing insanity," one

of the reporters whispered as Oteri continued his opening statement.

Oteri took time to not only explain how bright Tom was, but how degenerate his little brother Gerard was. As if the thirty-five-year-old Gerard was a member of the beatnik generation, Oteri reached back to the memories of the 1950s as he called Gerry a "booze hound." Then, flashing forward to scenes from a current public-service message, Oteri said Gerry had a "brain like a fried egg," from cocaine, marijuana, and LSD use.

"He's a typical screwed-up, rich kid who has never earned anything in his life. He's a poster boy for the 'Me Generation,'" Oteri claimed. It was here that Oteri outlined the one major flaw in Gerry's story—as Tom Capano saw it. While Gerry was right about disposing of the body, while he was right about buying gas, how much and where, while he was right about the types of screws that held the cooler lid in place, while he was right about even the most minute detail about disposing of Annie's body, according to Oteri he got one thing wrong: Tom never told Gerry in February 1996 that Tom might have to "whack" a couple of extortionists who had threatened his family.

That important bit of information, which could be used by the prosecution to show that Capano had planned Annie's death months before he carried it out, was all wrong. When Tom borrowed $8,000 from Gerry that same month, it was Gerry who implied that someone was shaking down his big brother. Tom just wanted to agree with Gerry in order to appease him, Oteri told the jury. According to Capano's defense team Gerry did that because he fancied himself quite the little gangster. He was a "Good Fella" or a "Wise Guy" wanna-be who loved the allure of breaking legs and muscling people.

Oteri said every fact could cut both ways and during the course of the trial this would be proven time and again. On the opening day Oteri let everyone know what that meant. Despite

Annie's diary entry, Tom Capano wasn't obsessed with her, he was her kindly confidant—her surrogate uncle or big brother—with whom, of course, she'd had sexual relations. But Oteri explained that away, as well. "We have no intention of besmirching Anne Marie Fahey, but she was not an eighteen-year-old kid just out of high school," he said.

Oteri saved his best venom for Deborah MacIntyre, pointing out that she'd lied repeatedly to the federal government before she struck a deal.

There was a possible explanation for the vitriol found in Oteri's opening statement—it wasn't all written by him. This was a fact Oteri later admitted to several reporters. "I had an opening statement all prepared and then the night before I gave it I had to tear it all up and start over again," he said. Capano knew what kind of evidence the state had against him. As Oteri had stated, there was no way to get around the cooler. No way the defense could argue that little brother Gerry with his "Swiss cheese memory" as Tom Capano would later testify, could make up all that stuff that was so well corroborated. So Capano told his lawyers he would concede the biggest part of the case—the part the prosecution admittedly could not prove—Anne Marie Fahey was dead. Tom Capano was the last person to be seen in public with her alive, and during the trial he publicly admitted he'd dumped her dead body.

The only thing left in contention after Oteri's arguments was what happened from about 9:30 P.M. on June 27, 1996, until 6 A.M. the following morning when Tom Capano pulled up in his brother's driveway.

It amounted to little more than an 8½-hour gap, and the prosecution and defense would take about three months to argue over what happened that night. Admittedly, the prosecution could not explain what had happened, but they were still asking for a guilty verdict and the death penalty for Tom Capano. The fact that no one in Delaware had ever been given such a penalty in such a case did not deter them in the slightest.

There was a good reason behind that. As much as Tom Capano had given away in the opening statement, there was cause to suspect he might give away much more, for Capano had claimed there was only one other person in the world who could corroborate his story.

Knowing the case as well as they did, Wharton and Connolly had every reason to believe that person to be Deborah MacIntyre. That meant there was an extremely good chance Tom Capano would have to take the stand in his own defense. Deborah MacIntyre was going to be a prosecution witness. It would be reasonable, with everything her attorney had said in the media already, that Deborah would deny being at Tom Capano's home the night Annie died. After all, Tom Bergstrom, her new attorney, had already said she was at home with her two children on June 27.

This all meant that Tom Capano would have to take the stand and refute MacIntyre's story. After the opening statements it looked more and more like a showdown was looming in the future—pitting Tom Capano, the urbane and supposedly intelligent attorney, against Deborah MacIntyre, an admitted liar and a woman he referred to as a "doormat" in some of his letters.

Capano would appear to have the upper hand in such a confrontation. But as everyone was to learn in the course of the trial, appearances were in no way related to reality.

The first witness the prosecution called to try and prove their case was Brian Fahey, who described his sister as a bit of a neat freak. Despite her emotional problems and an eating disorder, Brian said his little sister had come a long way from her skittish childhood and was extremely happy with MBNA Corp. executive Michael Scanlan, her new boyfriend. Six days before her death Brian had seen the couple holding hands and looking very happy.

On cross-examination Joe Oteri delved a little deeper into Annie's emotionally disturbed childhood and got Brian Fahey to admit that his sister had a "bad temper," and at one time may have chased after her father with a hockey stick.

Three other witnesses were called on the first day of the trial, including two secretaries from Governor Carper's office who said Fahey was fairly happy on June 27 and was preparing for a day off on Friday, which would include a massage, pedicure, manicure, and maybe some reading in the park.

Jacqueline Dansak, the next witness, was the waitress at Panorama who served Capano and Annie the night Annie disappeared. According to Dansak, the dinner was a very somber two-hour affair. Capano ordered Fahey's drinks and her meal without consulting her, and neither Capano nor Fahey spoke to each other throughout the dinner.

Dansak also told the jury on direct examination that Fahey was wearing a floral-print dress that night, and not the black "jet-setty" fashions that most of Panorama's female customers liked to wear. "She looked haggard, gaunt, her hair was unkempt. She looked tired," Dansak also offered.

On cross-examination by Charles Oberly, Dansak admitted she really only observed the pair for about fifteen minutes of the two hours they spent together and admitted she'd never seen Annie nor Capano before. However, she defended statements about Annie's appearance that night saying "her hair wasn't kempt by any standards."

That following morning as the trial resumed, Judge Lee welcomed the jury with a cheerful smile and began a ritual that he'd carry on until the end of the trial. He asked the jury if anyone had come into contact with any information through the media, or other means, that had to do with the trial. In unison the answer was no—as it would remain until the last day.

With that said, Connolly and Wharton called Dr. Neil S. Kaye, Annie's psychiatrist. Just moments before Annie planned to go out with Capano on June 26, she met with Dr. Kaye, and what he had to say, the prosecution hoped, would show Annie's fear of Capano.

The rail-thin Dr. Kaye, with short hair, intense eyes, and a short-cropped brown mustache, approached the bench, with a cowboy hat in hand, as congenially as he might approach a park bench. He seemed comfortable and capable. He appears in court several times a year.

He knew what it was all about. He looked at the judge, the jury, the attorneys, and even the spectators as he walked in— seeming to absorb all the details and to project an air of authority and dignity. Perhaps he didn't know that one man in particular was looking back at him with a bemused look of satisfaction on his face: Joe Oteri.

On direct examination Dr. Kaye told about meeting Fahey just prior to her dinner with Capano on June 27, 1996. He testified that she was "afraid of his [Capano's] rage and anger" against her.

According to Dr. Kaye, Annie had tried to let Capano down gently, but was finding that difficult to do because of her own fear of him and her fear of being alone. "I can't be lovers with you anymore," Fahey told Dr. Kaye she had told Capano. "But we can try to be friends." Dr. Kaye said he didn't think that would be possible in Capano's case and he noted that Annie had told him about threatening e-mails and letters Capano had sent her. It seemed to be damning evidence against Capano, but the crafty Oteri saw something else.

"Nice hat you've got there, Doctor," Oteri began on cross-examination.

Dr. Kaye smiled and thanked Oteri for the compliment and then went on to explain he collected wooden hats. His off-white cowboy hat was a $750 fashion statement he bought in a specialty shop that had been lathed from a single block of wood.

"Interesting," Oteri replied.

Forever after, Dr. Kaye became known to the defense team as "Dr. Wooden Hat." Some of the jury members muffled a slight chuckle, and even those who didn't like Oteri said they watched in awe as "two old pros," Kaye and Oteri, went at it in the courtroom.

Oteri caught Dr. Kaye off-guard when he made the esteemed psychiatrist confess his private passion was wooden hats, a fact that would later lead to a feature in a local newspaper. But, after that, the jurors believed Dr. Kaye gave as good as he got. "I thought it was some of the best cross-examination of the trial," said Juror #8, a young, beautiful, brown-haired woman who found as the trial wore on that she had more in common with Anne Marie than she felt comfortable discussing. "These were two professionals at the top of their game. It was very interesting to watch," she said.

Oteri asked Kaye to read his notes from the different meetings he had with Fahey, and each time he did, he also pointed out Kaye had not mentioned Capano by name in the notes. "You won't find the name Tom Capano in my notes," Kaye replied. But, he also said, that didn't mean much. Oteri pressed Kaye to show in the e-mails between Annie and Capano where the defendant had ever threatened Annie as Dr. Kaye had stated on direct examination.

Kaye couldn't point to many specifics but said at one point Fahey told Capano that he "freaks her out" by calling every half hour. Annie at another point said she could only "offer you friendship. I hope you understand." And finally Capano said he desperately wanted "to talk to you and will be out of my mind," if he couldn't.

Oteri got Dr. Kaye to admit that he had treated Annie only eight times including the day she died. The grand total of those meetings added up to about three hours of personal contact.

"You didn't know her all that well," Oteri said. It wasn't a question.

But what Kaye did know about Annie brought her suffering

into sharper focus. She first came under psychological treatment in 1986. She was just twenty years old. At the time of her death she was being treated for depression, anxiety, panic attacks, codependency, and anorexia—the pains of which she had carefully detailed in her diary. Kaye explained how Annie had tried to wean herself from dependence on laxatives. She used up to fifteen of them a day to try and control her weight.

"We were trying to help her gain power and control over her life, to be independent and to take her life anywhere she wanted," Dr. Kaye told the jury. "She was bright, attractive, and had an engaging personality. She had a lot of potential."

The words cloaked the courtroom. Tom Capano looked on indifferently.

Dr. Kaye went on to describe how Annie's problems were rooted in her traumatic childhood, with her mother's death and her father's slide into alcoholism. The father drank the family into poverty, Dr. Kaye explained, and abused Annie both emotionally and physically. She periodically lived with friends rather than at home. Dr. Kaye recounted the Faheys' economic problems brought on by the alcoholism that included the lack of electricity, heat, and telephone. Dr. Kaye also talked about Annie taking hot showers at school and finally how Mr. Fahey later lost the home at a sheriff's foreclosure sale.

All of that contributed, Dr. Kaye said, to Annie's fatal attraction to Capano. Capano was older, wealthy, powerful, and showered her with attention and gifts. In many ways Annie saw him as a father figure.

The next witness was someone Annie eventually came to see as her lover and potential husband: Michael Scanlan. Annie's boyfriend at the time of her death talked about how "she was the best thing that ever happened to me in my life." Capano didn't seem impressed. He sat like one of Dr. Kaye's wooden hats throughout Scanlan's testimony.

Colm Connolly walked Scanlan through his initial introduction to Annie, which had come by Governor Carper playing matchmaker. In 1995 the governor wrote down Annie's name and phone number in a letter he wrote to Scanlan, who then called her in September 1995 and they met at happy hour at O'Friel's Irish pub. The pair eventually began dating steadily, and Scanlan, a devout Catholic, recited to the courtroom their date to see a Mass celebrated by the Pope at Baltimore's Camden Yards. Scanlan also discussed other nonsecular dates like a Luther Vandross concert, as well as a ballet and an opera.

Annie eventually trusted Scanlan enough to tell him about her troubled past, including her problems with anorexia, and with Tom Capano. Scanlan had been supportive. He remembered Annie with a smile, recounting how he had surprised her by sending her flowers on a whim in early May.

"She called me right away. She was very happy," Scanlan said modestly.

Part of the defense strategy, which emerged this first week, was to deride Annie's relationship with Mike Scanlan. Oteri asked, during his cross-examination, if Scanlan had agreed to date Annie in order to "placate" Governor Carper, who'd arranged the date.

"That's not correct," Scanlan said.

"Is it true your relationship with her wasn't sexual?"

"Correct."

Oteri then asked Scanlan if he'd ever offered to pay to fix a small ding in Annie's windshield or replace her broken air conditioner. He had not.

"I never bought a girlfriend," he said. "And I never intend on buying a girlfriend."

Under redirect Scanlan also answered the lingering question as to why he and Annie had not had sex. Scanlan said Annie told him she didn't approve of premarital sex and he assumed she was a virgin.

Connie Blake, who lived in the apartment below Annie's, also testified that day and talked about the sounds she heard the night Annie disappeared.

Kathy Fahey-Hosey read her sister's diary from the witness stand, pointing out the strange twists Annie's affair with Tom Capano had taken. Annie was at first enamored of him, later in love with him, but also repulsed that she, a good Catholic girl, was in love with a married man.

Police detective Robert Donovan got to leave his seat at the side of Connolly and Wharton to climb on to the witness stand. He would eventually make more than a dozen appearances there, both for the prosecution and the defense.

In light of Capano's admission that he'd dumped Annie at sea, Donovan introduced in the first week of the trial the fact that he now knew Capano lied to him during the course of their first interview together, which occurred June 29, 1996. Capano had said he thought Annie had gone to the New Jersey shore with friends that weekend.

Donovan said the next day police were supposed to meet Capano back at his house, yet found him pulling out of the garage of his wife's home. When Capano saw the police he was, in a word, agitated. That was when Capano told the police he was upset with himself for disclosing so much information earlier that morning. Capano did escort the police back to his house where they searched for Annie but didn't find her.

Jack O'Donnell, on cross-examination, pointed out that Capano had indeed told him some things that were true that day. "He told you things that were true and other things that were lies." Donovan agreed, and could have pointed out where the biggest lie was told, but O'Donnell saved him the trouble: He pointed out that one example of a lie was when Capano "told you he didn't know where she was."

"That's correct," Donovan replied dryly.

Donovan put Annie's downstairs neighbor in perspective, as well, that first week. He testified that only Annie's keys, a ring, and a red-and-white sweatshirt and jogging suit were missing from her apartment. Perhaps that night she'd run into her apartment, changed quickly, and then left. After all, the floral-print dress had been found lying out, as if Annie had left in a hurry. But, again, the prosecutors did not know. It was only speculation.

Finally, during the first two weeks of the trial, psychologist Gary M. Johnson appeared to talk about Annie's problems. He'd treated her from July 1995 to February 1996. While Annie never mentioned a name, she did tell him that she was having an affair with a prominent man, who once held her captive inside her apartment for three to four hours.

Johnson went on to talk about the earlier incident and how the unnamed man had taken back gifts he'd given Annie, gifts he later returned. He also threatened to tell Michael Scanlan about their relationship.

"She perceived she was trapped in her apartment. She was quite terrified," Johnson said.

Annie told Johnson she was worried about this man showing up at public places where she was and seemed most terrified about an episode at the "Grand Gala," an already described Wilmington social event. This man also persistently sent Annie e-mail and letters.

"The relationship was very intense. The man was pushing her and was having a great deal of control over her life. She wanted to pull away, but he was not willing to let her," Johnson testified. Annie finally told Johnson the man was married and she was "profoundly ashamed" of that. No name was ever mentioned, so there could be some doubt about who this man had been.

Psychologist Michelle Sullivan removed that doubt. She treated Fahey from February 28, 1996, until the day she died. Annie described similar problems to Sullivan and named Capano as the problem back in March 1996. That's when Sullivan tried to convince Annie to report Capano to the Attorney General's Office, and she had not.

Annie told Sullivan that Capano had shown up at her apartment unannounced on numerous occasions—sometimes causing a scene. Other times Annie said Capano called her as often as twenty-five times a day.

Oteri on cross-examination went after Annie's character yet again, in his effort to show that she was still involved with Capano at the time of her death.

"My picture of her is different than yours," Sullivan said.

"There is no doubt about that," Oteri offered.

Sullivan did say it was possible Capano got some "false messages" from Fahey, but that her inability to completely cut Capano out of her life was part of her accommodating nature. She didn't like to hurt other people, Sullivan said, and was extremely vulnerable to Capano and his manipulative ways. According to Sullivan, the manipulation included harassment, threats, and gifts; a new air conditioner, car windshield, clothes, and trips to tony restaurants. At one point in time Annie Fahey told Sullivan she feared Capano might try to kidnap her.

Sullivan didn't consider that a serious threat until Annie disappeared. Then she came forward and spoke not only to Robert Fahey but to the police.

"I told them I was concerned about an abduction and thought Tom Capano was involved in it," she testified.

The defense had a different take on Capano's relationship with Annie during the final months of her life. They struggled throughout the trial during the cross-examination of prosecution witnesses and later on direct examination of their own witnesses to show that Capano loved Fahey, but accepted that their relationship could no longer be physical. Instead, the defense was painting the relationship in the final months as warm, friendly, and congenial. Tom Capano, the defense would maintain, had become Annie's surrogate father/big brother.

But after nearly two weeks of testimony the emerging portrait of Capano brought to the jury by the prosecution was not the staid, stoic, urbane man of wealth and taste he'd projected for years in Wilmington. Rather, a manipulative, craven monster was being described in great detail by those who knew Annie and had treated her for her various disorders during the final months of her life.

Chapter 11
Gerry Again

During the previous two weeks the prosecution had done its best to show the monstrous side of Tom Capano while the defense had done its level best to show Annie's flaws and to paint Capano as a caring friend.

But it meant nothing compared to the added dimension of brother against brother that took over the courtroom on November 9, 1998. The testimony pitted Gerard Capano against Tom Capano.

Joe Hurley, Capano's previous lead attorney, had already vilified Gerry as a "drug dealer" who made up all of his testimony to save himself against an illegal weapons charge. Oteri just called him "a liar, a junkie and a stone-cold bum."

His family wasn't too pleased with Gerry, either. He'd effectively been ostracized from it, causing him untold amounts of grief and pain. All of this occurred because Gerry had chosen to come forward. He'd gained some respect and empathy from courtroom spectators because, at the risk of great personal loss he'd stepped up to the plate and told the world the truth. As others pointed out, though, he kept silent for more than sixteen months and only came forward when he'd literally had a gun put to his head.

Still many saw him as a figure straight out of a Greek tragedy, and as Gerry Capano climbed on the witness stand on November 9 for the first of two days of testimony, there was no question that he was going to go back over the same ground he'd covered before.

"What did he say to you about a boat?" Colm Connolly asked him near the beginning of the trial.

"He said that if either one of these persons that was threatening to hurt his kids were to hurt one of his kids and he was to do something to them, could he use the boat," Gerry replied evenly.

"Well, what was this 'to do something'?"

"If they had hurt his kids and was to kill them, could he use the boat."

Tom sat as still as stone while Gerry gave his detailed testimony. Gerry described how Tom tried to get him to find someone to take care of the alleged extortionist.

"He was afraid that the guy was going to hurt him and he asked me if I knew somebody that could break legs, or, you know, beat this guy up and I said that I might."

"Did you ever talk to anybody?" Connolly queried.

"I did, but nothing ever came out of it."

Gerry had talked to an old friend to break some legs for his big brother. Just trying to help out a brother in need as Tom had helped him out of scrapes in the past.

For the rest of the day Gerry went through detail after grisly detail on how Tom approached him the morning of June 28, how his brother begged him and how he eventually came to help him dump Annie at sea. Tom Capano watched his little brother during some of his testimony, glared at him during some of it, made a bundle of copious notes and sometimes tried to ignore Gerry. Sometimes Tom Capano shot his little brother nasty looks, but if they were meant to rattle Gerry, they didn't seem to work.

"He said he had nowhere else to go," Gerry said as he recounted the moments that led up to the boat ride. "He said, 'Don't leave me flat. Don't leave me hanging. I need you, bro,' and that was it." As he testified, Gerry did not look happy. He looked like a broken man, reporters and spectators said.

Gerry went over the sight that greeted him when he arrived at his brother's home. "I saw a cooler with a chain wrapped around it and a rolled-up rug and some just normal garage stuff."

"What kind of condition was this cooler in?" Connolly wanted to know.

"Looked to be new."

"What size was it?"

"It was a big Igloo cooler, approximately 160-some quarts, fishing cooler kind of deal."

Gerry testified that he was afraid of the cooler.

"He wanted to put the cooler in my truck, and I said no."

"Why?"

"Because I just didn't want to do it."

Gerry went through the emotional upheaval that that day brought him. He outlined his actions in his drive to Stone Harbor, how he gathered fishing rods, how he drove out to sea, how he helped his brother dump the cooler in the ocean, and then the shock when he saw the cooler wouldn't sink.

Then he shot the cooler with a deer slug and watched in greater horror as not only the cooler didn't sink but a reddish liquid that looked like blood began to pour from the hole in the cooler.

Later he testified about the torturous ride back to Wilmington and how he helped dispose of the rug and a love seat in his brother's home.

"Would you describe this love seat for us. What you saw?" Connolly asked him.

"It had a stain on it, on the right, if you were sitting on it, on the right side about shoulder height."

"How big was the stain?"

"About the size of a basketball."

"What color was the stain?"

"I couldn't tell. The couch was maroon."

Gerry carried the love seat out of the room and at one point cut the stained piece of the love seat up and busted off a leg on the couch to make it look like it was "just an old, broken-up couch, and we threw it in the Dumpster."

"You say you cut up the stain . . . "

"Yes."

"What did you cut it with?"

"I always carry a pocketknife."

"When you cut it off, or when you cut into the couch, what did you see in the foam underneath the covering?"

"It looked to be something red."

Connolly then led Gerry through the minefield Oteri was sure to use against him on cross-examination: the raid on his home, the deal he signed with prosecutors, and his drug usage. Gerry admitted it all. He even said on direct examination that he began to use more drugs after Annie's disappearance.

"Why?" Connolly asked.

"For me it relieves a lot of stress," Gerry confessed.

He said evenly that he wasn't sure he was high on anything when Tom Capano told him about extortionists. However, the day he disposed of Annie's body, he distinctly remembered being stone-cold sober.

But it wasn't the drug testimony that caused the greatest commotion. After Gerry's testimony on Monday, November 9, 1998, Capano's attorneys asked for a mistrial. Almost two hours into his testimony, as Gerry was recounting for Connolly the raid at his house, he told the prosecutor that he had told his own attorney, Dan Lyons, the truth about what had happened on June 27, 1996, months before the raid. This was to argue against the defense contention that Gerry only made up his story after the raid to save himself.

"When did you tell him that last part of the story, that if your brother—about your brother asking you if he hurt somebody, could he use the boat?" Connolly inquired.

"When did I tell him that?" Gerry appeared nervous and confused.

"When did you tell Dan Lyons that, if you did at all?"

"I did tell him that."

"And when?"

"Before I went and took a lie detector test. . . ."

At that point Gene Maurer shot up like a rocket. "Object, Your Honor!"

The attorneys gathered for a sidebar near the judge and argued their points for several minutes while Gerry sat with his right hand covering his face as he shook his head from side to side. The objection came because in the state of Delaware lie detector tests are inadmissible. They've been found to be inaccurate too often to be relied upon. The mere fact that Gerry said he'd taken one was enough, Maurer and Capano's other attorneys thought, to dismiss the jury and bring in a new one. They wanted a mistrial. Granted the jury had not heard whether or not Gerry passed his lie detector test (he did), it was merely the fact the jury heard he'd taken a test that caused Maurer to ask for a mistrial.

The court reconvened at 2:30 P.M. that Monday and before the direct examination could continue, Judge Lee gave the jury very specific instructions. "I intend to deny the application for a mistrial and proceed," Lee told the attorneys. "I will give an appropriate instruction to the jury when they are returned to the courtroom."

The jury came in and the judge explained himself. "Members of the jury, immediately before the luncheon break the defense objected to the unresponsive answer of the witness to Mr. Connolly's question. The answer made reference to a lie detector test. Such a response is inadmissible, even though the witness did not indicate whether or not he had taken such a test, or if so, what the results might have indicated. The courts of this state, the federal courts, and those of every other state have consistently found such tests to be unreliable and therefore inadmissible as evidence.

"Therefore, you are to disregard the witness's response and you are not under any circumstances to speculate as to whether or not he took such a test, or what the results of such a test might have been. You are to in no way consider the witness's responses in your determinations.

"The previous answer is stricken, and Mr. Connolly may now proceed."

The moment had been seen as Capano's last, best chance to get off with a mistrial. Judge Lee had struggled to be fair and to make sure there were no procedural errors. If Capano was going to get off, the judge made sure throughout the trial that it wouldn't be on a technicality.

Shortly before 4 P.M. Joe Oteri got his chance to cross-examine Gerry Capano. Despite his public descriptions of Gerry's character, or lack thereof, Oteri went out of his way to be overly polite to him when he got on the stand.

"I was especially happy to see that," Juror #8 later said. "It showed some class."

It was not what anyone expected out of Oteri, given what Hurley had done previously and Oteri's own characterizations of Gerry being well-known. Oteri made reference to this during his cross-examination.

"They told me about your demeanor in court," Gerry said in reference to the preparations Connolly and Wharton had given Gerry for court.

"They told you I was going to be a bastard, didn't they?" Oteri said with a hint of a smile.

"No."

"Told you I was going to rip you apart, didn't they?"

"They may have hinted toward that."

"I'm not doing that. I'm a nice guy, right?"

In fact, as other attorneys later said, Oteri did handle Gerry deftly, but effectively. He started Gerry down the long road of destroying his credibility by asking him about his drug usage. He got Gerry to admit he got into arguments and insulted people when he'd tied one on.

"I'm not saying all the time," Oteri offered, "but occasionally you get across the line and you get a little rambunctious and have an argument with somebody?"

"I think that's fair to say."

"Okay. And occasionally you've kind of thrown a punch at somebody?"

"Occasionally."

"Okay. That's when you're drinking booze, correct?"

"Or doing the other."

Tom Capano still watched, saying little as his younger brother testified.

The cross-examination ended as Oteri showed the jury that not only was Gerry still using drugs, but the state knew it and had done nothing about it.

"You got busted in October for having a couple of grams, right?" Oteri asked.

"Yes, sir," Gerry replied.

"So you know it's illegal?"

"Yes, sir."

"Now, did Mr. Connolly or Mr. Wharton tell you to stop doing the drugs?"

"Yes, I believe they did."

". . . And did they tell you that you could get in serious trouble if you kept doing drugs?"

"They may have."

"Let me ask you the key question. Have you been arrested since you told them?"

"No, sir."

"Has anybody searched your house since you told them you were doing drugs?"

"No, sir."

"Okay. And, sir, you continue to do drugs, right up until this period almost up to today, right?"

"Trying my best to stay away from it, sir."

"But," Oteri started, then paused, "I understand that, Gerry. I mean, I'm not fighting, but you're doing them, right?"

"That's fair to say."

"And the government knows it, because you've told them. Right?"

"I did."

At that point Oteri asked the judge for a recess until the following morning, timing the break so the jury could digest the fact that the prosecution's star witness was not only an admitted drug user, but had admitted continuing drug usage to the government—a government that could but apparently hadn't busted him for his admitted felonious behavior.

The next morning Oteri got Gerry to talk not only about drugs, but his fascination with guns and shark, moose, and black-bear hunting, and the allegations of blackmail that Tom Capano had told him about.

Some of the conversations took place at Tom's home, where his wife lived with their children. Inside, just off to the right of the main entrance, is a large and lavish billiard room with dark wood walls.

"And you guys play some pool, don't you?" Oteri asked Gerry.

"We do."

"And while you're shooting pool, you drink some of that—I don't want to be racist, but some of that 'Dago Red'?"

"Homemade wine?" Gerry asked, evidently unsure of the meaning.

"Homemade wine," Oteri replied.

"That's right."

''That's powerful stuff?''

''Yes.''

''And these conversations could have taken place at Tommy's house while you were drinking Italian wine, and maybe you had done some cocaine?''

''Yes, sir.''

The implication was clear. Gerry, occasionally his older brother Joey, and brother Tommy had been drinking homemade wine, and in a drunken stupor they all said things they didn't necessarily mean. Oteri even kindly suggested that perhaps Gerry had first volunteered to give Tom a handgun to protect himself from the alleged extortionists.

He may have been drunk at the time, and apparently, Gerry was unsure. He told Oteri he may have asked if Tom wanted to borrow a gun to take care of himself.

Then Oteri got Gerry to admit that his older brother Tom repeatedly had to counsel him on his temper, and after Annie's disappearance became public Gerry admitted that Tom told him, ''Don't lose your temper and punch out any newspapermen.''

It looked like Oteri might be making inroads on shaking the foundation of Gerry's testimony, a point that was driven home by an exchange between Oteri and Gerry concerning whether or not Gerry considered himself a decent human being.

''Because you don't consider yourself a decent human being, do you?'' Oteri asked.

''I consider myself an okay human being,'' Gerry said softly.

''I can't hear you.''

''I consider myself an okay human being.''

''You said you thought this over. What would change? What would you not be any longer? Would you be decent? Would you be moral? Would you be law-abiding? What would change?''

''Probably all of them.''

''All of them. So you're not decent, you're not moral, and you're not law-abiding?''

''I haven't been in the past,'' Gerry admitted solemnly.

" . . . But in the future you're going to be?''

"I'm going to try my best.''

Oteri intimated that when Tom had come to Gerry, as Gerry claimed, and told him that he was being blackmailed, Gerry had not done right by Tom Capano, that, in fact, Gerry was not a decent human being.

"And when you find out that your brother's having these problems, didn't it occur to you that he was in serious trouble and the family should sound the bugle and kind of circle the wagons around him and help him?'' Oteri asked.

"I guess it did.''

"But, yet, you never went to the second oldest brother, Louis, and said, 'Louis, Tommy is in serious trouble. We got to get together and help him and see what's going on,' did you?''

"That was my mistake.''

"Say it again.''

"That was my mistake.''

" . . . And you didn't go to Joey and do that, either, did you?'' Oteri pushed.

A solemn Gerry could do no more than shake his head.

Then Oteri got to the meat of why Gerry was testifying against his brother. He led Gerry through the October 1997 raid on his home.

"How many officers showed up?'' Oteri asked.

"Twenty,'' Gerry said evenly.

"And how did they treat you?''

"Had a gun to the back of my head.''

Without saying it in so many words, the implications were clear. According to the testimony, it took a gun to Gerry's head, and later the threat of losing his kids, to get Gerry to testify against Tom. Without saying it, Oteri was also trying to show by the fact that Gerry never went to his other brothers to tell them about the extortionist that he had in fact made up the entire story.

This was driven home in the last exchange between Oteri and Gerry on cross-examination.

"... You were pretty mad, were you not, to suddenly find yourself in the papers accused of being an unfit parent?" Oteri began.

"That's a joke. I'm not an unfit parent," Gerry said as strongly as he'd stated anything from the stand.

"But you were upset by it, were you not?"

"You would be, too, I think."

"Gerry, you are absolutely right. I would be. But *you* were upset?"

"Sure, it's fair to say."

"Now, Gerry, do you remember making a phone call and leaving this message on February 9, 1998, to your mother? (This was just after his brother Tom's bail hearing.): 'Mom, this is your son Gerry. I called you but Katie hung up on me. Then I called again and her little asshole boyfriend hung up on me. You have ten minutes to call me back. If you don't, you can go fuck yourself.' Do you remember making that call to your mother?"

Gerry shifted in his seat. "I was drinking that day, and I remember apologizing afterward."

"But you did make the call?" Oteri pressed.

"I'm not saying I didn't."

"And you apologized for it afterward, correct?"

"It's not nice to talk to my mother like that. I was drinking and very upset."

"And you do things when you're drinking and upset?" Oteri asked, referring to Gerry's previous testimony about being a mean drunk.

"I made a mistake," Gerry said.

"How about the second call, Gerry. Do you remember this? Do you remember saying this:

'Mom, this is your son. Mom, your son Gerry. You better fucking call me. I'm tired of being the bad guy. If you don't fucking call me, you'll never fucking see me or my wife or my kids again. What? Are you pissed because I told the truth? Because Joe fucking Hurley couldn't break me down? As far as I'm concerned, you have three sons. One is a murderer in jail for fucking life, one you hate—and that's Louie—and Joey. Like I said, you can go fuck yourself. Did you really think that I would go to jail for twelve fucking years? If you thought I was bad on the stand, God fucking help you if this goes to trial. I'll think up even more shit to keep my ass out of fucking jail. And I'll make up fucking shit as I go along to keep Tommy in there for fucking life. I hate him. You got ten fucking minutes to call me back or you'll never see my kids again. I'm not threatening you, but if you don't call me back in ten minutes, you can go fuck yourself . . . '

"Did you make that call and make that statement, Gerry?" Gerry didn't flinch. "I'm sure I did, if you have it on tape."

"Thank you. I have no further questions, Your Honor."

Oteri had bloodied Gerry badly, pointing out his deepest pain and exposing his greatest weaknesses. He'd been outcast from his family, he was a drinker and drug abuser—but had he told the truth? Oteri had planted reasonable doubt all through Gerry's testimony. How would the prosecution respond?

On redirect Colm Connolly started with the raid. He pointed out that Tom Capano and his attorney Charles Oberly showed up at the conclusion of the raid.

". . . Did you ever tell your brother that you were thinking about coming in to the government?" Colm Connolly asked.

"I did."

"And what did he say to you when you told him that?"

"I think he said something like—he said something like 'act like a man,' I think is what he said. . . ."

The Faheys sat through the madness of the courtroom grimly at first, and then more openly critical of the proceedings as it wore on. For months they had prepared for "Annie's last fight" as they called the trial, but was anyone really prepared for how twisted the trial had become? They listened intently to Gerard's story, knowing most of it already.

Gerry spent most of the time on the stand, nervous and looking down, apparently, not wanting to meet the glare of his older brother Tom, who sat so silently during the course of Gerry's testimony.

As for the testimony itself, there were several questions left dangling in the air after Gerry Capano left the stand. The biggest, the defense attorneys said, was what would the jury believe about him? And what would they think about Gerard's nasty telephone calls to his own mother?

"Oteri certainly got the desired response out of the courtroom as he read the transcript of Gerry's telephone call. It drew gasps from the courtroom, and one female spectator, the local paper reported, exclaimed, "Jesus!"

Who knew what the jury thought of this? There was plenty of speculation from "Delaware criminal law experts" who were quoted frequently in the paper, but it was all guesswork.

It was obvious that Gerry was nervous. During one recess, for example, he stumbled from the witness stand and braced himself on the jury box before he took a breath and walked out of the side door. It was obvious Gerry had a drug problem. It was obvious Gerry had a temper problem. The one thing in his favor was that it also appeared Gerry did not have a problem telling the truth.

"He never did lie to us," Connolly later said.

The question was what would the jury take into deliberations? Did they see Gerry as a hopeless drug user, or as a man tortured by having to go against his family?

Many of Capano's family turned up for Gerry's testimony. His mother, Marguerite, sat quietly sobbing in her wheelchair, while two siblings, Marian and Joe, sat ashen-faced with cousins and friends during Gerry's time on the stand.

Also sitting on the sidelines, was Kay Capano. She, too, was called to testify, but because she was married to Tom she could only testify as to what she saw, not anything her husband told her.

She told the court that her husband arrived unannounced at her home at 7 A.M. on June 28, 1996, the morning after Annie disappeared, and that he took her Chevrolet Suburban and left his Jeep at her house. She said Tom appeared normal and had no visible injuries.

But when he appeared the next night, picking up her four daughters for the weekend, he appeared "agitated." She did not tell them about her conversation with Tom on their deck because it was privileged, but she did say since her husband's arrest last year, she had sent money orders to several prisoners at Gander Hill. By this time, Capano had been accused of soliciting hit men to kill Gerard and Deborah MacIntyre, so the jury was left with the impression that Tom was still planning and plotting from prison.

Finally, in the months before Annie's death Tom had told Annie and several of her friends that one of his daughters had brain surgery. Kay dispelled that as pure nonsense. She was not happy having to testify in the trial. She was unhappy with how her marriage had turned out, but Kay had finally done something about that. On November 13, just three days after Gerry finished his testimony, Kay began watching the trial with a new name: Kay Ryan. Her divorce from Tom was final.

They had separated in September 1995, long before Tom's lurid affairs became grist for the public mill, and she filed for divorce on February 10, 1998, just a few days after Judge Lee denied Capano bail. The divorce was uncontested.

* * *

By the fourth week of the trial Louis Capano was called in to testify against Tom. With tears in his eyes he told the court how he begged his brother Tom to tell authorities time and again about Annie's death. Louis even told Tom that he and Gerard would go to the cops if Tom didn't come forward, but Tom begged Louis not to do it.

"He told me the police didn't have any evidence," Louis said. "He didn't want to ruin his life or his daughters' lives."

Louis kept his word until just two days before he was to be hauled before a grand jury for the third time. By then it was too much for him, as apparently was the act of testifying. Louis excused himself briefly to gather his courage.

Under cross-examination he admitted lying dozens of times, but swore he was telling the truth now.

Louis said Tom drew him into the case on June 30, 1996, by asking him to come to his home. There his older brother told him police had questioned him that morning about Annie. Tom also admitted he was having an affair with her.

Tom Capano gave up part of the truth, telling Louis he and Annie had dined in Philadelphia the night before she disappeared, and because he was the last person to be seen in public with her, the cops suspected he'd done something to her. Tom steadfastly denied it and, as with Gerry, never said there was any horrendous accident.

"He said she was bulimic and suicidal and he had ended the relationship," Louis said.

Tom told Louis that after the dinner that night in Philadelphia he'd brought Annie to his house where she slit her wrists. The wounds were superficial, but she'd bled on Tom's sofa. Tom bandaged her wounds and then drove her home. He hadn't heard from her since, he told Louis, and Tom assumed she went to the Jersey Shore with friends.

Because the police had been probing, and he feared Kay and

his daughters would find out about the affair, Tom decided to dump the bloody sofa and some personal belongings Annie left in his house. Since he'd dumped the articles in a trash bin run by Louis's company, Tom asked him to have the Dumpster taken to the landfill as soon as possible.

Afterward Tom and Louis worked out a cover story and Louis agreed to commit perjury and say that emptying the Dumpster had been his idea. Louis then told his fanciful tale before the grand jury in August 1996, only he said because he believed in Tom.

"Anyone who knows my brother and his reputation knows he could not be involved in anything like this. I love him and tried to protect him."

Louis also said that months later he found out the truth from Gerard. He was shocked to learn from his little brother, who came to him in tears, about the trip *The Summer Wind* made on June 28. Louis was also shocked when he confronted Tom with the story.

"Are you happy now?" Tom said to Louis. Then he told Louis to leave Gerard alone, "Because you're stressing him out." It wasn't the fact that Gerard had helped dump a dead body at sea that stressed him out, was the implication, rather discussing the fact with a brother who didn't know about it was causing him all of his concern.

Over the ensuing months, as Louis fenced with the prosecutors, he said his little brother Gerry became a basket case. He often had nightmares. That's when Louis remembers distinctly asking Tom to come forward and confess. Tom wouldn't do it. After the police raided Gerry's home, Louis again begged Tom to come forward and told him Gerry was about to crack.

"Tell him to grow up and be a man," Tom replied.

Chapter 12

Here's the Story of a Man Named Brady . . . .

If someone wanted to get into the Capano trial to watch, he or she had to pass through a metal detector and two guards at the front door and then walk up two flights of stairs or take the elevator to the third floor to pass through a second metal detector and Kathi Carlozzi.

The Wilmington area during the last few years had been home to some strange, bizarre and high-profile criminal cases. Carlozzi was the "door warden." She made sure that only those who were supposed to get in to see the Capano trial could. She had to fight off her fair share of strange lunatics who seemed to be attracted to the Capano trial. One day she had to forcefully eject a man who screamed out Joe Oteri's name while he was questioning a witness.

"Jesus, my instinct was to duck," Oteri said. "That comes from getting shot."

Each morning Carlozzi allowed two sketch artists, Susan Schary and Bill Ternay, into the building first. After they were allowed in, Carlozzi ushered in Capano and Fahey family members, then the press, and finally she handed out tickets and allowed the general public into the building on a first come, first serve basis until the spectator gallery was full.

All had to wait outside in the hall, and everyone had to pass through her metal detector. At times the crowds were so thick that they resembled a New York subway at rush hour. Some of the members of the general public, who became regular attendees, had to show up as early as 6 A.M. to be guaranteed a seat for the court proceedings, which were scheduled to start at 10 A.M. Sometimes the single-file line of anxious locals stretched fifty people long and cascaded down two flights of stairs.

The press had it a little better. Regular press members with appropriate credentials could be assured of a seat each day, while infrequent press visitors would have to wait to see if there was room in the designated press rows, or take their chances and stand in line with the general public.

The families fared best. As long as there was room in the designated rows for the Fahey family, who sat on the right side of the courtroom, or the Capano family, who sat on the left directly in front of the press, the families got in. The Fahey side of the aisle always filled up. The Capano side was often near empty, many times on days when the rest of the courtroom was packed. Notable exceptions were the days in which Capano family members testified and the days the jury came back with the verdict and later with a recommended sentence.

The courtroom was not comfortable. The dark wood accommodations seemed dark and the courtroom was often oppressively hot. The judge addressed that issue on several occasions and made sure the audience knew the saunalike conditions were caused by the building's heaters and not the presence of so many lawyers and reporters in one courtroom.

The benches the audience were seated on were also less than comfortable. "They look like they were hauled out of a Catholic church,'' an Associated Press reporter was heard to remark. The benches were, many said, as uncomfortable as church pews.

Despite these discomforts, the audience was quite congenial. Capanos and Faheys met and mingled in the lobby and out in the hall with never a sign of open hostility. They were polite and cordial to one another, while inside the courtroom the lives of their loved ones were being laid bare, warts and all, for the general public.

By the fifth week of the trial the emotional distress was beginning to show on everyone's face. Capano had already acted up once or twice, many of the featured witnesses had admitted to lying at one point or another, and the Capano family dirty linen was getting a thorough airing as both Gerard and Louis had stepped forward to give the world insight into Tom Capano's mind and soul.

David Weiss, the Fahey family attorney, was sickened by what he'd already seen. ''Who could have feelings for Capano,'' he told an assembly of reporters one morning before Deputy Attorney General Keith Brady was scheduled to testify. Weiss was upset that Capano's attorneys had gone forward with a plan that seemed to trash Annie's memory. ''If it's an accident, why trash the victim? She was a human being. She did accept gifts, but she wasn't violent like they've portrayed her. All of that is completely unnecessary.''

But what had become necessary was to vindicate Gerard, the prosecution's most important witness. On Monday, November 16, Gerard Capano waived his attorney/client privilege, and his attorney Dan Lyons appeared in court to corroborate that Gerard had told him the story Gerard told in court months before his home was raided.

Lyons spent an entire day on the stand outlining what Gerard had told him and bolstering Gerard's contention that his brother Tom had mentioned extortionists and planned for months to kill Annie.

The next witness was Keith R. Brady, Delaware's chief

deputy attorney general, the second highest law enforcement officer in the state. He had talked to Tom Capano at about 8 A.M. on June 28, 1996. But Brady, although a friend of Capano's, was seen as a tangential witness at the time. Everyone wondered what the telephone call could've been about, but didn't have any other speculation as to why he would be called as a witness.

Brady was supposed to appear on November 17, but Colm Connolly had a bout of flu, so court was put off for a day. "We do not have alternate prosecutors," Judge Lee joked with the jury the next day. "So we didn't have court."

At 10:05 A.M. on Wednesday, November 18, 1998, prosecutors called Keith Brady to the stand. A tall, dark-haired man with wire-rimmed glasses, impeccably dressed, and with a trim athletic build, for some reason he approached the stand woodenly, quietly, almost as if he were walking to his own execution. "He must've really liked Capano to be that upset about testifying," a court spectator noted.

Brady testified that he'd known Capano since 1990 and that they initially had a professional relationship that became a close personal relationship. Capano told Brady in early 1995 that he found Annie to be "an attractive woman" as they both mutually admired her. Later Capano bragged that he and the young woman "were in a relationship." After telling Brady what a fine stud he was to attract such a beautiful and young woman, Capano also told Brady to "keep it confidential."

In the spring of 1995 Brady said Capano told him about a trip to a remote resort that he and Annie had taken together. It was significant in their relationship, because it was the first time Capano and Annie spent a "considerable amount" of time alone together. But just after the trip Capano told Brady that Annie had ended their relationship. "He expressed unhappiness," Brady said with no emotion.

On June 24, 1996, Brady said, Capano called him to set up a golf date, something they occasionally did. Capano eventually canceled and then called Brady on June 28. He didn't reach him. Two days later, on Sunday, June 30, 1996, Ferris Wharton told his boss Keith Brady that Anne Marie Fahey was missing and Capano was the last one to see her alive.

The next day Brady said he got to work and called Capano, getting his machine and leaving a message. Capano called back that day, but a game of phone tag had ensued. Capano left a message on Brady's phone saying that he thanked him for returning the call and saying he "wasn't doing too well." On July 2, Brady finally got a hold of his good friend Tom Capano on the telephone and took notes of their conversation. Those notes became the 133rd piece of evidence entered by the state.

Capano told Brady he was "blown away" by what had happened and that the cops had been treating him badly. Capano also told his good friend that the only thing that happened that night was they went to dinner and then "went back to his house after dinner."

"He then took Anne Marie back to her residence and carried some stuff back to her house," Brady said. Annie told Capano she wanted to take Friday off and didn't want to get involved in "legislative stuff." At 3 A.M. on July 1, Capano had been visited for the first time by Wilmington Police. Capano told Brady that the cops thought he was "hiding her (Annie) out" but Capano said she just "wanted some time off."

"Anne Marie is going to show up," Capano told Brady. According to Brady, Capano told him that Kim Horstmann had called him, and Capano told her, "I'm sure she'll stroll in on Monday," meaning that Annie would show up to work on time on Monday. Capano told Brady that he told Horstmann if Annie didn't show up for work on Monday, "I'd die."

Capano felt compelled, apparently, to say more about Annie. He told Brady that Annie was a "serious head case under psychiatric care," which Brady said shocked him because he had never heard Capano describe Annie as a head case before. Capano also offered that Annie had threatened to kill herself.

Reporters were busy scribbling away as it came to light that

Capano had spun events in another direction for a different audience. When talking to his brother Louis, Tom Capano said Annie had slit her wrists; when talking with Gerard it was a story of extortionists; and when talking with his good friend Keith Brady, he'd merely gone out to dinner with a head case who probably wandered away. There was a story and a new reality tailored for every audience, and Tom Capano could tell the different stories at the drop of a hat.

Colm Connolly shifted the questioning to Deborah MacIntyre.

Did Tom Capano ever arrange a sexual encounter with Keith Brady and Deborah MacIntyre? Everyone stopped taking notes and the court got eerily quiet. The Faheys looked on with small frowns. The jury perked up and seemed to lean toward Brady.

"Did Tom Capano ever arrange a sexual encounter with you and Deborah MacIntyre?" Connolly asked.

"Within the context of his relationship with Deborah MacIntyre," Brady said as devoid of emotion as the rest of his monotone testimony had been.

What the hell did that mean? The reporters looked at each other; the Faheys looked at their attorney; the judge stroked his chin and looked away; and Capano looked straight ahead. The one person who didn't act stunned was Joe Oteri who, after this startling admission of a sexual encounter, was going to get to cross-examine Keith Brady.

"I had to explore that," Oteri later said. "The prosecution didn't have to open that door, but once they did, I had to walk in. I couldn't let it drop."

The prosecution did have a plan in mind by exploring Brady's sex life. They planned to show that Capano was such a control freak, so manipulative that he had orchestrated his friend's and his mistress's sex life. Faced with the opportunity of showing Capano as a manipulative monster, or a sleazy pimp, Oteri said he opted for the latter.

Under cross-examination Oteri forced Brady to explain himself. At least now the packed courtroom knew why Brady approached the witness stand that morning like a condemned man.

"I have committed adultery on numerous occasions with three different women, not including Deborah MacIntyre. These were not relationships," Brady said.

He further explained that he wasn't resentful of Tom Capano for setting him up with Deborah MacIntyre and "considered him a mentor." In what way Tom Capano was his mentor, the audience could only guess. Brady did admit that after his relationship with MacIntyre his feelings for Capano, "cooled, but my relationship remained close."

"You mean you didn't let him know you were upset. You confided in him and he confided in you?" Oteri asked.

Brady agreed. In graphic detail Keith Brady explained how and why he ended up with Deborah MacIntyre and what, exactly, he meant by having had a sexual encounter with her "within the context" of her relationship with Capano.

After going out golfing with Tom one spring day a few years back, Tom introduced Keith Brady to Deborah MacIntyre and they all went back to MacIntyre's home, where Tom proceeded to have sex with her in one room while Keith Brady waited in another. All three of them naturally wanted to be comfortable in this environment, so Brady testified he, too, got naked. At some point during the course of this encounter Tom finished with MacIntyre and sat and watched porno movies while MacIntyre serviced Keith.

Three-way sex. Two men. One woman. The packed courtroom let out a collective sigh. "Sick bastards," one old woman said audibly from the back. Was Keith Brady telling the truth? There seemed to be little reason to lie about such an affair, especially after he described his encounter with Deborah MacIntyre.

"Deborah MacIntyre tried to arouse me by performing oral sex, but I could not achieve erection," Brady reported.

"No man in the world would lie about that," a court spectator offered. "He's telling the truth."

Oteri walked through the entire episode with Keith Brady providing running commentary and a play-by-play description. Later, in 1993, Brady admitted that he went out for a drink and met Deborah MacIntyre and she asked him back to her house. Being a married man, and yet a gentleman, Brady graciously declined. On redirect, Colm Connolly tried to make the point that all of this occurred at the urging, indeed because, of Tom Capano.

Oteri would have none of that.

Oteri attacked Brady's sexual morality, as well as his ethics, by taking notes of a conversation he'd had with Tom on the telephone shortly after Annie's disappearance.

"You made sneaky notes and didn't tell him," Oteri accused Brady.

"I made the notes because Tom was a good friend. It could've helped Tom. It could've hurt Tom. I didn't know at the time," Brady said in a rare display of anger. "I just wanted to have a clear recollection."

As for the threesome, Oteri got a second chance to cross-examine Brady. His point: Brady was in the room with Capano and MacIntyre of his own free will.

"That may be what happened," Brady said.

"You went in to join the party. You were thirty-nine years old. You were naked and doing the nasty. Did she hold a gun to your head, sir? You were there because you wanted a little action!" Oteri was beaming.

"I'm ashamed," Brady said woodenly with his head bowed in shame. "It has been a profoundly agonizing experience and I'm dealing with it with God's help. I'm extremely remorseful."

"When did your remorse start? It didn't start until you got caught, did it?" Oteri shot back.

"My remorse is genuine."

"But, sir, it didn't start until you got caught!" the fiery

Boston attorney let loose. Under the onslaught, Brady left the stand a broken man, just another body left by the wayside in the Capano trial the prosecution would argue.

The mood in the courtroom changed dramatically after Brady's testimony. While things had been described by spectators and reporters as strange or twisted before, with the state's second highest law enforcement official testifying that Tom Capano manipulated him into a threesome with Capano's long-time mistress, the prosecution had successfully turned a corner in their portrayal of Capano.

Prior to Brady, some of the members of the general public who'd been watching the trial were still holding out a pretense of reasonable doubt. Now, while still impossible to gauge what the jury was thinking—with notable exceptions they sat stone-faced through even the most sordid testimony—it was easy to see that among the general public at the trial, and in the community at large, Capano had lost what few remaining supporters he had.

Each day his family, which included four daughters and an ex-wife, had to listen and each day they said it became harder to do so. Capano's daughters occasionally watched the sordid testimony, sometimes with their uncle Joey and sometimes with their mother, Kay, in attendance.

Why, many members of the press wondered out loud, did Kay allow her children to listen to such lurid testimony? Kay said one day in court, it was because Tom wanted his daughters there as a show of support. Kay wasn't there for Tom, she was there for her daughters. "I've gone through enough pain in my life," she said through a veil of tears on the steps leading to the courtroom after a day of particularly salacious testimony. "And that man up there in that courtroom is responsible for a lot of it." She simply wanted to be there for her daughters, no matter what the price.

There was other fallout from the Brady testimony. Brady himself took an unpaid leave of absence from his job, his wife left him, and his reputation was essentially ruined. While the local Wilmington paper took great pains to protect him as much as it could—there was little mention of him at the time and even less mention of him in the specials the paper published upon the jury's guilty verdict—his life was in shambles.

There was great debate over who caused this destruction of a highly respected attorney. Some said Connolly had done it. He did in fact open the door in his direct examination of Brady. Some said Oteri did it by making Brady recount every seamy detail of his extramarital sexual activity.

But, Oteri and Connolly both pointed out that Brady was an adult—a well-educated, well-respected, and bright attorney. Oteri also pointed out that ultimately every man is responsible for his own actions, and indeed Brady had to answer for the choices he made. Connolly and Oteri merely had two different jobs to do and there was, as most legal experts took great pains to point out, no way the information was going to remain hidden once it became known. There was speculation that Brady, Wharton's boss, was the first to let the information be known—to Wharton. While Brady testified in court he never had anything to do with the investigation into Tom Capano's trial, he also testified he knew about the investigation. He had to know the possibility that his sordid secret would emerge under the scrutiny of a thorough federal investigation. Attorneys who studied the case also drew one other conclusion from Brady's testimony: If Tom Capano was going down, anybody he could take with him was going, too.

Chapter 13

Debby Does Delaware

Prior to Annie's death, few knew Deborah MacIntyre was engaged in a long-term affair with Tom Capano. After her testimony her name and his would be locked together forever.

"That MacIntyre woman? You mean the one who was doing that murderer Capano?" a Wilmington restaurant owner said one night after the trial. "They deserve each other."

For many years MacIntyre had hoped that would be true. But as she approached the stand on November 18, 1998, to testify in Thomas J. Capano's murder trial, it was the furthest thing from her mind. She was nervous, anxious, and a little scared. Her lover of many years was on trial for murdering a different mistress, and apparently, he had tried to murder MacIntyre, too.

Her testimony could be most damning to Capano. His own defense team had gone so far as to say she would be the "key" witness, but how would she stand up under the harsh light of public scrutiny, not to mention the oppressive environmental conditions of the courtroom?

Ferris Wharton on direct testimony talked her through all the preliminaries. She was a school administrator who lost her job in February because of the Capano case. She was a mother of two children, sixteen and twenty. She met Capano in 1977 and began her affair with him on that fortuitous day in 1981. They regularly got together at a Motel 6 on Route 9 under the shadow of the Delaware Memorial Bridge.

"Only the best," one of the reporters chimed in from his third-row seat.

MacIntyre said she and Capano had broken up once, in October a few years back, and it lasted for five weeks. Capano wanted to end it, but MacIntyre wanted to get back together.

Capano, she said, never talked about leaving his wife and she got used to a less than public relationship. "We both wanted to keep it quiet." But immediately afterward she admitted she "wanted something good to come out of it, like marriage."

Over the years she spoke to Capano once or twice a day and saw him once or twice a week. When Capano and his wife, Kay, split in 1995, he told MacIntyre he needed eighteen months of bachelorhood, but eventually he wanted to marry her. "I loved him very much," she said, adding that she knew from early on in her relationship with Capano that she loved him. She traveled with him a few times on business trips to Atlantic City, Montreal, and Washington, D.C., the last trip occurring about six weeks before Annie died.

In very quick order, Wharton got to the meat of the matter: the gun. In March 1996, MacIntyre said, Tom Capano came to her and asked her to do "something very special" for him. "He wouldn't tell me what," she testified. He renewed that request in April 1996 and at that time she said he asked her if she would buy a gun for him.

"What? Why?" She asked.

" 'Someone is trying to extort me. I'm not going to use it, I'm just going to threaten them. Besides, I'll give it back and you can use it for self-defense,' " she said Capano told her.

As she testified about the incidents that led up to the purchase of the gun, MacIntyre stared straight ahead, rarely meeting the gaze of her former lover, who sat staring through her from the defense table.

"Why don't you do it yourself?" she asked in response to him asking her to purchase the gun.

"I'd rather not," Capano told her. "I just need you to do this for me."

MacIntyre claimed she didn't want to do it, but agreed to against her will, so she went to the local Sports Authority and said, "I'd like to buy a gun for a friend."

The salesman refused. The type of sale MacIntyre had unwittingly tried to make is called a "straw buy" at the ATF, and is one of the most popular ways for felons to purchase guns. A friend buys the gun and lies on the form needed to purchase a gun by stating the gun is not being purchased as a present.

MacIntyre was embarrassed by the rebuke, turned around, and walked out of the store. But Capano was undaunted. On Mother's Day, 1996, MacIntyre said Capano asked her again to purchase a gun for him. On May 13, 1996, at 12:15 P.M., during a lunch break, Capano drove MacIntyre to a Wilmington-area gun dealer. MacIntyre got out of Capano's car, walked inside, and this time lied to the salesman saying she wanted to buy a small weapon for self-defense.

"He showed me a couple of different guns," she testified. She settled on a .22 Beretta. It cost $180, which she put on a credit card. She also bought a box of bullets. As she filled out the forms to purchase the gun, the dealer explained that it was a federal crime to purchase the gun for anyone other than herself. That didn't stop her, although it scared her.

"I was afraid not to (purchase the gun)," she testified. "I was afraid Tom would get mad. I was afraid he would leave me." As she spoke from the witness stand she seemed to gain strength while Capano, upon hearing her words, roped his attorneys into a conference at the defense table. MacIntyre said after she bought the gun she confronted Capano and explained her fears.

" 'It's ridiculous,' " she said he told her. " 'Don't worry about it. People do this all the time. I'll give it back to you.' "

She believed him. But, she said, he never paid her back for the gun and she never saw the gun again. In a three-page explanation entitled "Why did I buy the gun for Tom?," which was destined to become Defendant's Exhibit #1, MacIntyre gave lots of reasons. "The short answer—so he wouldn't get mad with me and threaten to leave," she wrote, which was fairly close to the testimony she gave.

At no point in 1996, according to her testimony and the written explanation, did MacIntyre ever connect the gun to Annie's disappearance. She did ask for it back, and on February 4, 1997, she claims Capano told her he "threw it away deep in the water."

"He convinced me that it had nothing to do with AMF (Anne Marie Fahey) and neither did he, of course. He told me he threw it away because he knew I really was not comfortable with guns and this was best for me," she wrote.

He gave her a cover story to tell investigators, which she claims she stuck to because of her "poor representation" and "naivete," and she said the government took advantage of both. "This scenario is a perfect example of the way our relationship progressed . . . forever, I have been starving for affection and I played right into his hands. I really believed that such control and manipulation was the way it was supposed to be."

Her explanation, far from just detailing how and why she bought the gun, also details some of the aspects of their relationship. She wrote about a time in 1986 or 1987 when she claimed Capano became physically abusive, shoving her head down on a bed and holding it there.

She also gave some additional details of their breakup that occurred in the 1990s. At the time of the breakup she said she became "hysterical and saw a psychologist," for counseling.

Finally she wrote about the Saturday night before Capano was arrested. MacIntyre and Capano were together at her home. Apparently, he never liked having the lights off and entered the home complaining it was too dark. He became threatening and then "he snapped—he shoved me out of the way, turned over a chair and threw a lamp on the floor."

MacIntyre still loved him at this point, she testified, and blamed his behavior on the stress of the case against him and the fact that he believed his two brothers had spoken to the government.

In what would later become Defendant's Exhibit #2, MacIntyre, like many of the other principals in the case, prepared her own time line as to what happened on June 27 and the days immediately following. Ferris Wharton, the calm and capable veteran prosecutor, walked her through all of it in court.

On the day Annie died, MacIntyre said Capano called her at work around 5 P.M. and told her he had to go to Philadelphia for a meeting, but would probably be back around 9:30 P.M. that night and would call "to say good night." That evening she claimed she went to a swim meet with her children, they got take-out food from a nearby restaurant, and headed home. They ate, and MacIntyre claimed she had some wine and then cleaned up and went upstairs, where she took a shower, got ready for bed, and then turned on the television set. She distinctly remembered watching *ER*, one of her favorite shows, and then called Capano at his home around 10:30 P.M.

She got the answering machine, so she left a message that ended with, "Don't get in too late. Love to hear ya," and then she hung up. As she left the message, she remembered seeing a close-up of Eriq LaSalle on television. Then she curled up into bed and said she drifted off to sleep during the beginning of David Letterman.

Then the phone rang.

"It jolted me awake and I jumped out of bed," she wrote

in her time line, "and walked into the other room to get my bearings so it wouldn't sound like I was asleep."

She picked up the phone.

"Hello," she said.

"Don't you ever leave a message on my voice mail," she claims Capano said to her.

That seemed puzzling, she testified, as she had done it many times in the past. "He was very irritated," she claimed. He told her he was just tired and had a long day. According to her testimony and her time line, he said, "I might want you to help me with something tomorrow morning. What are you doing?" She told him it was pay day and she had to go into work and distribute checks to program directors. "He got angry, very agitated," she said. He claimed that she always let her employer, the Tatnall School, take advantage of her. After about five minutes, she said, they ended the call, with Capano still being upset.

She said she tried to sleep, but couldn't. "I was upset. I tossed and turned for forty-five minutes." Then she called Capano back. She said the phone rang four times and there was no answer, so she hung up. She had wanted to speak to Capano, she said, because she "thought he could make me feel better." Within a minute of hanging up, she said her phone rang. It was one long ring and when she picked it up, no one answered. She hung up. Within seconds, she testified, the phone rang again and when she picked up it was Capano.

" 'I 69'd you,' " she said he told her (a reference to hitting *69 on a telephone to recall someone who'd just called). " 'Why did you hang up?' "

She explained to him that she was upset and couldn't sleep. They both apologized to each other and "had a nice conversation" about her work. Again she said he asked her if she might help him with something in the morning and she again said she had to go to work. "I could pick up the checks early and then help you out," she offered. The conversation lasted, she said, perhaps as long as thirty minutes and she hung up happy. Then, she testified, she immediately went to sleep.

On Friday, June 28, 1996, MacIntyre said she got up early and drove to work around 6:15 A.M. to get the paychecks for some one hundred summer employees. At 6:45 A.M., she testified, she called Capano from the faculty lounge at Tatnall School and told him that she was going to go home, shower, come back to deliver the checks, get organized, and try to take the afternoon off.

She said she could help him with whatever he needed. He told her, she said, that he no longer needed her help, thank you just the same. After that, MacIntyre said, she went back home, showered, and then drove back to Tatnall. On the drive up 17th Street near Tower Hill she claimed she saw a navy-blue Suburban parked along the road. She claimed she saw Tom Capano jogging there and he waved her down.

She slowed, stopped, and said she was ''surprised'' to see him. They kissed and commented on the ''coincidence'' of seeing each other. ''He looked hot and sweaty as if he had just walked,'' she said. They talked a little, her about her workday, and he about a golf game he was going to try and get together and then they parted.

He then called her at work, she testified, around 10:30 A.M. (her time line said it was ''about 10 A.M.''). This was the call that set investigators looking at her in the first place. At this point, she said, Capano told her that he was still trying to get in touch with a friend about a golf game and also was trying to reach Keith Brady for the same. He had plans for dinner— wanted to do something with his kids—but said he would like to see her that evening, probably around 9 P.M.

''Fine,'' she said and hung up. She claimed she didn't hear from him anymore that day.

He showed up, she said, overdue by about two hours and after she had already gone to bed. He had his own key and knew the alarm code to her house.

"He apologized, crawled into bed, and immediately fell asleep," she testified.

The next morning, she testified, they slept in and he left at noon. As he left, she claimed, she saw the blue Suburban parked in her driveway. "It was too big to fit in my garage."

The next day, she said Tom rang her doorbell, walked into the house with his hands on his head, and nervously told her, "I think someone has set me up."

"What's going on?" she asked.

" 'I can't tell you,' " she testified he said.

As she remembered it he was sitting in a chair in her living room and she was sitting on the floor at his feet. Slowly he explained that the police came to his house at 3 A.M. that morning to search it and he was "alarmed, frightened, and worried they would awaken his children," she wrote in her time line. She also testified that Capano gave her a bag containing three adult movies and told her to hide them. He offered her "no explanations," she testified.

He left her home shortly, only to return around 4 or 5 P.M. At that time, she said, he was "visibly upset" and "I don't ask him what is going on—still thinking extortion—and he will tell me when ready." He left and then called her around 9 P.M. that night and asked if she could come over for a while to watch TV with him. She did and then fell asleep in his home, leaving the next morning at 7 A.M. On Tuesday, July 2, 1996, Capano called her at work, MacIntyre said.

"I have something very shocking to tell you. You'd better sit down," he explained. She did.

"Do you recall reading in the paper about a woman who was missing . . . , " he began. "She was last seen out to dinner with a prominent Wilmington attorney? That was me."

"I was shocked," MacIntyre said.

Capano told her that he was a suspect in Annie's disappearance and that he had hired an attorney and he wanted to get out of town for a while.

"I was stunned, shocked, instantly cried, and was too amazed to ask questions," she wrote in her time line. ". . . He was very mechanical. . . . " Capano, she said, arranged for her to meet with Charlie Oberly, whom Capano had already hired, and for the first time that afternoon MacIntyre told an attorney about the events of June 26.

She said that night Capano called her from Stone Harbor, New Jersey, and she asked who Anne Marie Fahey was. "He said he had fallen in love with Anne Marie Fahey, but it was all over now," she testified. "He was telling me he loved me very much," MacIntyre continued. "I was very upset with this conversation. We were not exclusive, no, but he hid this from me."

She asked him how many others there were and he didn't answer. She didn't see Capano again, she claims, until July 17, when she got Italian take-out and went to his house. "It was the first time I noticed the changes in the family room off the kitchen," she wrote in her time line. "Upon commenting on the changes, he told me that he had spilled his brother's home-made wine on the sofa and rug by the table."

With Louis, it had been blood from Annie's slashed wrists. With Gerry, it had been the blood of an extortionist, and now with MacIntyre, the story was spilled wine.

That's where MacIntyre's time line ends and where Wharton chose to stop discussing Annie. From there he led MacIntyre through the potentially devastating testimony of her involvement with Capano, from the early days through their sexual trysts.

Capano, who stonily watched her testimony concerning Annie's death, put his head down and shook it from side to side as MacIntyre recounted her early meetings with Capano, their New Year's Eve huddle in a bathroom, and their brief eventual sexual encounter on Capano's desk at work while MacIntyre's husband worked in a nearby office.

"He got me on his desk, hugging me and kissing me," she

said of Capano. "I enjoyed it. It made me feel good. But I stopped it because someone could walk in."

She talked about her arrangements on Memorial Day in 1981 to meet Capano at his home, and then later, after making love, they set up a pattern of meeting and loving in the shadow of the Delaware Memorial Bridge at the nearby Motel 6.

"He cared for me, he listened to me. He enjoyed my company. He made me feel good about myself. I really did want to spend all of my time with him. I became satisfied with less and learned to live with that because he made me feel so good," she declared in a strong, steady voice from the witness stand.

About ten years ago Capano convinced her to have sex with a man she'd had a crush on in high school. The man had moved away to Boston but was back in town for a school reunion. MacIntyre testified she took the man back to her house and had sex with him in her living room.

"Tom arranged it and watched it from the window," she said evenly.

The courtroom again became disturbingly quiet as MacIntyre haltingly described the sexual encounter. "It was all Tom's idea," she said. "I did it because he wanted me to do it."

With some difficulty MacIntyre also described the Keith Brady threesome and her later encounter with Brady at a restaurant. While she said she had a drink with him, she also said she did not invite him back to her home.

MacIntyre then went through her grand jury testimony and admitted she misled the grand jury about when she and Capano first became intimate. She also testified that after Annie disappeared, Capano told her that since Annie could speak Spanish she'd probably gone to Mexico or "some Spanish-speaking country and would be able to survive for a long time."

She said Capano told her he was being extorted by a man who had tried to extort him years ago. He drove a blue Cadillac, and Capano even supplied MacIntyre with a name, which she didn't remember.

Finally, Capano told her to tell investigators that she had bought the gun for self-defense and for home protection, but she became nervous that her children would find it, so she threw it away.

After Capano was arrested, he had a good deal of time on his hands being locked down for twenty-three hours a day, so he spent a lot of it writing to Deborah MacIntyre. She said she threw away some of the letters, but kept quite a few, as well. She even wrote him back, and once she became a government witness all of the letters that could be found were entered as evidence. His letters were state's exhibits, while her letters became the first joint exhibit, and many found their way into local, regional, and national newspapers. Some of the more lurid aspects were even featured on television news-magazine shows. It is obvious by the intimate and sometimes crude nature of the letters that this was not the original intention of either Capano or MacIntyre.

It is also evident by the letters that Capano is an articulate human being. His handwriting is easily readable—all of his letters because of the confines of jail are handwritten—and he is verbose. He often wrote multiple-page letters, some of them upward of a dozen pages. It is also evident that he considered himself quite the wordsmith. "You ever notice how he doesn't strike anything out?" Ferris Wharton mused after the trial ended. "It's as if everything he writes is perfect the first time he writes it." Certainly, there are few corrections on Capano's handwritten letters, which are complete with detailed, written directions and very purple prose.

Wharton had MacIntyre read excerpts from some of the letters on the stand. Capano's letters are full of venom and he saved his strongest dose for Colm Connolly—whom he constantly referred to as a "snake," a "weasel," and a "Nazi."

But the letters were not void of sexual references or even, as Jack O'Donnell later pointed out, subtle instruments of tor-ture by MacIntyre. "I walked around the house and sent an e-mail to [my daughter] completely naked—cooled off in twenty minutes and am now writing to you . . . , '' she wrote on January 16, 1998. '' . . . I am so proud of you for being so strong and you must be mentally healthy if you can spend so much time alone and confined,'' she added. O'Donnell often pointed out how such characterizations would torture an imprisoned man.

This early letter also still clearly finds MacIntyre believing Capano. ''It sounds like your dream team (Capano's attorneys) has cost about half a million already. Well, I think it is worth it and always will be worth it. Obviously you are lucky to have money, but I know you never intended to spend it this way. Write a book and get it all back. Would you do it?''

MacIntyre also lashed out against Capano's brother Louis. '' . . . I am so glad you have made Joey trustee. It would have been a disaster to have Louis involved, even if this hadn't happened. He is so ruthless. . . . He is the one responsible for all of what has happened. Your younger brother (Gerard) is much too stupid to have come up with such a scheme.''

She also wrote on January 16 of being there for Tom at the upcoming bail hearing, if he needed it and said she missed him quite a bit. She ended her letter by saying Capano's voice was ''like a drug'' to her.

She wrote to Capano again on January 20 and January 21. In the first she talked about drinking with a friend and buying a rug. In the second letter she claimed she had a ''pretty bad day'' because Bob Donovan and another plainclothes detective showed up at work and handed her two subpoenas. ''I had no reaction,'' she wrote, ''but was really mad. Wrecked my day, and I made all kinds of mistakes thereafter as a result.''

She also told Capano that her attorney at the time, Adam Balick, and Colm Connolly got into a shouting match on the telephone the previous evening. ''I'm not scared, as I have nothing to hide, but I am very unhappy about having to go over it all again . . . , '' she added.

On January 22, 1998, she again wrote to Capano and told him not to feel guilty about her having to spend money on lawyers. MacIntyre also took a swipe at Kay Capano in the letter and expressed her concern about Kay's ability to take care of Capano's children. "It is amazing to me that Kay is being so difficult. If she gets the money outright, she will certainly go on a spending binge, compromising your kids (sic) future."

On Friday, January 23, MacIntyre wrote Capano again, and told him about her sick son and the daily problems of raising two children. On Saturday, January 24, 1998, MacIntyre wrote in the first of two letters she sent to Capano that day, telling him that she wondered what she wrote about the previous day because she got so drunk. She told Capano she would be home around 6 P.M. the previous evening to take a telephone call from him at Gander Hill prison, but she stayed at a bar with a friend to drink.

"God knows how much I drank, but I really got drunk I believe," she wrote. Meanwhile, her son whom she suspected had mononucleosis was at home by himself. Her sick son fielded the call from Capano. "I hope you didn't mind 'wasting' a call on him," she wrote.

She blamed Capano's brothers for being "such liars" and ended with a bit more description of her sexual nature and Capano's. "I bet you were thinking about what I was doing last night too and hoping for the best for me. Did that get you going again?" She signed that letter "All my love, Deb."

But MacIntyre's night out caused some conflict between her and Capano, or at least she thought so because she wrote in her second letter, dated January 24, 1998, that Capano hung up on her when he called. She apologized for getting drunk, but said she'd tried to find some stress release because she was "getting ready to be publicized soon after this hearing and I hate it," she wrote.

She was still firmly in Capano's camp, according to the letter, because she also wrote, "As for Connolly, of course I don't trust him. He has no reason not to like me as I have always cooperated before. He doesn't like what I've said, I know. And even though he told me he believed me, I am sure he still doesn't. Very frustrating for me because the truth is all I know."

On Sunday, January 25, 1998, MacIntyre made reference to the coming bail hearing. "It is easy for you to tell me what to do, but I don't think it will be that easy, as they have not been at all accommodating to date."

MacIntyre was concerned about being forced to testify at the bail hearing scheduled for February 2, 1998, and asked Capano numerous questions about what she would face. MacIntyre was worried about there being an audience in the courtroom and wrote that if there was, then "maybe I won't wear my glasses." She also wondered if the Faheys will be allowed to be there.

The letter Capano wrote on Wednesday, January 28, 1998, was entered into evidence. The date was a pivotal one for MacIntyre. On that day she had been interviewed under oath, and the interview had been taped. The most important question prosecutors had for MacIntyre concerned her purchase of the gun.

Some have speculated Capano wanted to write to her on that day to make her feel good about herself, give her a chance to know that lying under oath about the gun was done for a good cause. "It's 11:57 P.M. and with any luck your (sic) naked right now on all fours with your dinner date making you come like crazy doggy style . . . so he can admire your magnificent body on your knees."

Capano also confessed that learning about a recent date MacIntyre had caused him to masturbate twice. He referred to these masturbation episodes as "relaxation" therapy.

But things weren't all sexual escapades in Capano's world at that time. His seven-page letter detailed a number of other things in his life, and on the second page he finally got to what he needed from MacIntyre. "The bad news is that we—that means I—need you to testify next week." Capano explained what he needed MacIntyre to do, outlining why he and his attorneys believed she should testify in his coming bail hearing.

"Debby MacIntyre is an important witness for us but, maybe more importantly, she's an impressive witness. We want Judge Lee to see and hear this very credible and honest woman because she will make a very positive impression on him (once she gets over the jitters which will take two minutes). We don't have many witnesses like her who have relevant and important things to say and is on our side," Capano wrote in his letter. He said this characterization of MacIntyre was the opinion of his attorneys, but he concurred.

He also took time to warn MacIntyre against taking her sister with her to court. He ended the letter with X's and O's.

Despite the candor in her letters, MacIntyre was not totally convinced that her private correspondence with Capano was remaining private. She believed Connolly, Donovan, and Wharton had access or were intercepting her letters. "So, if they are reading this, Hi Assholes," she wrote. When she read the sentence in court, Juror #2 laughed.

Her letter of January 29 showed how she seemed to be on an emotional roller coaster. "I've changed my mind now and do resent you for all that I am going through," she wrote, but by the end of the letter she was "praying harder and harder for you and myself," and ended the letter with "All my love, Deb."

In Capano's letter, written on the same Thursday, he expressed his discomfort with MacIntyre's attorney and Colm Connolly. Connolly in particular always seemed to draw out Capano's temper. Connolly, he claimed, cannot be trusted, "and unfortunately I am always right." Later on in the eight-page letter Capano again vented his frustration with his nemesis: "Why can't people understand Connolly is a snake, can't be trusted, and has to be fought every step of the way."

Part of Capano's fight against Connolly was over the gun Capano had MacIntyre purchase. In many places in several of his letters he meticulously outlined MacIntyre's cover story as to why she bought the gun and what happened to it. ''I told Charlie (Oberly) that I knew you had bought it and I was against it; that you showed it to me and it's possible I touched it; why you bought it; why you got rid of it—because of [your son] and his friends. Hey, that's not the first time nor will it be the last time you make an impulsive purchase—just remember the house fiasco last year—and then realized it was a mistake. Apparently you used your credit card, so it's not like you were trying to hide anything. And as for them having the actual gun—which we doubt—so what? They've got to connect it somehow and Charlie doesn't think—and I agree—they can even if it does have my print on it somewhere. So what if I touched it when you showed it to me?''

Later Capano spent nearly three pages giving MacIntyre detailed and very explicit instructions on what to say when she showed up in court. ''REMEMBER TO KEEP YOUR HEAD HELD HIGH,'' he wrote. ''Be sure to swim the day you testify,'' he added.

Later he described for MacIntyre how to walk, to expect to pass through a metal detector, and then offered her a choice of walking or taking an elevator to the third floor. The courtroom, he said, can be intimidating, but he added that he'll be sitting there ''at a table with my guys.''

''Try to answer most questions either yes or no, but sometimes you'll have to explain things . . . Connolly will try to put words in your mouth, so don't let him,'' Capano coached her through the intricacies of testimony and then told her to expect objections, sidebar conferences, and estimated she would be on the stand for about an hour. After she testified, Capano said, she should leave and get a drink at a local Italian restaurant.

On Friday, January 30, 1998, MacIntyre was still concerned about testifying before the bail hearing and she showed concern for Capano's diet, hoping he got a chance to eat his favorite foods.

But the new public emphasis on MacIntyre's relation to Capano was starting to affect her. "I don't imagine that I will ever be friends with your kids now, or for that matter any of my old friends. It does bother me that my life has been publicized and should be private. I am ashamed to tell you the truth and blame you for it all happening to me," she wrote.

For the first time she also talked about testifying not just for Capano, but for the government: ". . . I don't even understand how immunity works," she wrote.

For more than fifteen years Capano had controlled MacIntyre, down to the point of telling her what to drink, where to go to dinner, who to walk with into court, and who to have sex with and where. Although she was still a month away from signing up with the government, as January came to a close, Capano had to realize her growing resentment was a real threat to his beating the murder rap hanging over his head.

With that in mind he wrote to MacIntyre on February 1 in a very placating manner.

"You were a little testy tonight (on the phone) but I understand. I hope you stick to agreeing with me about your schedule and the other things."

Capano was referring, among other things, to the long list of detailed instructions he gave to MacIntyre for her possible trip to court. He also instructed her to allow a friend of his to drive her to court. Then Capano launched into another theme: the cooler.

By now it was well-known that Capano was suspected of using the cooler to dump Anne Marie Fahey into the ocean. But it was important for the prosecution to show that Capano bought the cooler months in advance of the murder specifically to be used as Fahey's makeshift coffin.

That would indicate advanced planning, and would help bring a death sentence against Capano. Advanced planning would also be a good reason to keep Capano in jail before the trial—something he was desperate to avoid. "Maybe you didn't pay attention," he urged MacIntyre in the letter. "But when you said 'what the hell is that' I told you what it was—a fish cooler for Gerry's new boat . . . I can't imagine they asked you about it last week at the interview, but if they did and you forgot about it, then you can instruct Adam (Balick, her attorney) to send a letter clarifying things. It's important." Capano then told MacIntyre his attorney would come by her house and coach her on her testimony, and "if Adam gives you any grief at all or disagrees or tries to talk you out of things, fire him on the spot and Joe (Hurley, his attorney) will suggest another lawyer."

He finished his letter by tugging at MacIntyre's heart strings by saying he was stuck in prison during his little girl's birthday. He signed off with: "Love you. Follow my suggestions. Please. Tom."

MacIntyre's letter on February 1, 1998, was uncharacteristically long for her and a bit confrontational. She claimed Connolly confronted her about her statement she'd made on January 28: ". . . Connolly had checked on something I said and it didn't match—another bluff because he was wrong."

She was also increasingly agitated with Capano, though she still professed to love him, stating she was unsure she could live up to his high expectations. She was also irate about losing her privacy.

Later, Capano sent this letter back to her with passages underlined and an accompanying note that read in part: "Deb—please mail this letter back to me. I want to keep it to remind me of the good things and the way you once felt about me." He promised to neither call nor write to her again.

However, on February 2, he wrote to her again. "How many times in the course of our relationship did I tell you to dump me, to move on, to make a life for yourself? Obviously you should have listened. Yes, I feel guilty and sorry and I've told you that frequently lately,'' he wrote. ''You didn't do anything wrong and you have nothing to be ashamed of so don't let your obsession with privacy distract you from what matters.''

Capano wrote to MacIntyre about the importance of her testimony and ''that stupid gun. . . . They are trying to twist the gun you bought into something other than what it was. Christ, how many single women own guns for self-protection during record crime waves?''

Although Capano seemed obsessed with the gun and getting MacIntyre to testify about it during his bail hearing, she never did. Somewhere along the way MacIntyre decided she couldn't do it. She refused to go to the bail hearing and lie for Capano. Her feelings about that were expressed in her letter of February 2. She'd previously put up a brave front concerning her January 28 interview with Colm Connolly but finally admitted it was horrible for her and the scare tactics had worked. She said her attorney, Adam Balick, had chastised her for continuing to support Capano. For the first time MacIntyre told Capano, ''No.'' She even admitted as much in her letter and begged for his forgiveness. She ended by proclaiming her undying love.

Capano replied on February 3 that he was ''quite literally numb'' by her decision. But he continued to try to get MacIntyre to see things his way, and to drive home the idea that he needed MacIntyre very badly, he tried guilt. ''Monday's icy letter makes it clear that you are ready to put me behind you and move on with your life. . . . As I said, I didn't expect it to be so abrupt or for the axe to fall this week when I'm at my low point.''

In MacIntyre's letter of February 3 she expressed her fear and said she was ''really shocked'' and ''scared'' by the possibility of facing criminal charges because she purchased the gun. The prosecution made much of Capano's alleged telephone harassment of Annie when Capano was apparently trying to manipulate her, and in MacIntyre's letter she said Capano often made numerous telephone calls to her, as well.

In prison Capano had extremely limited access to the telephone and lost some of his phone privileges because he had manipulated other prisoners into making calls for him. Despite that, MacIntyre wrote him she had five phone messages from him when she got home the night before.

She added a lengthy postscript to her letter—apparently after she successfully connected with Capano on the telephone the night before. In the postscript she confronted Capano's previous day's letter and swore she wasn't selling him out or giving up on him.

But the damage was done. To protect herself MacIntyre had refused to go into open court and lie for Tom Capano. He had specifically asked her in the letters and on the telephone to lie about how and why she bought the gun, as well as lie about seeing a cooler in his basement.

In letters dated February 5, 6, and 8, she wrote complaining about the media attention she had received, how it was worse than Capano ever described, but how she still loved and believed in him.

Meanwhile, Capano took a much nastier tone with MacIntyre in letters dated on February 4 and 9. In his letter of February 4 he'd already gone to the bail hearing and heard through his attorneys the story MacIntyre had told the authorities. "You fucked up," he told her at one point.

"You were my most important witness," he finally said, adding that she should dump her lawyer and sue him for malpractice.

His next letter started out with: "A few additional points by way of farewell;" and then listed on two pages, ten different points on why he was telling MacIntyre "good bye." He said he would throw away any future letters she writes, advised her the government won't offer her immunity because she can only help his case and that he wished her peace and happiness.

There was about a two-week break in the letters. By the end of February, MacIntyre had lost her long-held job at Tatnall, because, she said, the publicity from the trial overshadowed everything she'd done there. Capano broke his two-week silence by writing to her and urging her to fight the Tatnall School. His ten-page opus was filled with optimistic advice. At one point he urged MacIntyre to sue the local paper for libel. He also made sure he told her quite often how wounded he was by her actions and was devastated to find out "that your love and devotion for me did in fact have limits."

MacIntyre had lied in a sworn statement for Capano, bought the gun for him, and had covered for him since July 2, 1996, when she claimed she first learned about Annie's disappearance. It was only in late February 1998 when it became apparent to her that she, too, could be charged with a federal crime for making false statements on an ATF questionnaire, and perhaps charged with perjury because of statements she made on tape and under oath at the end of January 1998, that she decided her love and devotion for Capano had some limits.

MacIntyre's last letter entered into evidence on February 26, 1998, was four pages, and like all of her letters save two it was single-spaced and printed on a computer printer. "You think I have betrayed you—I have not—I have told the truth and we must both live with the truth. I know completely, for sure, without a doubt, you love me . . . I have been walked over most of my life, and by you for sure. I guess I let the man of my life walk over me more than anyone else."

It was a kiss-off, and Capano knew it. "Why do I get involved with these women," he later told fellow Gander Hill inmate Nick Perillo, who in turn talked about it on network television. His last, best ally was finally ditching him. MacIntyre hadn't testified at Capano's bail hearing. She had dumped the attorney he set her up with and gone with her husband's suggestion, Tom Bergstrom—"That loathsome attorney," as Capano had called him. MacIntyre was to be granted immunity and become a witness for the prosecution. Inside Gander Hill, prison guards and inmates said Capano went nuts. He tried to wrangle himself greater access to the telephone, but couldn't do it. He broke at least two rules trying to do it, got caught and was punished.

He wrote to her three times on February 26, just before she was to become a government witness, and promised her he'd spend the next thirty years with her, even intimating he'd ask for her hand in marriage. Then he pled with her to fight for him.

In his letters, Capano built MacIntyre up in one paragraph, only to tear her down in the very next one. The letters often mention Capano's children, as well as MacIntyre's, and even talk about how close Capano came to being the father of her son. In his last three letters he used this yo-yo approach several times.

His distaste for MacIntyre's new attorney was still evident. "Lawyers are a dime a dozen. True love is rare," he advised her. Then after three letters of pushing, plodding, pleading, and prying, he put it on the line to her: "You must now prove your love to me," he warned. "This is my ultimatum and this is your choice: me or your lawyer."

She didn't pick Capano. The day after Capano's letter Deborah MacIntyre signed her immunity agreement.

In Capano's January 27 letter he said MacIntyre had "destroyed" him. "My world just ended," he began after he found out about her defection. Later on in the letter he talked about putting a letter she wrote to him "next to my heart. Debby, I was going to keep it next to my heart until we were together again. It was going to give me the strength to survive, to overcome to come back to you."

He lashed out against Connolly, and said the prosecutor tried to get his own brother Gerard to wear a wire in order to entrap another brother, Joey, in some lies, then returned to his emo-

ATTEMPT TO LOCATE
MISSING PERSON

ANNE MARIE FAHEY
WHITE FEMALE 30, DOB 1/27/66, 5'10", 128 LBS ,
RESIDENCE: WASHINGTON ST.,WILMINGTON, DE.

SUBJECT ANNE MARIE FAHEY WAS LAST SEEN ON
THURSDAY, JUNE 27, 1996 AT   WASHINGTON STREET, AT
APPROXIMATELY 2200 HOURS. SHE HAD DINNER EARLIER
BETWEEN 1900-2100 HOURS AT A RESTAURANT IN
PHILADELPHIA. HER VEHICLE, WALLET AND CLOTHING WERE
FOUND AT THE RESIDENCE. NO CONTACT HAS BEEN MADE
WITH ANY MEMBER OF HER FAMILY OR FRIENDS.

IF LOCATED PLEASE CONTACT:

DET.DONOVAN - WILMINGTON POLICE DEPT - (302)571-4512
LT.DANIELS - DELAWARE STATE POLICE - (302)323-4412

Ann Marie Fahey disappeared on June 27, 1996 after
breaking off a three-year love affair with Thomas Capano.
(Courtesy Wilmington, Delaware Police Department)

Sign outside the local pub where the Fahey family and
friends first organized the search for Anne marie.
(author's collection)

On November 12, 1997, prominent attorney
Thomas J. Capano, 48, was charged with the
murder of Anne Marie Fahey.
(Photo courtesy Wilmington, Delaware Police Department)

Thomas Capano killed Anne Marie Fahey in the house he was renting at the time. (author's collection)

Capano used his brother Gerard's boat, The Summer Wind, to bury Fahey's body at sea.
(Photo courtesy Wilmington, Delaware Police Department)

Security photo of Thomas Capano at ATM machine on
June 28, 1996 helped corroborate Gerard's testimony.
(Photo courtesy Wilmington, Delaware Police Department)

Thomas Capano
denied any knowl-
edge of Fahey's
whereabouts for
over two years
before he was
tried for her
murder.
(Photo courtesy Bob
Weill/ The Review)

Capano's longtime mistress Deborah A. MacIntyre.
(Photo courtesy Bob Weill/The Review)

Kathi Carlozzi, Court Administrator, with the 162-quart cooler that once contained Fahey's corpse. (author's collection)

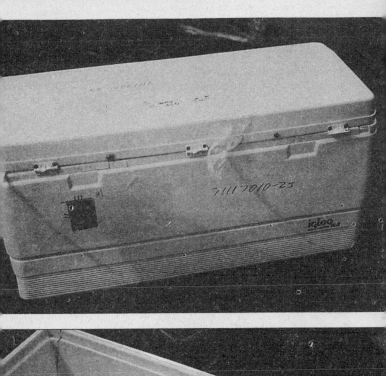

Witness for the State, the youngest Capano brother, Gerard,
(right) and his attorney Edmund D. Lyons, Jr.
(Photo courtesy AP/Wide World Photos)

Second oldest brother Louis J. Capano, Jr. took over the day to day operation of the successful Capano family business after his father died.
(author's collection)

Joseph Capano, the third oldest brother.
(author's collection)

Assisted by her granddaughter Christy, Marguerite Capano leaves her son Thomas's trial. (author's collection)

Thomas Capano with prison escort. (author's collection)

Members of Capano's defense team were (left to right) Eugene J. Maurer, Jr., John F. O'Donnell, Joseph S. Oteri, and Charles M. Oberly III. (Photo courtesy Bob Weill/ The Review)

Delaware Attorney General M. Jane Brody, State prosecutor Ferris W. Wharton and Federal prosecutor Colm Connolly (left to right).
(Photo courtesy Bob Weill/ The Review)

Superior Court Judge William Swain Lee.
(Photo courtesy Bob Weill/ The Review)

Attorney David Weiss (left), Ann Marie's older sister
Kathy Fahey-Hosey and members of the Fahey family.
(Photo courtesy Bob Weill/The Review)

Park bench dedicated to Anne Marie Fahey.
(author's collection)

tional distress caused by her defection. "We swore to each other that we'd stand together so I could beat this thing. You swore you'd always be there and never desert me. When did that change?"

Then Capano wrote (now on page seven of this particular letter) how the other inmates in Gander Hill were mocking him and saying his girlfriend "turned rat" and was a "snitch."

At this point there were no other letters entered into evidence. Later the jury would find out that the correspondence had continued. Prosecutor Colm Connolly had objected to having letters submitted in the case after MacIntyre became a witness for the government because Capano began hinting in the letters that MacIntyre had killed Annie. The only way the public would see or hear from some fifty other lengthy Capano letters would be if Capano himself took the stand.

Wharton's direct examination of MacIntyre continued. Wharton presented to MacIntyre as an exhibit a very accurate floor plan of her home and of her alarm box, complete with the alarm code and details of her bedroom, including a mirror in front of which she testified she and Capano often had sex.

MacIntyre seemed slightly shocked as she identified it all.

Wharton ended his questioning: "Did he (Capano) ever tell you he'd thrown Anne Marie Fahey's body in the ocean?"

"No, he did not," she replied.

"Did he ever tell you she died because of an accident?"

"No, he did not."

The whole courtroom breathed a collective sigh of relief as the direct testimony came to an end. It had led so far away from the original crime that if the Fahey family had not kept their courtroom vigil, there had been a risk that the reason everyone was assembled in the courtroom would've been forgotten.

A seamy, tawdry lifestyle, the newspapers said, had been exposed through Deborah MacIntyre. Here, the prosecution later argued, was evidence of Capano's obsessive, controlling nature at its most venomous. For close to twenty years Capano controlled every detail, no matter how minuscule, no matter how disgusting, no matter how personal in MacIntyre's life.

Now it was the defense's turn to explore that testimony.

Chapter 14

Colitis, Menstruation, and Blood Remover— Oh, My!

Deborah MacIntyre's letters and testimony were crowded with references to her sexual proclivities as well as Capano's. They were also filled with scatological references and comments about Tom Capano's undershorts. For days the jury, the judge, the attorneys, and the public got to see, read in the newspapers, listen to on the radio, watch on television and discuss over the watercooler Capano's most personal habits. But the strangest of fiction did not match the facts laid bare in the Wilmington courtroom.

There appeared, many reporters said, to be no end to the depths to which the trial would sink. In one letter to MacIntyre, Capano made reference to his bloody shorts, caused by his colitis, and joked that he should maybe invite Colm Connolly down to his cell to see if the prosecutor wanted to gather some evidence. In some of the earliest notes that Donovan took, colitis is frequently referred to and it was the topic of discussion in not just MacIntyre's testimony but other testimony, as well.

Why all the concern about Capano's bleeding anus? It was

the excuse he gave for buying the blood remover that was found in his and MacIntyre's houses—blood remover prosecutors suspected Capano used to get rid of bloodstains caused when they said Capano shot Anne Marie Fahey.

By the time it was mentioned in the MacIntyre testimony, nasty hygiene problems weren't the worst of the dirty Capano linen to be aired.

There was so much more, and Eugene Maurer had to cover all the bases as he got up to cross-examine MacIntyre. It was a tough cross-examination. MacIntyre sat, obviously in emotional pain, for several hours giving her direct testimony and reading her letters to Capano. She huffed; she drank water; her voice quavered; and she presented as sympathetic a character as she could to the jury.

She dressed like a conservative librarian, wore wire-rimmed eyeglasses, and had the prim and proper air of a schoolteacher. Despite the sexual, scatological and embarrassing personal testimony, she'd kept a stiff upper lip throughout most of it. When she seemed close to tears as she read passages in the letters about her love for Capano, it seemed, most observers agreed, natural—not forced nor rehearsed. Maurer was facing someone who projected enough dignity into a very disgusting situation to give her some sympathy with a jury. Still, she was no saint and had admittedly lied dozens of times—that was where she was vulnerable—and that's where Maurer chose to begin his attack.

With a cordial "hello," Maurer quickly got MacIntyre to admit she'd lied in her January statement to the prosecution. MacIntyre at one point said she and Capano had been just close friends and only began dating in 1995, after his separation from Kay.

"That was a flat-out lie, was it not?" Maurer asked.

"That is correct," MacIntyre replied.

"I lied from the beginning about the nature and length of

our relationship," MacIntyre admitted, adding that she'd lied as recently as August 1998.

"I am telling the truth today," she stressed.

Maurer also got her to admit she lied repeatedly about the length and breadth of her relationship with Capano—as recently as August 1998.

"I never lied about our relationship intentionally," she said of her statements at an August hearing. "That was a poor choice of words. I was embarrassed for myself."

"You were lying to protect yourself," Maurer said.

"Yes, and Tom Capano."

"That is something you are capable of doing?" Maurer queried.

"Yes."

"You are capable of lying to the federal and state government?"

"Yes, I am."

Then Maurer took MacIntyre back through years and layers of lies.

In 1981, Maurer pointed out, MacIntyre was good friends with Kay Capano. They went shopping together and saw each other. They were, in his words, "trusted friends." So, when Capano and MacIntyre began seriously flirting with each other, "Did you go to Kay?"

"No, I did not."

She testified she never told Kay that her husband came on to her and admitted that she liked their chance encounter at Capano's office in the spring of 1981 and didn't complain to her husband about it, either.

"You wanted to have an affair with him?"

"Not in April. But on Memorial Day it was mutual," MacIntyre offered politely.

MacIntyre also admitted the duplicitous role she played with Capano's wife, saying she showed up in social settings with her spouse Dave Williams and saw Kay Capano—all the while keeping it a secret that she was having a torrid sexual affair with Tom Capano.

She recounted her trips with Capano out of town on business outings, her plans for the future, and again stressed how she got used to less from her relationship with Capano and how initially she was a little upset that they weren't in a monogamous relationship. But, she said, she never knew about Annie, and nothing ever caused her to think Capano was seeing Annie or any other woman.

Maurer went after her about Keith Brady and other sordid aspects of her character, and for the next hour or so in court she took Capano's advice and kept her answers exceedingly short. She limited herself to saying "That is correct" or "No, that is not correct" more than eighty times.

Eventually she admitted she didn't have any suspicions about Capano being a murderer until January 1998, and at that point in time she became worried because she had lied on an ATF form. She was assured, she testified, by Tom Capano that the gun she'd bought was not used to kill Annie. "I was in denial," she claimed. "I wanted to believe what Tom Capano told me."

Among the other things MacIntyre said she wanted to believe was a statement she told Bob Donovan in a March interview. She had told Donovan that Capano told her that Annie's blood was found in his home because he had accidentally struck her in the nose when she violently fought with him as he tried to get her into a psychiatric hospital.

Maurer made a point of showing MacIntyre's duplicitous side as he went through those very same letters the prosecution had combed through in MacIntyre's direct testimony.

In her letter of January 20, 1998, for example, she wrote how she had "nothing to hide."

"Was that the truth?" Maurer asked.

"No. I wasn't thinking about the gun," MacIntyre explained.

Maurer then approached the witness and almost whispered at her: "Were you thinking about June 27?"

"No. Just other aspects of the case."

Maurer had taken the time as he began his cross-examination to write on a large easel situated in front of the jury, "The truth is all I know," which MacIntyre had told Capano in her letter of January 24, 1998. The poster-sized proclamation sat there for the entire length of his cross-examination and was a point he returned to often.

"You have not told the truth many, many times," he charged.

"Correct," MacIntyre replied in her customary monosyllabic monotone.

As Maurer continued to nibble away at her credibility, MacIntyre claimed she was getting confused. "I was confused by the rambling . . . ," she stated at one point in an apparent swipe at Maurer. From the bench, Judge Lee stifled a laugh.

"Yes, I lied under oath," she finally admitted with more stridence in her voice. "I told a lot of lies under oath."

"If I told you," Maurer said, "that you lied sixty or seventy times, would that be about right?"

"I would believe you," MacIntyre replied.

Shortly thereafter, Judge Lee spoke up. "I'm sure everyone in the courtroom believes it's time to quit." The jurors nodded in agreement. It was time for the weekend break in the trial.

Only two days had elapsed while MacIntyre went through the sticky details of her life and read out loud from the letters she and Tom had exchanged. For many in the courtroom it seemed like months. The hope in the general public was that Maurer would finish up soon.

Court was scheduled to reconvene at 10 A.M. on Monday, November 23. It started late the following Monday, but by 10:15 A.M., Maurer was again attacking MacIntyre's credibility.

Central to Maurer's theme was that, far from being under Capano's control, MacIntyre often acted on her own, sometimes in concert with Capano but often acting out against his advice—as a normal, free, supposedly rational, and mature adult would. For example, Maurer looked at the gun purchase.

"Did Tom ask you to buy bullets?" Maurer asked.

"No."

"He didn't discuss with you the bullets, type of gun, method of payment, etc., before you made the purchase?"

"No."

MacIntyre reiterated that it was Capano—not her—who wanted the gun, and while she never discussed the specifics of the gun purchase, it was Capano who drove her to the gun shop and Capano who asked her to buy the handgun.

Maurer then walked MacIntyre through about a dozen interviews she'd had with police and federal investigators in the wake of Annie's death. It came to light then that she'd first spoken to police at the end of July 1996, and she'd come to put together her own time line and position paper on why she purchased the handgun for Tom Capano.

She told Maurer that by the end of January she was "ambivalent" about Capano and afraid of the government's "scare tactics."

"Nothing specific," she said when asked by Maurer what she meant by scare tactics. "It's just the whole interview was frightening to me."

Why, then, pressed Maurer, was she referring to the government's efforts as scare tactics?

"My lies were scaring me," she said.

Maurer continued to probe that, and asked why in her letter of February 3 she agreed with Capano about seeing the cooler at his home, when she in fact had not. "I was being hammered about it," she offered.

"Once again you were doing what he said?" Maurer asked.

"I was trying to pull away, but yes . . . I just wanted it to go away."

If Capano controlled her and manipulated her as she claimed, Maurer argued, why were there times when she fought with him?

" . . . There were times you completely disregarded his advice, didn't you?"

"Yes," MacIntyre offered.

On three occasions in his letters Capano made reference to a house MacIntyre had put a $1,000 down payment on—only to change her mind later. Capano used this as an indication that MacIntyre was flighty, as well as evidence of the fact that she disregarded his advice on occasion.

Maurer went to another portion of a letter, dated January 20, 1998, when MacIntyre poked fun at the idea of Capano controlling her.

"You felt walked on?" Maurer said, after pointing out that MacIntyre herself had dismissed such a notion in the letter.

"I had been for many years," she said with tired disgust lingering in her voice.

But Maurer wouldn't let go. He pointed out in a letter dated January 24 that MacIntyre had no guilt for whatever it was she did and didn't care what others thought. This thought was echoed in her letter of January 27 when she said "fuck all the others" who weren't her friends.

Maurer looked at the jury, feeling he'd made his point that MacIntyre was not controlled by Capano. Charlie Oberly sat with a yellow highlighter at the defense table marking through a document. As he had months earlier to Joe Hurley, Capano—seemingly oblivious to the ongoing testimony—turned and said something to Oberly who immediately stopped using the highlighter.

Maurer finally got around to Keith Brady.

"This threesome, if you will . . . ," Maurer began as he questioned MacIntyre about her escapades with Capano and Brady. How did it come to pass Maurer wanted to know. MacIntyre said she knew Brady and Capano were coming over to her house. Tom had asked her to put on a bathing suit. Luckily, she said, her children weren't home. As for Keith Brady, she testified she never thought about Brady being married. Not for a moment. "I was scared. Better to say I was embarrassed," she said.

"I was afraid not to do this, because I thought he (Capano) might leave me."

Maurer seemed stunned. "You were afraid if you didn't have three-way sex he would leave you?" The surprise in his voice was as apparent as the smattering of grins on the faces of those gathered in the courtroom.

"That is correct," MacIntyre offered.

Maurer seemed to mentally shake out the cobwebs and move on to another by now infamous sexual encounter. In 1988 MacIntyre apparently told Capano about a high school boy she'd had a crush on, but with whom she'd never had sex. She claims at her high school reunion Capano urged her to correct this matter, so she attempted to seduce the man. Capano, she said, liked the prospect of her making love with her old high school buddy, "because he wanted to watch."

She successfully got the man to come back to her house, and she admitted to having sex with the man there in her living room—while Capano eagerly watched from the window outside her home.

"There was nothing to keep you from calling it off," Maurer chided.

"I didn't think I had that option," she said. "I was afraid to do something Tom didn't want me to do."

Apparently, she testified, Tom didn't want her conquest to know there was a voyeur at the window enjoying the sex show the unnamed man was performing with MacIntyre. It was a little private matter between her and Capano. Her old high school flame was just there to perform like a dog in a circus— without the benefit of knowing there was an audience admiring his technique.

"It was bad. What I did was wrong," MacIntyre offered as an apology.

"You don't think there was an element of deceit involved?" Maurer asked.

"Yes."

"You admit that?"

"Yes."

"You derived no pleasure from that situation?"

"No, I did not. I agreed to do it because he (Capano) wanted to do it and because I was afraid not to."

That point withstanding, Maurer succeeded in getting MacIntyre to admit she was a liar, engaged in deceit, and she had sex with at least two married men, while in at least one of those occasions, remaining a duplicitous friend of the man's wife. MacIntyre's morals were attacked—rather successfully, many of the jurors later said—and whatever sympathy she seemed to elicit from the jury also seemed to be crumbling. Capano watched with a glint in his eye and occasionally a smirk on his face as Maurer deftly handled her. That's when he got to MacIntyre's immunity deal.

"You walk scot-free, don't you?" he asked.

"It's fortunate," MacIntyre replied.

"You Walk Scot-Free, Don't You?" he said again, seeming to verbally capitalize each word.

"Yes."

It was obvious as Maurer went through MacIntyre's time line for June 27 that he didn't think she should get to walk away from the case a free woman. It was also apparent he didn't believe much of what she said occurred that day and the days immediately afterward.

For example, she testified that she only remembered in September, just a few short weeks before the trial was to begin, that Capano asked her to "help him out" with an unnamed chore the morning after Anne Marie Fahey disappeared. Presumably this meant Capano wanted her to help dispose of Annie's remains. She didn't remember this detail until very late in the game.

"You mean you woke up and, like a vision, you remembered?" Maurer said in a sudden display of emotion.

"That is correct," she said. "I imagine I suppressed this memory subconsciously."

"You do that?"

"Yes."

"Do you close your eyes and these things come to you?" Maurer taunted at another point.

MacIntyre said she just suddenly remembered. As an example, she said, on the preceding Sunday she suddenly remembered Capano coming to her house with porno movies after Fahey's death.

"I did not remember until then," she offered.

MacIntyre later told reporters that she likened her sudden recollections to "a volcano going off" in her head. She remembered crucial details, some of them just days before the trial when "I started thinking with my brain and not my heart."

Maurer and the defense team had another interpretation: They thought she was lying and making up testimony as she went along. Maurer then asked her about the morning telephone call she received from Capano on June 28, 1996. This call occurred while he was in the process of getting Annie ready for disposal at sea.

"In fact, didn't he say, 'Everything is going fine with what I'm doing . . .'?" Maurer said with more than a hint of accusation in his voice.

"No," MacIntyre said. "He never said that to me."

While MacIntyre claimed this call—which occurred at Gerry Capano's Stone Harbor home—lasted for a couple of minutes in length, Maurer pointed out through telephone records that she was either lying or mistaken. The call lasted less than a minute.

Maurer let that revelation work on the jury's collective psyche as Capano openly grinned. Maurer then moved on to another

subject: the day MacIntyre claimed she found out about Anne
Marie Fahey.

Was she upset? Yes, she was, she admitted.

"How upset?" Maurer wanted to know.

"I was upset."

"Angry?"

"I was upset."

"Extremely upset?"

"Yes, I was."

Then came the outright accusation.

"Didn't you in fact find out about Anne Marie Fahey not
on July 2, but on June 27 or 28?"

"No, Mr. Maurer. I never heard of Anne Marie Fahey until
July 2."

"Didn't you go to [Capano's rented home] June 27 to 28
with a firearm to visit Tom?"

"No, sir. I never left my property from the time I returned
from the Arden Swim Club [where she'd gone with her children
for a swim meet] until the next morning when I went to Tatnall."

"Didn't you have your firearm at Tom Capano's house on
June 28, 1996, when you first learned about him and Anne
Marie Fahey?" Maurer asked with force.

"No. I did not," MacIntyre replied with equal force.

"And you deny that your firearm discharged that night in
that house, striking her?"

"I don't know what happened to that firearm. I gave that
firearm to Tom on May 13, 1996."

"You deny that you discharged that firearm?"

"I deny that I discharged that firearm."

"Are you absolutely certain about that?"

"I am absolutely certain about that."

Chapter 15
Slick Nick

The trial of Thomas J. Capano now limped toward the Thanksgiving holiday. In the real world outside the packed Wilmington courtroom, there was talk of impeachment and presidential sexual shenanigans. The world, it seemed, was awash in sordid tales of sexual encounters, backstabbing and corruption. It paled in comparison to the Capano trial and was barely talked about in Wilmington.

"Who cares?" was the common reaction to the ongoing presidential story.

The MacIntyre testimony put the Capano trial over the top in terms of what many called seedy, immoral behavior. Who, it seemed, wanted to talk about the President when in gossipy, staid Wilmington the topic of conversation everywhere was that people who'd once been so highly thought of in their conservative, little town were, in the words of one restaurant owner, "sex freaks" and "murderers."

Anne Marie Fahey's death seemed very far away when compared to the general lack of morality displayed by many of the principal witnesses, all of whom testified they were in therapy. Some, like Capano, were being treated with an assortment of chemicals that many addicts would pay top dollar for on the street.

Deborah MacIntyre's testimony brought the "morally repugnant" aspects of the case into sharp focus. While MacIntyre herself could certainly be seen as another manipulated victim of Capano's, she also appeared flawed and not without some guilt.

"I wonder if she ever knew she bought the gun that killed my sister," Robert Fahey mused often during these times in public.

The Faheys had limited sympathy for MacIntyre, as did the general public. With newspaper headlines like "Thanks for Sharing" and proclamations like "Debby Does Delaware" floating through Wilmington, clearly people weren't entirely sympathetic to MacIntyre's involvement in Fahey's death. MacIntyre herself remained closeted, staying at her Delaware home and trying to ride out the storm. News crews and reporters regularly knocked on her door during this time—especially after the sexually titillating testimony was made public. She kept all but a few at arm's length, often refusing to even open her door for reporters. She was clearly having trouble with her newfound popularity and was taking few chances with her reputation in public.

Capano himself seemed to be having trouble with her testimony, as well. During Maurer's cross-examination when he accused MacIntyre of pulling the trigger and killing Annie, the trial was halted because according to Joe Oteri his client Tom Capano "is under some medical and physical distress." He explained Capano's problem could be rather messy and smelly, and the courtroom was quickly cleared.

Several jury members, before being led away, said they saw Capano pull his legs up under him in a fetal position as he sat at the defense table. At least a few thought Capano's distress

had little to do with his physical distress and more to do with
the emotional distress MacIntyre's testimony was bringing him.

Outside Oteri met with reporters and came to the point.
"He's shitting his guts out with colitis," Oteri said, painting
a mental picture many reporters hadn't anticipated and didn't
want.

After the break MacIntyre continued saying she wasn't "hiding anything," but Capano was no longer eager to hear her
testimony. He sat at the defense table with his head down for
most of the afternoon.

There was no redirect by Wharton or Connolly after Maurer's
cross-examination, but the prosecution did face the challenge of
corroborating some of the key points in MacIntyre's testimony.

The first person they chose for this was Nick Perillo, the
same Nick Perillo who Capano had told MacIntyre in a letter
on February 27, 1998, was near tears after finding out MacIntyre
had ratted Capano out.

Perillo, a silver-haired petty thief with a history of burglary,
forgery, theft, and drug addiction, was well-known in the Wilmington criminal community. After the trial he became a minor
Wilmington celebrity in his own right, appearing on ABC's
20/20 and occasionally popping up in local bars greeting well-
wishers.

"Perillo is quite a character," one jail guard said of him.
"He's doing life on the installment plan."

Perillo readily admitted to his reputation, but in court also
admitted to being part of the Capano puzzle. As Perillo told
the story, in early March, right after MacIntyre signed her
immunity agreement and agreed to testify for the government,
Capano secretly plotted with Perillo to break into MacIntyre's
home, burglarize it, and vandalize it in an attempt to terrorize
her. Evidence already showed Capano was, at the same time,
telling MacIntyre how much he loved her.

Perillo, or "Slick" Nick as defense attorney Jack O'Donnell
and a host of other prisoners called him, had been arrested on

two burglary charges in January. He faced a possible life sentence as a habitual criminal, but his own attorney Tom Foley later said he probably would have faced closer to five years for his charges.

Perillo said after he was arrested on January 12, 1998, he lied to prison authorities to get a better bunk in prison. Perillo said he needed protection from another inmate because Perillo was going to testify against him. That lie would keep Perillo from sleeping on the floor in general population "in deplorable conditions" as he had during his previous stay at Gander Hill. "I hoped I would get a cell and a bed," he said.

It worked, and Perillo was placed in solitary confinement on the "1F Pod," home of Thomas J. Capano. Shortly after Perillo's arrival, he testified that Capano was placed in a cell next door to his own. They struck up an easy talking friendship by speaking underneath their cell doors, and a short while later, Capano asked Nick to do him a favor.

Perillo "played" the new "fish" in the tank—Capano. Perillo appeared to go along with Capano, but as early as February 27, the same day MacIntyre signed on with the government and Capano swore to her in a letter that Perillo was distraught over her defection, Perillo wrote to his own attorney telling him that Capano had told him MacIntyre had bought the gun for him. He asked Foley to keep the information private for the time being because he didn't know yet what to do with it.

"Jesus, I think the bastard killed her (Anne Marie) and he's trying to destroy anyone that gets in his way . . . ," Perillo added, asking for advice from his attorney about what to do about the conversations he was having with Capano.

In an additional correspondence, also written on February 27, Perillo said Capano was becoming increasingly agitated with MacIntyre because she wouldn't take his advice. "He said he always gets involved with head cases like Fahey," Perillo claimed. "He called her (MacIntyre) a stupid dumb bitch time and time again." Perillo also said Capano paid him $25 for his efforts, which had been deposited in his commissary account by Capano's estranged wife, Kay. She never knew why the money was placed there—but did it after Capano asked her to do so.

The very next day, Perillo agreed to place a call to MacIntyre for Capano.

"He asked me to call you to see . . . to see what your schedule was," he told MacIntyre when she answered the phone.

"He misses you . . . ," he also said.

"Oh, God, don't he, you know, oh, it's past that for me," MacIntyre said.

"Okay."

"You can tell him that."

Perillo and MacIntyre exchanged some pleasantries, including the fact that Perillo had called previously and spoken with her teenage son.

Then Perillo slipped into the conversation a question Capano wanted him to ask.

". . . he wants to know if the rumor is true. I don't know what that means," he said.

"I don't know what that means," MacIntyre replied.

They apparently both knew what that meant.

They changed the subject to the current edition of the local newspaper, which featured MacIntyre's picture on the front page with an accompanying article.

Perillo didn't mind talking about that, but keeping in mind what he'd already written about to his attorney, he had a question of his own for MacIntyre.

"Yeah, he, he, I guess, heard rumors, uh, about, I think it was, it had something to do with the, what was supposed to be in the paper today."

"Yeah. Well, that was there. It was in the paper. There's a picture of me and everything, so . . . ," she replied.

"That he . . . ," Perillo began, which was met with a long sigh by MacIntyre. " . . . He asked you to get that?"

"What are you talking about?" she asked.

"The, the gun."

"Yup," she said.

"Yeah, that's what, that's what he said."

From two different sources, the only two in the world who would know, Perillo had confirmed the truth about why MacIntyre had purchased the gun. She'd done so for Capano and he had encouraged her to lie about it.

A short time later, after Capano told Perillo he had MacIntyre buy the gun that prosecutors say was used to kill Fahey, Capano had another favor to ask. On March 4, Perillo said, Capano asked him if he knew of someone who would burglarize MacIntyre's home. "He said it would be 'easy pickings' " because MacIntyre would be away on a ten-day vacation. He added this conversation to the second correspondence begun on February 27, along with his growing concern about being around Tom Capano.

In this same correspondence Perillo again asked for advice, and said in blunt terms how he considered Capano volatile and dangerous. "I am sick of hearing this tale and will help in whatever way I can," he said

On March 4 Perillo also wrote to Ferris Wharton, telling him, "I have some information pertaining to Mr. Capano and his dealings with Debby MacIntyre that I'd like to discuss with you. . . ." Wharton received the letter on March 10.

Perillo told this to his attorney on March 8 and said some "crazy" things were going on in prison. Foley originally thought Perillo's story was too far-fetched and speculative. "They are never going to want to use a guy like this," Foley told himself. He finally decided to approach Connolly with Perillo's story.

Three days later, on March 11, prosecutors met with Perillo. He walked into the prison meeting with a five-page diagram, which included a road map to MacIntyre's home, a diagram of her burglar alarm—complete with alarm code, a detailed floor plan of MacIntyre's house, and a page with thirteen written instructions that outlined specific items to be burglarized and vandalized in MacIntyre's home.

"Total of five TV's. Best one in master bedroom," said instruction #9.

"Must shatter floor to ceiling mirror on wall in master bedroom. Absolutely required."

"Must locate and remove plastic bag with sex toys and videos in a closet in master bedroom suite or under bed," read instruction #11. All the art in the house was original "and valuable" and must be removed or destroyed, it was explained. Perillo said Capano gave him the road map and instructions on March 5 and told him the best time to hit the place was between March 18 and 28. Perillo, by now tired and evidently scared of Capano, wanted nothing to do with it and gave the entire package to the prosecution.

The floor plan of the home was so exquisitely detailed that it pointed out where hidden valuables were in certain closets, advised that there was nothing of value in other storage areas, and even advised there were no motion detectors, so the burglar wouldn't have to worry about being caught once inside.

Rumors and reports of such activity on Capano's part had been known for several months. Nonetheless the detailed nature of the instructions, first mentioned by Wharton during MacIntyre's direct testimony, showed to what great lengths Capano would go to strike back against MacIntyre. The ramifications were astounding to many in the courtroom.

Jack O'Donnell, whose task it was to cross-examine Perillo after Ferris Wharton had laid out the plot with such great care on direct examination, faced another daunting task.

Perillo admitted he'd spent fourteen of the last eighteen years in prison and denied he ever came forward because he thought he could get a deal for himself. He said he did it because he feared for MacIntyre.

"It never occurred to you that if you set Tom Capano up,

you could eat Christmas dinner outside prison?'' O'Donnell asked.

Perillo never got upset, even as the defense sought to tear him up. He just chuckled lightly. ''That's ridiculous,'' Perillo replied.

It was clear to see the jury enjoyed Perillo's roguish performance. He seemed genuinely disturbed by Capano's actions, and while an admitted criminal and felon he clearly didn't find Capano's behavior in any way desirable. He was, many later said, a breath of fresh air in the courtroom. He laughed, he was animated, and he seemed grounded in reality. More importantly, the judge, the jury, and the courtroom laughed with him. He was a felon, but he still knew right from wrong. That was something that many spectators said seemed a unique character trait among many of the principals in the Capano trial.

But O'Donnell continued to accuse Perillo of making a deal and setting Capano up to do something Capano normally wouldn't do. Perillo admitted he was addicted to cocaine and heroin. O'Donnell got him to talk about his past as a ''snitch'' for law enforcement and also got him to admit he burglarized the home of his former attorney, who was also his ex-wife.

Thanksgiving came and went. The Faheys celebrated it without their youngest sister, and Capano celebrated it behind bars in a cold and lonely cell. The prosecution was winding down its case now. It still had to corroborate portions of MacIntyre's testimony and there were a few other important witnesses to see, but the general mood as the public came back was that of renewal.

Chapter 16
The State Rests

The prosecution had a lengthy list of people to get to as court reconvened. Still hoping to bolster and corroborate MacIntyre's testimony, the state called Mary Ann White, Tatnall's assistant business manager. Although she testified she was with MacIntyre a little later on June 28, 1996, than MacIntyre herself claimed, White testified that she was together with MacIntyre in close proximity for nearly forty-five minutes from 7 A.M. to 7:45 A.M. the morning after Annie's death. MacIntyre seemed "fine," she said.

Leigh Anne Cassidy-Chesser said she talked to MacIntyre and had a "pleasant" conversation with her that afternoon around 2 P.M. about her children attending Tatnall's extended day-care program.

Joan Brady (no relation to Keith Brady) testified she was MacIntyre's assistant at Tatnall. She saw her on June 27 at the swim meet and again the next day at work, and she appeared "normal" both times.

Brady apparently had MacIntyre's ear, because MacIntyre

confided in her about her romantic liaison with Capano, and on July 2, the same day MacIntyre claimed she found out about Annie, Brady said MacIntyre seemed upset. "She took me into my office and closed the door and said Tom Capano was the last person seen with Anne Marie Fahey. She was upset."

The prosecution hoped to show that MacIntyre couldn't have anything to do with Annie's death because there was no way she would have conducted herself the way she did immediately after Annie's death.

The defense hoped to show that all of the telephone calls between Capano and MacIntyre the day of the murder and immediately following showed collusion and cooperation on something relating to the murder. Taken out of context, the prosecution would say, it could've been seen that way. But in the context of the fifteen-year relationship Capano had with MacIntyre, it was not all that unusual for them to talk several times during any given day.

After the Thanksgiving break another issue had to be addressed by the prosecution. One of the theories advanced by Capano was that the blood found in his apartment that belonged to Annie was there because during sex she'd bled on his floor due to a heavy menstrual flow.

Dr. Scott Hawkinson testified Annie never complained of a heavy menstrual flow and that she said she was not sexually active from 1993 through 1996.

Capano's time line was introduced by Kevin Shannon after the break, as well. Shannon, an FBI agent, testified that he seized a file from the law offices of Capano's partner. It was the early alibi prepared by Capano, and his attorneys fought to keep it from being introduced as evidence, saying to do so violated attorney/client privilege. However, since Capano sought to hide the file, Judge Lee admitted it as evidence.

Brian Murphy testified about the press release he and Capano drafted and never sent out to the public. In another attempt to explain the bloodstains found on the floor of Capano's home,

Murphy testified that Capano had told him that one of his four daughters might have cut herself while running around his house.

This all occurred on November 30, during the seventh week of the Capano trial. The next day, December 1, 1998, the trial entered its third month and brought the public a view of yet another Capano mistress.

Susan Louth, a petite, pretty blonde dressed in black, approached the stand with all the energy and enthusiasm of a high school cheerleader. It was obvious to everyone that Capano enjoyed watching her enter the courtroom.

Her testimony added another shock to a trial that was already quivering from Perillo's and MacIntyre's testimony. Louth testified that even while Capano was trying to rekindle his romance with Annie, stringing along Debby MacIntyre and busy breaking up with his wife, he was also dating her between November 1995 and July 1997. She said the two of them shared a nonexclusive sexual relationship. "It was like a challenge for me. I liked that," she told the jury.

"How in the hell does he do it?" several of the male jurors asked during the break.

As he had with MacIntyre, Capano corresponded with Louth from behind bars—beginning one letter with the affectionate sobriquet "Dear Slutty Little Girl."

The letters to Louth were as ribald, if not more so, than those he'd sent to MacIntyre, the prosecution showed. "You are, after all, dumb, you flatbacked your way through school and you never learned to count," Capano told her in a letter dated Thursday, February 12, 1998.

Capano also talked about getting fan mail "from young chicks who want to get together when I get out. Can't wait. One of them will probably send me sexy pictures soon and in her last letter talked about oral sex. Perfect."

Capano seems not to have had a problem writing about

everyone's sexual preferences, especially Deborah Mac-Intyre's, or insulting people.

Capano wrote MacIntyre's son about the upcoming court trial and how his mother had a new "unethical," "sleazy," "disgusting," "scumbag" lawyer. "I cannot stop loving," MacIntyre, Capano wrote. But "I'm about to say something you may not like, but it's true. Your mom is not very strong, so people are able to intimidate her and force her to do things she doesn't really want to do. There are times I'm sure, when I did it (although I really can't think of any) but at least I love her and care about her." He also told him to tell his mother to "be extremely nice to Tom Shopa because he has what she needs and can be trusted to be very private and is definitely interested in helping her take care of it, but is too shy to ask so she'll have to ask him."

On the same day of the Louth testimony, Shopa came forward and said that Capano, a longtime friend, asked him to go over to MacIntyre and sexually service her. "He said she was very needy," Shopa, a divorced accountant, told the court. "I was shocked and very upset by it."

Considering the testimony of previous witnesses, the prosecution made sure it pointed out Shopa never followed through with Capano's wish. Capano's letters to Louth also discussed the problems he'd been having getting along with the guards in prison. He said he'd been labeled a "troublemaker" and would probably be moved to a maximum-security prison elsewhere in the state. He told Louth he wanted to "get even" and asked her to test the waters on a theory that people might buy about Annie's death. "Maybe you also heard that a couple TV stations — but not the *News Journal*—reported that I was going to say she (Deborah MacIntyre) killed Anne Marie and I covered it up for her. I can't tell you or anyone where we're headed, but if you talk to anyone, why don't you say it makes a lot of sense for a lot of reasons." Capano told her that by floating that scenario she might influence his potential jury pool.

He said he'd pay for Louth's testimony if she'd travel from the Virgin Islands, where she was living, to Wilmington to testify for him. He apparently wanted Louth to testify that it took two of them to move some heavy furniture he'd given her, because the prosecution was alleging Capano moved Annie's body all by himself after she died. He was going to say it was impossible to do.

Capano also raged against the system in his letters to Louth, saying he beat the prosecution in court at the bail hearing, but Judge Lee wouldn't give him a fair shake and was convinced Governor Carper put political pressure on everyone to keep him in prison.

On December 1, 1998, there was a small cadre of other witnesses, including Chris Hancock, a Blood Bank of Delaware donor advocate, who said they retrieved Fahey's donated blood (she had donated it in April 1996) from the Swiss Red Cross. Alan Giusti, a DNA analyst at the FBI laboratory, said there was only a 1-in-11,000 chance that blood found in Capano's house came from someone other than Anne Marie Fahey.

It was now December. The local newspaper reported a forty-five-year-old woman was stopped by Newport police on Monday, November 30, after they clocked her driving 47 mph in a 30-mph zone. She apparently didn't handle herself too well because the police decided to search her car. They found a small wooden pipe with marijuana in it and a small amount of cannabis sativa in her car. She was a juror in the Tom Capano trial, and when she reported for jury duty on December 1, she was removed from the case by Judge William Swain Lee.

On Thursday, December 3, the prosecution rested, but not before the 235th piece of evidence was introduced: the cooler.

The prosecution prefaced its introduction with testimony by several people who showed just how lucky the state had been in recovering the cooler. Ronald J. Smith told the jury he remembered that a friend of his, Kenneth Chubb, had found a cooler with bullet holes and no lid while fishing in the Atlantic Ocean on the Fourth of July weekend in 1996.

When Chubb showed Smith the cooler, Smith said he looked at the holes in it and told Chubb it had been shot with a 12-gauge shotgun slug. Smith, after reading about Fahey's sea burial and the discarded cooler, called the FBI and said, "I'll tell you a story and you tell me what you want to do."

The fact that the cooler had been shot had never been revealed in public. Detective Bob Donovan said he drove to Chubb's vacant trailer near a Delaware beach and found the cooler in a shed, where Smith said it would be. FBI forensic expert Michael W. Ennis then took the stand and told the jury that bullet holes, in the side and bottom of the cooler, came from a single lead slug. Then Colm Connolly and Ferris Wharton slowly reached under the evidence table, picked up the cooler, and like pallbearers marched the cooler (described as Annie's "coffin") before the jury and put it down. A few of the jurors leaned forward to get a closer look.

Then the last witness was called, and Kenneth Chubb, a middle-aged fisherman and seemingly affable fellow, got on and told the story of how he found the cooler, patched the holes, put the lid from an old cooler on the new one, and added a handle. He'd used the cooler on his boat to hold fish and stored it during the winter in his shed.

The day after Capano was arrested, Chubb's old friend Smith called and said, "They are looking for your cooler."

That ended the prosecution's case.

Close to eighty witnesses had been called, and 235 different pieces of evidence had been introduced. After seven weeks of testimony, Wharton's contention, first espoused at the bail hearing, "If Capano couldn't have her, then nobody could," was the motive both Wharton and Connolly said drove Capano to kill Anne Marie Fahey. The onetime prominent attorney and social scion from one of the wealthiest families in Wilmington had been portrayed as a sexual dilettante—a rich, spoiled man used to manipulating people and getting his own way, no matter what his kinky and perverse tastes demanded.

He was described as a monster. "I think there was a fight going on inside Tom Capano's head between good and evil," Colm Connolly later said. "And on June 27, 1996, evil won." He was not only portrayed as a murderer, but a man who tried to plan the perfect murder. Here was a man who claimed to be a good father, but the prosecution had painted him as a callous, ruthless man who would use anyone and anything to get what he wanted—forsaking his marriage vows for pleasure and forsaking that pleasure to commit murder. He was portrayed as a "control freak" who preyed on vulnerable women and both flattered and insulted them to get what he wanted.

The prosecution's case had been full of surprises, coming almost daily, as Capano's life became well-known and was intensely discussed in the tiny town of Wilmington, and up and down the east coast. Newspapers from Pittsburgh, Washington, D.C., Baltimore, Philadelphia, and New York regularly sent reporters to cover the increasingly bizarre revelations that escaped from the mouths of the major witnesses in the Capano case.

How did something like this stay hidden for so long in friendly, gossipy Wilmington, Delaware? That was one of the big questions. No one in the pubs seemed to know for sure. Everyone seemed to know something about Capano. One person knew he was stepping out on his wife, another knew he liked to impress women.

Susan Louth said when she went to work at the law firm Capano worked at, she was told by everyone to be careful of Tom Capano because he "was a big flirt." But everyone also said he was so friendly, so winsome, so helpful, and so charming. This was not the image presented in the courtroom. The two different Capanos seemed so far apart, it was doubtful whether one knew the other existed.

MacIntyre's testimony showed she'd seen both sides of Capano when she said no one could build her up as well as Capano and no one could trash her better, either. What became obvious was, at least just prior to Fahey's death, Capano was running his life as if he were the carnival performer who tried to keep all the plates spinning at once.

He was a middle-aged man, a former rugby player, and an outgoing social animal who'd split from his wife and lived all alone in a spacious, expensive home. The plates he had to keep spinning included being a father and friend to his four daughters; he was involved with MacIntyre, Louth, and Annie while his wife divorced him; he had the managing partner's job at one of the top local law firms; and he had social and political responsibilities and public appearances to make.

How could he keep it all going without having the whole thing crash in on him? As it turned out, he couldn't. The defense team said the prosecution had done a very good job of demonstrating that. What Connolly and Wharton could not and had not done was to show little more than circumstantial evidence of Capano's crime. There was still no corpse. The prosecution, while giving a good reason why Annie was murdered, had not endeavored to tell anyone how it was done. They couldn't. They couldn't even say for certain when Annie died. What the prosecution could do was give the jury the cooler.

Looking at that cooler sitting in court every day after it was introduced was a powerful emotional experience for members of the jury as well as the Fahey family. Mark Fahey still doesn't like to talk about it. His younger sister, Kathy, said it was upsetting to see and touch the cooler, but glad it was presented to the jury. "Anne Marie was shot," she said. "Anne Marie was stuffed in a cooler and I think it was important that got across."

Capano's kinky sex escapades meant nothing to Kathy Fahey-

Hosey, either. "I don't care who he slept with," she said about Capano. "He murdered my sister."

Other Fahey family members were equally vocal. Brian Fahey challenged Capano to come forward and testify, but said he didn't think Capano had "the guts" to do it and was too smart to make such a bad mistake. But Capano's own attorneys weren't so sure. Behind the scenes a monumental feud was brewing between Capano and his attorneys. Since Oteri had given the state Annie's murder and the body in their opening statement, Oteri and Capano and his other attorneys had been heading for a showdown. There was only one person who could adequately describe what had occurred in Capano's house the night Annie died, and that was Capano himself.

He admitted to being there, dumping the body and having dinner with her the night she died. There was talk in Oteri's opening statement about another person being present who could verify all this. It was widely assumed that MacIntyre was that person, and indeed Eugene Maurer had certainly pointed bluntly in that direction during his cross-examination. But Mac-Intyre had said she wasn't in the vicinity of Grant Avenue the night Annie died. She was at home. That left only Capano to explain what had happened.

There seemed to be little doubt he was compelled to testify, but Oteri was dead set against it, as were the rest of Capano's attorneys and they voiced their concern daily with Capano.

"My concern is a practical one about that," Oteri explained. "It's not just that we believed that Tom Capano couldn't handle himself. He actually did better than we thought he would do. But anytime you argue for reasonable doubt to a jury and don't put your client on the stand, then the burden is strictly on the prosecution. Did they prove their case? And it's easier to punch holes in that. But when you put your client on the stand, then you give the jury the choice of believing the prosecution or believing your (the defense's) story, and invariably, I think that weighs heavily against the defense."

But Capano wasn't buying it. Jack O'Donnell, who knew Capano for close to thirty years, said during this time it became extremely difficult to work with his old friend. "This is not the Tom I knew. That Tom is rational. This Tom is totally irrational. We told him not to get on the stand because we knew he wasn't playing with a full deck and couldn't handle it," O'Donnell said. "He didn't make one single rational decision during the course of this trial. He spent over a million dollars for his lawyers and he rejected our advice daily."

Chapter 17

The Scalpel v. The Chain Saw

What everyone expected when they assembled in the court-room on a balmy Pearl Harbor Day in Wilmington, Delaware, is not what everyone got. December 7, 1998, was supposed to be the first day of Tom Capano's defense against the charge that he planned and carried out a murder on Anne Marie Fahey. But Capano decided to drop a few bombs of his own on Pearl Harbor Day, and they had little to do with his actual defense. Instead, he was upset with the people who were defending him.

Judge Lee began the morning session with his usual pleasant-ries and was about to bring in the jury, but didn't. Joe Oteri stepped forward and announced to the judge that the defense team and the defendant had "serious strategic differences."

Those differences, Oteri said, were "deep," and they had attempted to resolve them and they could not be resolved. As a result of those differences, Capano said he wanted to conduct his own defense, with Charlie Oberly remaining merely as an advisor. Capano, in other words, wanted to fire the counsel on which he had spent more than one million dollars. The attorneys, in turn, had come to the court and asked to be removed from the case—sickened with Capano's attitude. Capano stood up in court and said his defense team had reached "irreconcilable differences," but while Oteri said the divisions were deep, he claimed Capano's description was "not entirely accurate."

The judge had quite a problem. On the one hand, Capano was an accomplished attorney. On the other, the old adage that someone who represents himself in court has a fool for a client, is often true. This was a capital murder trial, which made Capano's request even that much more problematic. The judge shook his head and quoting the old adage about self-representation asked Capano if that in fact was what he wanted.

Capano said, well, no, he didn't "want to relieve" his attorneys. As he explained it to the judge, he wanted to use "every legitimate weapon available," to him to defend himself. "I don't want to be sitting in jail three years from now for something I didn't do, saying, 'I should have done this, I should have done that.' I'm on trial for my life."

The judge nodded that he understood that, but still. . . . As the judge started to explain, Capano looked over at his attorneys and "shushed" them, then turned back and looked at the judge. In calm, measured tones, Capano explained his plight. "I am like a soldier in a foxhole surrounded by the enemy. I want to use all ten grenades I have, but my attorneys insist on using five."

There is no question the tension between Capano and his attorneys had been building since the trial began. Oteri and Maurer had both voiced their concern about Capano's unwillingness to take advice. Even O'Donnell, who'd been tight-lipped in the beginning, had opened up and discussed the difficulty in dealing with his old friend.

Capano told Judge Lee that his lead attorney, Joe Oteri, wanted to proceed with "a scalpel. Joe believes less is more. I want to proceed with a chain saw." This comment drew some gasps from the audience, and was delivered in the same monotone as the rest of his speech.

The judge noted that Capano was at least "an attorney, an experienced criminal attorney . . ." "I'm not all that experienced," Capano interrupted. "I worked twenty-two years ago in the Attorney General's Office for a very short time."

"You have taken great pains and considerable expense," the judge noted, to hire his defense team. "Perhaps you should listen to their advice," he warned.

"I have great confidence in them," Capano returned. "Joe Oteri is almost like a father to me." But Capano said he owed it "to my kids. I have got to fight to the best of my ability. I can't do that with one hand tied behind my back. Why hold back when the stakes are this high? This breaks my heart." With that, the Fahey family, watching in as much shock as the rest of the audience, stifled a laugh.

The judge still didn't want to allow Capano to fire his attorneys.

"Has it occurred to you that you will be presenting yourself as the prosecution contends?" the judge asked, in reference to the idea that Capano's firing his attorneys would make him look like an egomaniacal "control freak."

"I know he's going to try and twist it," Capano said, pointing to Colm Connolly, but not naming him. "Everything is already twisted. I don't expect anything different with this."

Still, the judge wasn't inclined to grant Capano's request. The normal rules of criminal procedures would remain in effect, the judge said, and he observed that "this trial has produced a lot of surprises," and this was probably the greatest of all.

"I'm not inclined to grant a mistrial," the judge warned.

"I'm not asking for one," Capano replied.

Capano argued that he had the absolute right to defend himself, if he so wanted, but the judge said he wasn't so sure he had that "absolute right" once the trial had already begun and counsel was in place. It looked like the judge was going to rule against Capano, so the defendant tried a different tactic. How about a hybrid defense? Under his first request, Capano would retain Maurer and O'Donnell as paralegals who would chase down witnesses and deliver subpoenas but never appear in court. Only Oberly would remain in court, but only in an advisory role. Oteri apparently would be free to leave town a wiser and richer man. Under the second scenario, the defense team would present Capano's case their way and then Capano would ask witnesses additional questions and present other evidence and testimony. He wanted the best of both worlds. "That's a pretty unique request," the judge said.

Oteri shook his head and said he wanted to have nothing to do with such a circus. "It would be a Pinocchio show. We'd all look like a bunch of fools in front of the jury," Oteri said with emotion. "The jury will convict him immediately and it'll look like a bunch of fools up here."

"This is a unique situation. Unique in many ways. Mr. Capano is a practicing member of the bar," the judge said by way of reply. "Mr. Capano can fire you, but I don't have to let you go. I personally don't think it is in his best interest." Then the judge addressed his attention to Capano, who stood in his dark-black suit looking as if he were arguing a case on someone else's behalf.

"That scalpel, chain-saw analogy is a little scary to me," the judge said with a wry look on his face. "You'll be wielding the chain saw. Have you thought how that will look to a jury. You're on trial for your life and you'll be wielding the chain saw. How will that work?"

Capano said he understood; Oteri said he had no intention of sticking around to do paralegal work for Capano and then have Capano change his mind again. "I haven't fired them," he said.

"What have you done? You didn't fire them?" the judge asked.

"No."

"Did you relieve them?"

"No."

"What the hell have you done to them?" the judge asked to a smattering of laughter in the courtroom. Capano couldn't explain all that well, so the judge encouraged someone to speak up. With bemused looks on their faces, Connolly, Wharton, and Donovan sat relaxed at the prosecution table watching the fireworks. They turned their eyes, as indeed all eyes in the courtroom shifted to the defense team, looking for someone other than Capano to speak.

Gene Maurer got up. "We have chosen to say we would not do that (either of Capano's requests). We have made a decision not to pursue that course because of the negative ramifications. It is his life, but we will not present the defense he wants," Maurer tried to explain.

"It's not a matter of style," Capano offered. "It's more, it's more numerical. My attorneys, they are refusing to do things which are necessary to save my life. I want to use every rock I've got." By now it was coming up on the lunch hour and Judge Lee decided to take an extended break to ponder the questions Capano had brought to him. "Although you've given me many opportunities to make new law, I wish to do it the way it's always been done," Lee said. He'd get back to everyone after he looked up case law and had some lunch.

After a nearly 3½-hour lunch break, Judge Lee came back with a definitive ruling on the possibility of a hybrid defense; "No." On the possibility of firing or dismissing his defense team, the judge was also inclined to say "No" to that, but wanted to talk about it some more.

"For someone who hasn't tried a case in twenty-two years, this is a very challenging course of actions," Judge Lee told Capano. "You hired four really good lawyers and the vote comes out four to one against you, maybe you ought to listen." The judge also told Capano if he decided to represent himself he would not be able to address the jury and tell them why he was doing so. There would also be strict limits on what Capano could ask. For example, he could not say to a witness, "Well, you knew I really loved Annie, don't you?"

Capano thought some of the judge's decisions "seem incredibly prejudicial," he said with a big sigh. The judge said, "We're past the opening arguments. That was months ago." He admonished Capano that the trial would not start over anew for him. The judge would give a brief explanation that Capano was now representing himself, and that would be all that was said.

As Judge Lee and Capano continued their dialogue in court, Capano's attorneys sat silently at the defense table. Maurer looked angry, Oberly indifferent, Oteri sat silently, and O'Donnell sat looking amused at the whole thing. Connolly, Wharton, and Donovan, who hadn't had to say a complete sentence at all during the day, looked on in fascination as Capano appeared to publicly self-destruct.

"The fact that you haven't represented a case in twenty-two years and now want to represent yourself is a little less considered than the image you wish to project," the judge warned. "I've tried to cut you some slack and I failed."

Capano stopped to eat a muffin and to take his medication before he continued. "I understand you are making a decision of great importance," Capano explained.

However, the judge and Capano weren't even on the same page. "I've been trying to figure out what the hell you want," the judge told him. Indeed, it had vacillated during the day. He had fired his attorneys. He hadn't. They wanted out. They did not. Capano wanted a hybrid defense. He didn't. Finally the judge told Capano to sit on it overnight, meet with his attorneys again, and come back the next morning with a final decision on whether or not Capano actually wanted to fire his attorneys, and the judge would proceed from there. With that, court adjourned. It was a complete waste of a day in terms of putting on a defense. But in terms of finding out what Capano was really all about, it was an eye-opener for everyone involved.

"If Tom Capano can't play his way, he doesn't want to play," David Weiss explained. "That's clear."

Capano's attorneys seemed as upset as everyone else as they filed out of the courtroom. Television crews followed them over to Gander Hill as they went in to talk to Capano. News crews videotaped them entering and leaving, and provided little clue as to what the disagreement was all about. The meeting, also attended by Tom Capano's brother-in-law Lee Ramunno, was described as "stormy" and "tempestuous."

"We just tried to get him to listen to reason," Ramunno later said. "Sometimes when you're so close to a situation, you just can't see things all that clearly."

The prosecution team left the courtroom with their usual "no comment" to the media. Clearly, they were not damaged by the aborted affairs of the day. They'd made points and injured Capano deeply with their case, that much was established and corroborated by Capano's reaction in court. The reaction was something that made many shake their heads. Capano used terms like "hand grenades" and "chain saws" in the most cavalier manner. The gruesome reality of Capano's statements in court took many by surprise, even as they tried to figure out what the disagreement between Capano and his attorneys was all about.

At the core of the disagreement was the speculation that Capano wanted to commit perjury, or perhaps already had done so. There was also speculation that the disagreement surrounded Capano's desire to take the stand in his own defense.

O'Donnell still won't say specifically what caused the monumental dustup in court that day, but said it was something "significant."

"We had a strategic difference of opinion on which way we could go. So, we needed time to do some more investigation. And it became abundantly clear after we did that investigation that there was only one way to go and that was the end of the discussion," O'Donnell said.

The next morning, court reconvened. The tension was palpable. Oteri, usually omnipresent outside to talk with reporters before a session began, was nowhere to be seen. Neither were the other defense attorneys. Just after 10 A.M. they all showed up in the courtroom with Tom Capano following shortly thereafter. Everyone stood as the judge entered, and then everyone sat. The judge asked the question on everyone's lips.

"Is it your contention to represent yourself, Mr. Capano?" he asked the defendant, who stood at the defense table.

"No."

"And you're satisfied with their representation?"

"Yes, I am. Quite satisfied. We had a meeting last night and I'm satisfied. There were some misunderstandings on my part."

What they were, Capano did not say.

Chapter 18
Really Good Friends

The defense started out by trying to poke holes in a key prosecution theory that pointed to Capano's motive for killing Anne Marie Fahey. Connolly and Wharton, through a variety of witnesses, described Annie's final months as bliss with her new boyfriend, Michael Scanlan. Capano's inability to handle Annie's newfound happiness without him drove Capano to kill her.

The first witness, Michael Hare, got on the stand and told everyone that both Annie and Capano were supposed to separately attend a campaign fund-raiser he had in an unsuccessful Wilmington City Council race on June 27, 1996, the day Fahey was killed. She was supposed to attend with Michael Scanlan, according to Hare, but neither she and Scanlan nor Capano showed.

The next witness, Al Franke, the director of operations of a company that owned a local hotel and popular restaurant, testified he was a close friend of Annie's and they often "confided in each other." Franke said he did not know Michael Scanlan, but knew of him, and Annie had told him there was no physical contact between Annie and Scanlan. "She thought the relationship was going nowhere. She never said she was in love," and Franke never asked.

Denise Frawley, Capano's secretary at Saul, Ewing, Remick and Saul, testified in the February bail hearing that Annie frequently called Capano's office and she noticed no decrease in those calls in 1996. Frawley was sick and unable to attend court, so her testimony was read to the jury.

She said in her testimony that Annie and Capano had a "nice relationship and cordial." They were, according to her, very good friends.

Jerry W. Brady, the manager of Philadelphia's Mann center, testified in an affidavit that Capano purchased Jackson Browne concert tickets on June 27, 1996. He purchased the tickets the day Annie died. Could Capano have planned her death if he planned to take her to a concert? The defense noted that the concert occurred six weeks after Annie's death and indeed, as Capano would later testify, he did plan to take Annie to the concert. Certainly, the defense implied, if Capano were *planning* to kill Annie he wouldn't buy tickets to take her to a concert scheduled to occur after the day he planned to kill her.

The defense was laying its groundwork. How could Annie and Capano be enemies or at least not friends if she was calling him every day? Why would he kill her if they were friends? Why would he kill her if he was buying her tickets to a concert? What motive could he have for planning her death if her relationship with Michael Scanlan had been going nowhere?

The next few witnesses attempted to shoot holes in the testimony provided by one of the prosecution's main witnesses, Deborah MacIntyre. To do it, the defense called back to the stand two of the prosecution's own witnesses: Bob Donovan and FBI Agent Eric Alpert.

Donovan admitted under direct examination that when he first interviewed MacIntyre she claimed that Capano and she were just "very good friends." She didn't say anything about their sexual relationship, nor did she admit that she and Capano slept together the night after Annie disappeared. Donovan next talked to MacIntyre on September 6, 1996. In that interview she said she became Capano's lover in September 1995, just after Capano split with Kay. That was a lie, because she later admitted they'd been lovers since May 1981. Donovan suspected MacIntyre was lying about the 1995 date, but claimed he didn't have any proof to the contrary, so he let it be.

Again, in a February 4, 1997, meeting, MacIntyre gave the September 1995 date as the time her relationship with Capano became sexually intimate, but then contradicted herself and said she had sex with him in 1993 when he visited her home with Keith Brady. She conveniently left out the crucial bit of information that she'd had sex with Brady while Capano watched.

Not until January 28, 1998, did MacIntyre finally tell Connolly, Donovan, Alpert, and Wharton that her affair with Capano began much earlier, although she was still lying about purchasing the .22-caliber Beretta pistol she later said she bought for Capano. She finally came clean about the gun after she signed her immunity waiver in February, but Maurer continued to question Donovan and Alpert about how MacIntyre's testimony had changed since then. Not until April 25 did she say Capano had called her the night Annie died and asked for help with something the next morning.

Maurer took delight in pointing out that MacIntyre seemed to remember more and more in "visions" that came to her after she became a government witness. Her story changed, too, in regards to seeing Capano jogging early the morning of June 28. Originally, she didn't remember seeing Kay Capano's Suburban there that morning, but later did remember it.

Finally Maurer pointed out how she testified about Capano bringing pornographic tapes over to her house on June 30, 1996. She'd only remembered that nugget of information mere weeks before the trial began. The embarrassing part of that information, at least as far as MacIntyre was concerned, was that she failed to mention that the pornographic tapes belonged to her!

When Maurer got outside of the courtroom he spared nothing on Deborah MacIntyre.

"She lied to protect herself, not Tom Capano," he told reporters who had assembled for the daily news-briefing the defense team often gave. "None of the lies had anything to do with protecting Tom Capano. It was all about her."

The defense read into the record testimony given by Jack Healey, a friend of Capano's. Healey said he saw Capano and Annie together in a Philadelphia restaurant just three weeks before Annie's death and they seemed cordial and friendly.

On December 9 the defense went to work on "Slick" Nick Perillo. First, to establish how Perillo and other inmates communicated with Capano, the defense team played a videotape that showed Capano's austere living conditions. The videotape showed a small cell painted in a neutral color with a thin strip of a window that overlooked the prison yard. There were vents at the top of the wall that inmates often employed to speak to each other. The tape also showed a red line painted on the floor several feet outside of Capano's cell.

Prison guards later testified that the red line was there because of Capano. The urbane lawyer had been testing his limits in prison regarding matches and cigarettes. The prison had to change its policy and some of its rules because of Tom Capano. The red line kept inmates free to roam around the pod from getting too close to those inmates still locked down in their cells.

Fred Lane, one of the correctional officers, testified to the prison's ability to monitor the twenty cells on 1F-pod where Capano lived. Granville Morris, another corrections officer, testified that Perillo confessed to him that "he's working on something."

Twenty-year-old David Lee Lawhorn, a prisoner doing ten years of a fifteen-year sentence for robbery, said Perillo told him Perillo would use the Capano case to get out of jail early. "Nick's a pretty decent guy. Easy to get along with," Lawhorn said. "He's just a jailhouse snitch basically." Inside prison, Lawhorn said Perillo first observed and then sized up Capano. "He (Capano) ain't as smart as he looks," Lawhorn said Perillo told him. Lawhorn had been cellmates with Perillo for only two weeks, but also said Perillo told him that Capano was naive, a point with which Lawhorn agreed.

Lawhorn said Capano was okay, though, and Capano had given him shower slippers and cigarettes. Ferris Wharton made much of the purchase of the shower slippers, intimating that Capano had perhaps bought some testimony.

"These weren't eighty-dollar shower slippers, were they?" Oteri asked Lawhorn, who replied, no, they were worth only a couple of dollars.

"Just about all the money you have in the world, isn't it?" Wharton pointed out quietly.

Outside of the courtroom, Lawhorn got to show what he thought of Capano. As prison guards took him out the back door of the courthouse and placed him in a police van for transportation to Gander Hill, Lawhorn with all of his exuberance stuck his fists out for the television cameras and shouted "Capano Rules!"

There were other convicts paraded before the jury, as well as other prison guards. James Johnson, doing a two-year stint for burglary, assault, possession, conspiracy, and theft, said Perillo told him "Capano is a free ticket out of jail." And then, repeating the most oft heard words concerning Perillo, said "Nick is kinda slick." He also called Nick a snake and slimy, but apparently never did so to his face.

Wayne Lee Cropper, also doing time at Gander Hill, testified that he heard Perillo offer to do a favor for Capano. "I'm gonna break into her home," he testified Perillo said to Capano one night in prison.

"Forget it. You're nuts," he said Capano replied.

Cropper also referred to Capano as "Mr. C."

"Mr. C is all right," Cropper said.

The defense called Perillo back and grilled him about trying to set up Capano in prison. He was quickly accused by the defense of saying, "I'm gonna use this fish," to another inmate, who was in prison for killing an informant.

"I don't know where you come up with this stuff. I mean really," Perillo said as if he'd just ordered a cheeseburger. "It would be pretty stupid to tell a guy who's in jail for executing one informant that I was another informant."

Perillo seemed to be many things, but somehow "stupid" didn't seem to fit the profile—at least to the jurors, many of whom later said they not only enjoyed Perillo's time on the stand, but believed what he had to say.

The bottom line was no matter how slick "Slick" Nick was, he had diagrams and instructions written in Tom Capano's hand. The details were so precise and the work put into those instructions appeared to take so much time to complete, that it would be hard to dismiss the entire episode as an attempt by Perillo to set up "a fish" like Capano.

When it came down to a question of whom to believe, Capano the social scion and prestigious attorney, or Nick Perillo, perennial con man and heroin addict, the jury overwhelmingly chose the latter.

The defense had a similar problem with Deborah MacIntyre and tried to put witness after witness on the stand to discredit her. After running through a parade of convicts, they also brought in Capano's former attorney, Joe Hurley, to attack MacIntyre's credibility. Capano's first "lead attorney," who'd quit the case in April, strolled into the courtroom, flashed an avuncular smile as he climbed on the stand, and looked at Gene

Maurer. "You've been waiting for this all your life," Hurley said.

Hurley briefly explained his role in the case and took a jab at Deborah MacIntyre's testimony. The bottom line was that, according to Hurley, not only did MacIntyre omit several facts when earlier interviewed by prosecutors, but Hurley said she'd omitted them when he'd talked to her, as well. Clearly, the defense was making the case that MacIntyre just couldn't be trusted.

Later, jurors would say they made that point very well. What it would boil down to was the crucial question of who was lying about the night Annie died. Would the jury believe MacIntyre or Capano? The case was quickly and inevitably heading for that showdown. The eighth week of the trial ended on that note.

The next week began with testimony from another Capano brother: Joey Capano. Called by the defense team, Joey was the only brother to testify on Tom Capano's behalf during the guilt phase of the trial. Joey, a swarthy, slightly balding man with thick hands and deep furrows in his brow, was also the family member who spent the most time attending Tom Capano's trial. His mother, his ex-wife, his daughters, and even one of his girlfriends made appearances for Capano, but it was his brother Joey who stayed loyal until the very end.

Joey's main testimony seemed to be about an anchor he got for his younger brother Gerry's boat and about the cooler his older brother Tom purchased—the same cooler that would be used to temporarily house Annie's remains. But Joey also took time to go after his brother Gerry's reputation. Gerry had moved in with Joey after their father died and Gerry, Joey said with chagrin, was "a bit of a hell-raiser."

"He does things to extremes," Joey said, shaking his head. He never raised his voice and tried hard to show brotherly concern about Gerry, whom he said he loved deeply. But, according to Joey, Gerry's biggest concern was about "his next boat."

"He's always talking about buying his next boat and constantly thinking and talking about his next purchase." Joey also testified that Gerry considered himself an outdoorsman and a "tough guy," but he was really loving and caring. "He tends to get things twisted frequently," Joey testified. Gerry's drug problems came out in court again as Joey said he tried one time to get Gerry into rehab.

It was not a pretty family picture painted by Joey. He was a developer, who competed with his brother Louis for jobs. "I don't get along with Louie, although we share office space," he said. Gerry was thought of as the problem child and didn't get along with his family, Joey maintained, although he stressed how good-natured Gerry was and how much he loved Gerry.

Joey knew Annie, too, saying he'd met her in December 1995 and found out about her affair with his older brother Tom through a mutual friend who saw the couple together at the Philadelphia International Airport. Joey confronted his brother in the spring of 1996 about the affair and when he asked him if he was having an affair with Annie, Joey said his brother said one word: "Yep."

Joey said in the spring of 1996 his brother wanted to buy a gift for Gerry because Gerry had treated Tom's daughters so well. Tom had no knowledge of fishing or boating, but Joey said since Gerry was always in the market for a boat and loved the outdoors and fishing, hey, why not "buy him a cooler." Joey said in August 1996 he picked up an anchor for Gerry's boat after Gerry told him he'd lost his. There was no diabolical plan, Joey said. He just went to Rehoboth beach and got an anchor, no questions asked.

Inside the courtroom the defense case appeared to gain some momentum. Joey's testimony made it appear that the cooler, far from being bought and paid for as part of an elaborate plan to kill Annie, was simply an innocent gift. Gerry could be dismissed, according to Joey, because he was often mistaken.

The defense next called Robert "Squeaky" Saunders—

another "good friend" of Tom Capano's. Saunders, a certified AIDS caregiver and legal brief writer, wore a kufu hat and his best prison whites into court. He'd been incarcerated for twenty-two years for a murder in 1976.

He had shot a man in the back of the head and tried in vain to dump the body in the ocean. He was prosecuted and put in prison by Thomas J. Capano. Squeaky looked like he would have enjoyed being anywhere other than in the courtroom, but perhaps his wide-eyed look was more appropriately ascribed to being out of stir for a day.

He testified that he'd known Nick Perillo for about ten years and that Nick was known as a "company man" in prison, tempted to curry favor with the guards and prison management in order to lighten his own load in the joint.

"He doesn't deal in honesty," Saunders said, claiming that Perillo once sidled up to him at Gander Hill and was tempted to talk to Saunders about Capano. Squeaky said, "You can be cool with me because, you know, Capano put me in jail."

So, he claims Perillo opened up to him and said, "I have something in mind."

What Perillo had in mind, according to Saunders, was the idea to take advantage of the "fish," Tom Capano.

What is a "fish," Joe Oteri wanted to know.

"A new person, you know, has no knowledge of the system," Saunders explained.

Saunders said he had no idea why he was showing up in court that day and had only found out he was coming the day before. "I know I've been in so long I ain't got no open charges," he volunteered.

"I told you when I talked to you I was a righteous dude," Oteri said for no discernible reason.

"Yeah," Saunders replied.

"Did you believe me?"

"No, sir."

Oteri laughed and Saunders issued a very small grin, but the joke went over most people's heads.

In the cross-examination the prosecution tried to show that Saunders was still a jailhouse lawyer, after twenty-two years of time inside. He'd filed a writ of mandamus in his case as late as 1997. If Capano could support some of Saunders's claims, might Squeaky not have a better chance at a new trial? Squeaky denied it, but the lingering doubt was there as the ninth week of the trial came to a close.

With Saunders's declaration that he'd only been notified the day before that he'd have to go to trial, plus some other testimony that showed a flurry of activity by the defense team in the last few days, coupled with the outburst and turmoil in court between Capano and his lawyers the previous week, there was indeed a shower of speculation among members of the press and the general public. It began to be bandied about— especially by some of the courthouse regulars who knew all the reporters and every witness by first name—that the defense team hadn't done much for Capano.

This was in error. Oberly had been faithfully plodding along since the beginning, Maurer since January, and while O'Donnell and Oteri had been on the case the shortest length of time, they'd all put in a great number of hours investigating and defending Capano.

The appearance of a hurried defense was brought about, those close to the case said, because of Capano's obstinance, and his attorneys having to shift gears to adjust to that and the unique nature of the case. "We worked our ass off for him," O'Donnell later said. "Being four guys thrown together like that, we worked together incredibly well. And we did an incredible amount of work." Part of the problem for the defense became not only Tom's obstinance, but his constant note-taking, visible to everyone in the courtroom.

"We got to the point where we would ask each other, me, Gene, Charlie, and Joe, I mean, for suggestions after we got done with a witness,'' O'Donnell said. ''You know, I'd lean over and say, you guys got anything else I should ask.''

O'Donnell said each attorney got used to doing that and benefitted from the other. But what was unwelcome were Capano's suggestions. ''We tried very hard not to take Tom's suggestions. He got each of us good,'' O'Donnell explained. ''Every time we asked a question he gave us, we had our ass handed to us. If he had 500 suggestions, there were ten that were good. He had Joe (Oteri) ask about the trip to Homestead (Kim Horstmann testified about a long weekend trip Annie took with Capano). The witness said it was the worst weekend of her (Annie's) life. Joe came back (to the defense table) and said, 'Thanks, Tom, that was a great question, you got any more?' And Tom said, 'Yeah, I got these five.' Oteri said, 'Yeah, right,' and sat down with no more questions. It got to the point where (Colm) Connolly and (Ferris) Wharton knew which questions were Tom's.'' So could members of the audience.

The contentious behavior between Capano and his attorneys never abated, although at times it was not as close to the surface as when Capano nearly fired them. Clearly, however, the defense was troubled, and those troubles showed themselves plainly in the next witness the defense called to the stand, Dr. Carol Tavani.

Chapter 19

Seven "Undies" and a "Blankey"

Central to the defense claim that Annie had died of a horrible and tragic accident was the contention that Capano had not planned any murder. The cooler was a gift, the anchor serendipitous, the testimony by Gerry—where it could be questioned—was bullshit.

For the next two days, Dr. Carol Tavani, Thomas Capano's prison psychiatrist, would try to hammer home the last point. In the process she brought into the court some disturbing mental images that shocked an already numb public.

Court began late on December 14, as it always seemed to do. By the time it got under way just before 11 A.M. the courtroom was already restless. As the weather got colder, the courtroom seemed to get hotter, making people restless in the morning, listless by lunch, and somnambulant by the end of the day.

Dr. Tavani entered the courtroom just after 11 A.M. A short, red-haired woman, she looked like Dr. Ruth Westheimer's cousin and dressed like a naval admiral. Her blue suit was complete with brass buttons, epaulets, and gold braided chevrons on her arms.

She, like Dr. Kaye before her, brought an impressive resume into court, and for some fifteen minutes everyone heard about it. She had spent time as an emergency room physician and currently dealt with drug addicts and drug abuse problems. "Sixty to eighty percent of all inmates have substance abuse problems," she explained.

She first met Tom Capano on November 14, 1997, just two days after he was taken into custody. "He smokes a pack" of cigarettes a day, she remembered, and "has a chronic spastic colon," for which he took a nonprescription drug.

Her extensive notes, entered in as defendant's Exhibit #28, outlined her months of visits and treatment plans, as well as information about Capano. Apparently, he wasn't having too good a time in prison. On that first visit Dr. Tavani noted that Capano was "upset his brothers have turned on him. He wished he had a fatal heart attack," but she noted that he was not suicidal.

On November 17, 1997, Dr. Tavani saw Capano again as he was put into solitary confinement. During the next several months after his bail hearing and before his trial, Dr. Tavani saw Capano many times. He even specifically requested to see her on at least one occasion. Her notes detail Capano's vexing concerns as his fortunes and hopes changed while inside prison. In the beginning he was taking a medication for his colitis while also taking Wellbutrin, Paxil and Xanex for his depression and other psychological problems.

In March, Capano's chart shows he was depressed because he was "betrayed in a special relationship."

"He was in control (of himself)," the doctor said, but "things could change." This was the time Capano was trying to hire Nick Perillo to vandalize MacIntyre's home, as well as hire another inmate to clip both MacIntyre and his brother Gerard.

"He was doing things he knew was self-defeating, but he couldn't stop," Tavani said of Capano at this point in time. " 'I can't help myself. I'm not in control,' that's what he told me," Tavani testified. She had wondered if there was a "less restrictive prison" for Capano to be in.

In April, Tavani said Capano felt "compelled" to reach out to Deborah MacIntyre and couldn't stop himself. Tavani said seeing Capano like that even tortured her. She said she "genuinely" cared about him. She testified she not only wanted to treat him but take care of him. Tavani said Capano was suffering from anxiety and general depression, became dependant on the prescription medication, and worse, his "stress was beyond control of his medication." By April, Dr. Tavani said, Capano's heart was racing, he had panic attacks and was sleep deprived. She didn't increase his medication because she "didn't want to blast the guy into being snow."

Was Dr. Tavani describing a man who was stressed out over a horrible accident, or a man consumed with guilt over committing murder? Capano would have something to say about that later, but for now Dr. Tavani was concerned about his stress level for a variety of different reasons. Would he take his own life? She didn't seem to think so, but she said he was beginning to waste away and was lashing out against friends, family, and prison officials.

He got in trouble when she first began treating him because he had one too many writing pens, and in May 1998 she noted that he got in trouble again while in stir and was denied phone calls and visits. Dr. Tavani likened it to "sensory deprivation" and noted by June 1998 that Capano looked drawn and hadn't shaved. "He's even more depressed," she said. Again, Capano confessed to her that he was still writing to MacIntyre and said he couldn't stop himself from doing it.

In July 1998 Capano told Tavani he was fighting with his own attorneys, had few "lucid moments" and was feeling "very blah." Not much emotion at all, Tavani noted.

"Did you ever feel Tom Capano manipulated you?" the defense asked.

"No," Tavani said with all the passion she could muster into her petite frame.

After detailing the horrible conditions Capano had lived under during his months of incarceration, Tavani then was led through the minefield of a psychological term called "confabulation."

It is, according to Tavani, "a well-known neuro-psychiatric symptom" in diffuse and organic brain diseases. She said gaps occur in memory like "holes in Swiss cheese" and that the brain struggles to fill those gaps with something it feels must've happened—or what was suggested by someone else to have happened. "The hybrid becomes the new reality," she explained with muddled clarity. To many it sounded like "confabulation" was a psychiatric term for lying, but Tavani said the confabulator actually believes in the fiction he creates and cannot discern it from reality.

The whole "Swiss cheese" analogy sounded to the prosecution like the psychobabble sometimes used to introduce plot twists in poorly scripted television shows, but Tavani assured the reporters outside the courtroom this was not the case. Dr. Tavani also told the courtroom that Gerry Capano had taken such a massive amount of drugs in his lifetime that it caused him to confabulate.

"A confabulator tells you about stuff and you don't know whether it's true unless you corroborate it," she said. At that point Ferris Wharton and Colm Connolly appeared to turn to each other and let a small smile pass between them. The good doctor had driven home a point as well if not better than Wharton and Connolly—on every important issue Gerry's testimony had been painstakingly corroborated. No matter how many relatives, doctors, and friends came forward to dismiss him as "twisted" or as a liar and drug addict, they could not get around the important fact that Gerry did not lie about the events of June 28, 1996.

The doctor saw Gerry's actions in a completely different light. Using psychiatric terms and very vivid descriptions, she called Gerry a "demented brother," and said "he could suffer from dementia." Gerry's drug usage had so addled his mind, according to Dr. Tavani, he couldn't even do simple arithmetic. At one point in time Gerry Capano testified that a gram of cocaine cost him about $80 and that he had bought 3½ grams for about $150. This was an indication, according to Dr. Tavani, of some cognitive dysfunction. "It seems to indicate a problem with simple math," she said, noting that if a gram cost $80, then multiplying three and a half times would be much more than $150.

Then Dr. Tavani segued into another topic of which she was going to offer her expert testimony: the e-mails sent between Tom Capano and Annie in the months prior to her death. These e-mail messages, while introduced earlier in evidence by the prosecution, did not have the emotional impact of the letters between Tom Capano and Deborah MacIntyre, possibly because most of the e-mail messages between Capano and Annie were saved by Capano and tended to show him in as favorable a light as possible.

Dr. Tavani said the e-mails were an example of a healthy, giving relationship and "a warm, friendly, jocular, mutual caring" relationship full of concern for one another. According to the e-mails, testified Dr. Tavani, far from being a manipulated pawn of Tom Capano's, Annie was able to set limits. "They both had needs and they used each other to achieve those needs." She also said Capano was "very generous to her (Annie)."

"It's a positive relationship evolving into something," she added.

As Tavani said that from the witness stand, Juror #11, a middle-aged, white woman who often wore a crucifix to court, openly sneered. She sneered again moments later as Dr. Tavani noted that Annie was "emotionally intimate with Tom Capano." As for Annie's diary, the doctor said it showed Annie's "dark side."

"She (Annie) was distorted and delusional in the way anorexics are," Dr. Tavani testified.

At this point Colm Connolly finally objected. He was later in the ball game than Judge Lee, who'd sat rolling his eyes at most of the doctor's testimony. "She's making judgments any layman could make," the judge said in sustaining the objection.

Joe Oteri quickly finished up on the direct testimony, covering the final and most damning entry in Annie's diary. Dr. Tavani admitted the last entry, which called Capano a control freak, was "180 degrees" from the rest of the diary entries. "Sounds like an angry entry," she said in what many considered the greatest single understatement of the entire trial. "Sometimes you have to be mad to separate," she concluded.

The doctor wrapped up with calling her assessment of Annie and to some extent Gerry "psychological autopsies," wherein she made professional assumptions about their character as she didn't have the opportunity to interview them both in person.

Tavani's testimony stretched into a second day, during which Ferris Wharton would cross-examine her. During a break in her first day of testimony Dr. Tavani stood outside talking with reporters, concerned she would have to reappear the following day. She made it clear it was just professional concern. "I'd rather be curled up at home with a blankey than be here," she told a female reporter.

On the second day of her testimony Dr. Tavani showed up in a solid-green outfit with as many brass buttons as the naval academy uniform from the day before. She waited as did everyone for what turned out to be a monumental delay by even Capano trial terms. The session did not begin until 11:30 A.M.

"Gentlemen, we can't do this every morning. I'm serious," Judge Lee said. Mel, the tall, thin head bailiff, looked on sternly as if to emphasize the judge's point. It was getting close to the Christmas holiday, and the trial still looked like it might never end. The judge apologized to the jury and the public for the interminable delays and then allowed Ferris Wharton to conduct his cross-examination after a final bit of direct testimony.

Wharton began with a disarming question about how Tavani observed people. Can you observe people and make an educated guess from watching them as to what their body language means, Wharton wanted to know.

"Yes," Dr. Tavani said unequivocally.

As Wharton stood in front of her with his hands folded in front of him he asked her if she could offer an opinion on his body language.

"Seems a bit defensive," Tavani offered with a smile.

The jury laughed; the judge, attorney, and spectators giggled. Wharton laughed perhaps the loudest. Even Capano offered a bit of a giggle.

The point had been lost on most everyone, but not Ferris Wharton. Soon he showed the jury and the rest of the courtroom that he was not just making a joke at his own expense. He pointed out how Tavani had diagnosed both Annie and Gerry Capano without ever seeing either one of them and he got Tavani to admit that it was best to interview people in person, in order to see their body language and to fully evaluate what it is they say and how they say it.

For the rest of the day Wharton systematically, yet very graciously and with the ability of self-deprecation, eviscerated Dr. Tavani on every major point she made.

Wharton showed Tavani the directions Capano had drawn up for the planned burglary at MacIntyre's home. Tavani admitted that the split with MacIntyre caused "major stress" for Capano and that the directions were an "emotionally charged directive." About the words Capano underlined, she had written: "Emotionally charged and very important." Tavani's notes about MacIntyre show that Capano couldn't see that letting her go would be better for him—"better than trying to control her," the doctor testified.

Tavani further admitted under cross-examination that on August 16 Capano denied to his doctors that he had any knowledge of Annie's disappearance. Capano also told the doctor that he and Annie would only have intercourse during her menstrual cycle, and that was why the FBI would find blood in his apartment.

Wharton had Tavani read a report by Dr. Joseph Bryer, Thomas Capano's former psychiatrist, which showed Capano lied to him about Annie's disappearance nearly two months after Capano dumped her at sea. Capano told Bryer in August 1996 he wasn't responsible for her disappearance. "He told Dr. Bryer that he took Anne Marie Fahey to her apartment [June 27, 1996] and he heard nothing more from her," Tavani said. He also told Bryer his former lover might have been a victim of random street violence, committed suicide or, perhaps, gone on a trip. But if she committed suicide Capano said he had no idea why the body hadn't shown up.

Tavani said Capano talked about Annie in the present tense on a couple of occasions and went back and forth deciding if she was still alive, but "he's angry at her and blames her," for whatever happened.

Tavani gathered all of this information from interviews with Capano and notes from other doctors who'd seen Capano. For Annie she referred to diary entries and e-mails, as well as testimony provided about Annie and doctors' notes. She admitted she never even interviewed one person who knew Annie. For Gerry she had done essentially the same.

It amounted to guesswork—at least that's what Wharton showed during his cross-examination. Was it good guesswork? Dr. Tavani admitted at least four or five times that there is "no substitute for a face-to-face interview."

She also admitted that Capano continued to try and "control Deborah MacIntyre" from prison and got upset when he couldn't. Wharton also gracefully attacked her with facts she couldn't refute. She'd met Capano fifteen to twenty times in jail and developed a special rapport with him. She let Capano "ventilate." But Wharton had something else to use to question Tavani's credibility.

She had testified she was an "in the trenches" doctor from an emergency room and specialized in drug addiction cases.

"Ever heard of an eight ball?" Wharton asked her in a very casual manner.

Did the good doctor, who specialized in drug addiction, know that Gerry Capano was accurate when he said he purchased 3½ grams of cocaine for about $150? Apparently not. She had simply multiplied 3½ by the going price of a gram, $80, and had come up with a higher figure than Gerry said he paid. She assumed something was wrong with Gerry's mathematical abilities. Her "in the trenches" work, apparently, didn't reach to the street level, for she didn't know about volume discount in the drug trade. Three and a half grams is known as an "eight ball" in drug culture, and buying more can cost less.

It was a devastating blow to Tavani's credibility, at least to a couple members of the jury who had more street smarts than Tavani. She didn't recover from the blow on redirect, either.

At one point she talked about Capano's life in prison and referred to the fact that he only had "seven pairs of undies" that he had to wash out in his sink to keep fresh. "Undies?" Were they lace? Even the judge turned and looked at her when she made that comment.

After two days the judge had had it. At the very end of the second day of questioning, when Colm Connolly objected to a question asked by Oteri, the judge could control himself no longer. "We have an expert witness that hasn't been used as an expert witness," he said. Lee was also at wit's end with the entire "confabulation" theory. "I can't say the word and hope never to have to deal with it again," he candidly offered from the bench.

* * *

Underneath the trial's sometime jocularity, there was the increasing speculation about strife in the Capano defense team. Walking in one morning for court, Oteri placed his briefcase on the floor next to the door and excused himself in public because he had to go talk "to the nitwit."

Maurer was still sore about the humiliating public attempt to fire him and had become less open with the press. O'Donnell, always acerbic, was particularly sour. Only Oberly seemed to remain the same, and that was because he didn't socialize much with the press prior to court. Also, dealing with his increasingly ailing wife kept him focused on other things. There was, of course, a major battle brewing. It was the cause of some of the morning delays, and the major source of irritation by the members of the defense team. Would Tom Capano testify. "Who knows?" Joe Oteri said whenever questioned. He was still set against it. For all the reasons he'd told reporters for weeks, he was convinced putting Capano on the stand would be the quickest route to a guilty verdict. Weeks into the trial it was obvious to most that the government's case was largely circumstantial. There were so many questions left unanswered Oteri was convinced he had a real solid chance at a hung jury at the very least. But Capano couldn't resist a captive audience, and his attorneys were still struggling to talk him out of testifying. But the suspense had been building as to whether or not Capano would testify from the day he was arrested, and it reached a feverish pitch as December rolled on.

That was the currency Tom Capano had. He *knew* what really happened the night Annie died, and while everyone expected him to tell a story that would suit his own purposes, all concerned thought there might be enough facts sprinkled into his testimony to discern what *actually* had happened.

After Tavani left the stand, there was anticipation in the courtroom that Capano himself would next be called as a witness. Instead there was another small parade of convicts to tell everyone, again, how slick, "Slick" Nick Perillo was. It was overkill and according to one of the defense attorneys an example of Capano's influence.

It also seemed clear as court recessed on December 15 that the trial was sure to go at least a week or two more, which would mean because of the coming holidays, the trial would not end until sometime in January 1999—more than 2½ years after Annie died.

Through the turmoil the Faheys kept their vigil, their patience, and their character. Brian Fahey became especially adept at verbal stingers in the newspapers aimed at Capano, but he never lost his cool, nor did any of the other family members as they had to wade through the onslaught of lurid, graphic, and seemingly nonsensical testimony.

Some of the friends of the Fahey family openly speculated about how they were handling the trial. Kevin and Mark, the two oldest, had remained the most quiet and some thought were the most volatile. Mark had certainly expressed his concern about seeing the cooler and still didn't want to talk about it, but Kevin seemed like a rock throughout the trial.

Robert, most of their friends said, was the pillar. He had been stoically present for most of the trial, giving quotes to reporters, answering questions like sister Kathy and brother Brian had, and joking and drinking with reporters. Most considered him straightforward and honest. Fahey family friends said there was little chance that Brian Fahey would "go off," either. Quick-witted and with an omnipresent smile, he took things in stride well.

The question was how well would the family take it if Capano got up and trashed the memory of their dead sister from the witness stand. At the end of the day on December 15, it was apparent the defense had little else to do. It was put-up or shut-up time for Capano.

Chapter 20

"I didn't do it."

December 16 dawned with the longest lines yet to get into court. As early as 6 A.M. some had shown up outside the courthouse to try and get inside to see Tom Capano take the stand. For more than two years he'd remained silent. Now would Capano come forward and tell everyone what he said had happened?

The defense opened the day with housekeeper Mattie Coleman, a woman whose clients included Capano and his mother Marguerite. Oteri, who had complained about "wacky hearsay laws" in Delaware, didn't hesitate to use them to his advantage. Coleman testified she had a conversation with another of her clients, Sharon Purzycki, who told Coleman that her son told her that his friend had seen a weapon at his mother's home. That mother was Deborah MacIntyre. The testimony was hearsay and designed to try and raise reasonable doubt. However when she got on the stand, Sharon Purzycki said she never had any such conversation with Coleman. Her son was called to the stand and said he never spoke with MacIntyre's son about a gun. That prompted the defense to call MacIntyre's son. The towheaded, athletic-looking sixteen-year-old looked like the proverbial deer caught in headlights as he approached the stand. He also denied the story.

The main event would be Capano. Wednesday, December 16, 1998, at about 10:47 A.M., court reconvened.

"I wish to testify," Capano told the court, shocking no one, but certainly not pleasing his attorneys who'd advised strongly against it. With those four words Capano began an eight-day odyssey that spanned two calendar months and two different years.

The judge wanted to make sure Capano understood what he was up against. "You will be subject to a lengthy and intense cross-examination," the judge forewarned Capano.

"No doubt, Your Honor," Capano replied. Capano explained how he had discussed testifying "on and off" for the last six months. He admitted he coerced his attorneys into allowing him to testify.

Oteri wanted to make sure that point was driven home. Oteri made Capano get on the stand and reiterate it was all his own idea. Capano said he "loved" Oteri and the job the whole defense team was doing. "His (Oteri's) opinion is that the defendant should never take the stand. The majority opinion is I shouldn't do this," Capano told the packed courtroom. "This is the decision I've been allowed to make ... all the garbage that is going to be thrown at me I'm aware of," he assured the judge.

Capano appeared lucid, contrary to the description made of him by his doctors, and contrary to his own descriptions in court of his mental state. But he was fidgety. As the graying, bespectacled former attorney strode confidently to the stand and sat down, he eyed the jury, the judge, the prosecution, and finally his own attorneys. He couldn't get comfortable with the microphone at the witness stand. It had given other witnesses problems, as well, and he actually broke it off its handle. The bailiff came over and quietly helped him to adjust it.

"Thirty seconds up there and you've already wrecked things," Oteri admonished.

It served to break the stiff and tight mood. Capano began by saying he was on a cocktail soup of chemicals and consequently, "I ramble."

"Calm down and take your time," Oteri told him.

Capano did.

"I've been portrayed as a spoiled, rich kid . . . , " he began.

"I object." Connolly wasn't wasting any time. Capano looked at him with enough venom that the entire courtroom could see his anger. The objection worked.

"I come from a blue-collar background," Capano continued after the objection and a new question was put to him by Oteri. "My father was a carpenter. I come from people who worked with their hands. My dad was proud the first thing he built was an outhouse."

"Not a minute into the testimony and we're already in the toilet," a Philadelphia television reporter said from the press row.

Capano went on to chronicle his family story of humble beginnings as his father became one of the richest men in Wilmington, where he went to school, and who his brothers and sisters were. "My father believed in working at an early age. I went to work at thirteen and moved lumber, poured concrete . . . lots of manual labor."

He testified how he got married, had children, bought the former bishop's house from the local diocese, and how his oldest daughter, Christy, went away to college in New York City at a "place I didn't want her to go." He was just a humble, self-effacing, devoted family man, he told the jury when "this nightmare began."

Oteri carefully tried to walk Capano through his life, pointing out how his taxes were done, who he worked for, and how he toiled his entire life to get to where he was now.

Along the way, as Capano outlined his rags-to-riches story, he took a subtle swipe at the prosecution contending there was no way he would make a deal with Squeaky Saunders. "Nothing I could say twenty-two years later would make any difference. A plan is ridiculous," he said and then shifted gears back into telling the world about his early life as an attorney and how he turned away from the family construction business because he wanted to make his life count for something.

His humble beginnings enabled him to become the city solicitor and then become Wilmington city government's chief of staff. Capano talked about his political connections with the former Republican governor and in one of the case's many ironies talked about how he got part of the funding for the Gander Hill prison extension.

"Now, sir . . . , " Oteri began as he took another line of questioning.

"It's Tom, not sir," Capano said with a smile as sweetly and softly as he could.

Capano wanted to talk more about his resume, but Oteri wanted to talk about the cooler. Oteri wanted to know if Capano had used a credit card and used his car when he went to purchase the cooler at a local Sports Authority. "You can't have too many coolers," Capano said. He claimed, as his brother Joey had, that he bought the cooler as a present for Gerry and hid it in a crawl space of his home with some "screens and stuff," and "cans of paint."

Although he hadn't bought Gerry a present in years, and admitted his family didn't exchange birthday gifts, Capano said he was going to give the cooler to his younger brother as a present on the Fourth of July weekend for all the nice things Gerry had done for his daughters.

Capano had a different version of what happened as far as the loan Gerry gave him, as well. He could not deny the loan was made as there was the check to prove it. Capano claimed he borrowed the money to give to Annie to help her out with her eating disorders. He didn't tell Gerry what the money was for, and Capano said his younger brother got "newsy" and began asking him questions like, "Are you okay?"

"I said fine, I just need the money," Capano testified. That's when, according to Capano, Gerry put on "his tough-guy role," and said, "Are you being threatened? Are you being blackmailed?"

"I said, no, no, no." Capano claimed he never told his brother he wanted the money to pay off extortionists. Gerry came up with that himself. Capano said his younger brother Gerry also volunteered to find someone to break some legs for brother Tom. "It was not my idea to solicit leg breakers," Capano said with equanimity from the stand.

When Gerry couldn't muscle his older brother into hiring some leg breakers, Tom Capano testified that Gerry gave him a gun. "It was his idea," Capano testified. "I didn't want anything to do with it, but I went along with it." Capano admitted he told Gerry he felt a little uncomfortable being all alone in a big, empty house, but "I never fired a gun in my life but once. It was a shotgun." Capano said he wouldn't feel too comfortable with a gun for protection. He never liked guns, he said, and would "probably end up shooting myself," by mistake.

"Gerry, I don't want a cannon in my house," Capano told his younger brother when offered a shotgun, so he decided to take a small handgun instead, a gun Gerry had to show him how to operate. Then the two brothers talked about Tom's children. In very direct tones Tom Capano testified he could kill someone if he had to. "Anybody hurts my kids, I'll kill them." The courtroom was deadly silent as Capano said it. He enunciated each word clearly and the voice he used to say those words sounded as hostile, jury members later said, as anything they heard in court.

"Now that's just conversation," Joe Oteri offered in an attempt to mitigate what Capano had just said. But his client didn't get it.

"No. I mean it," Capano said.

He'd just told the jury he was capable of murder. Granted, according to him it would only be to protect his children, but if the jury was looking to see if Capano could take such drastic action, for any reason, he just gave them the answer. It was not the answer Oteri wanted to hear.

Capano quickly went on saying he gave the gun back to his younger brother less than a month after he got it. He claimed it was "uncomfortable," and Capano thought a "baseball bat would do," if he needed home protection.

Capano then recounted how "sweet" Gerry was when he was a child and how everyone "doted" on him, but by adolescence, according to Tom, little brother Gerry got heavily into drugs, was expelled from school, and went to reform school. Gerry had no interest in working, Capano testified, "One thing we learned from our father is a strong work ethic, but Gerry didn't get that."

Instead, Gerry was—at least according to Tom Capano—a bum, a drug addict, and a lowlife who lied often, got out of work whenever possible, and brought shame to his family. He was a "mean drunk" who occasionally fought with members of his own family and left nasty messages for his mother. He used the "F" word, Capano testified, in front of his own mother and sister: "Everyone. My dad would never do that."

Shortly thereafter, testimony came to a close for the day.

December 17 dawned a cloudy, mild day.

Back on the stand Capano began talking about his longtime lover Deborah MacIntyre. "She didn't tell you the truth," Capano said about the way he and MacIntyre became intimately involved.

"Everybody kissed everybody else at midnight," Capano said of the incident at a New Year's Eve party where MacIntyre said they first became attracted to one another. "She said I told her that night that I loved her. I did not. She was wrong on that. She was very aggressive with me."

According to Capano, it was MacIntyre who was the aggressor. This was not entirely inconsistent with MacIntyre's own testimony, nor with what Capano's own daughter saw. MacIntyre said she did go out of her way to visit Capano in his law office. But Capano said she was much more aggressive than that.

"She testified I called her. That's a lie. She called me," he explained, saying he wasn't all that much interested in MacIntyre at first. "Debby was by far not the most attractive woman there, and I wouldn't fool around with her. I could get fired."

MacIntyre, Capano explained, was a spoiled, little girl. "I may have mentioned she came from a very wealthy family as opposed to Anne Marie," Capano said. The petite, blonde MacIntyre was a swimmer with a healthy body, who only married to get out of the house and away from a "dysfunctional family," Capano explained.

On the early spring day when MacIntyre visited Capano at his law office, he was very surprised, he said, and that she "shut the door and displayed her affection." The testimony MacIntyre offered about their subsequent sexual encounter on Memorial Day weekend in 1981 "blew me away," Capano said with a slight head nod. He was shocked because he claimed it happened nothing like how MacIntyre recalled. Oh, yes, they did make love at his home and she did arrive on her moped. But Capano claimed he never called her. That didn't make sense, he testified. After all, she was still married, and what would happen had he called and reached her husband instead? Capano said he was sweaty, dirty, and had just cut the grass. He was in no mood to have sex.

"I was pleased but happy to see her," he explained. But, "I told her this wasn't a good idea. I worked with her husband.

I didn't physically push her away, but she made all the advances."

Being sweaty, dirty, and having just cut the grass, Capano apparently couldn't fight off MacIntyre's repeated advancements and retired to his den with the needy, sensual MacIntyre. "And we made love." Almost immediately Capano told her he wasn't interested in leaving his family. This, said Capano, did not sit well with MacIntyre, and when his mistress found out Kay Capano was pregnant, "She physically beat me. She's a swimmer. She's all muscle," Capano said earnestly.

He lowered his head, and looking through the top part of his glasses to the jury, he said clearly and succinctly, ". . . And by the way, for the record I did not hit her back."

Capano helped MacIntyre financially, managing her trusts and inheritance to bring in higher yields. He gave her no money, but did occasionally give her gifts. He also testified about the business trips the two took together on occasion and then Capano apologized for "how this has degenerated into an X-rated, sexual sideshow."

The jury seemed to sigh. Perhaps the worst was over. After the apology Capano said Deborah MacIntyre was "the most aggressive woman, sexually, I've ever known." He just couldn't resist the sexual dynamo that was Deborah MacIntyre. "She has the strongest sex drive," he said with a straight face. "We had a very active sex life. She liked sex as much as I."

It was almost laughable and sad, Capano explained, that MacIntyre would blame him for the sexual threesome they'd enjoyed with Keith Brady. After all, according to Capano, it was his fantasy to have sex with two women and it was her fantasy to have sex with two men. "It was her idea," he said with a straight face. Joe Oteri, who seemed as shocked as anyone else with Capano's sexual candor, finally got a question in on point.

"Did Mr. Brady take part voluntarily?" Oteri asked.

"Well, it had to be voluntary because no one forced him," Capano said.

As for the former lover from high school, the man MacIntyre said Capano watched her have sex with from her living room window, Capano said that, too, was all MacIntyre's doing.

"The only thing I instigated," Capano explained, "was, you know, why don't you call the guy and let him escort you. I said hey, you never know, you might get lucky."

Capano said he was completely surprised when MacIntyre took her old high school flame home and engaged in sex. "She said she was satisfied several, several times," Capano explained. He testified he peered through a window and watched.

"I did. It may have been my idea or hers. Anyway, I left the house and watched. I did."

Capano explained he left his home after his wife Kay and his children went to sleep. Kay, he said, "always went to sleep early."

With his wife and children asleep, he walked the few blocks over to MacIntyre's house and enjoyed the show, Capano said.

"I'm very liberal, have a very liberal attitude toward sex, and I know Debby felt the same way," he offered by way of explanation.

After Deborah's high school flame was satisfied, Capano decided to waltz into her home and have "different sex" with her. Oteri did not let Capano elaborate.

Capano testified MacIntyre had obtained her father's porno collection, and Capano said his mistress "needed physical release." After he was arrested, he worried about her, and that was why he called up an old friend and asked him to go over to MacIntyre's home and "service her."

"She has an overpowering sex drive," Capano explained, which threw the courtroom into another shocked silence.

There was just no getting around the sexual testimony in the Capano case. Some laughed, some cringed, and some got angry about it. Some didn't know how to react. But all who listened couldn't help but comment on how far away from Annie's death much of the testimony had traveled. The Faheys said they didn't care less about who or what type of sexual travesty was involved. They just wanted to know what happened to Annie.

Capano got around to some of that when he began talking about the gun MacIntyre purchased. He said he wasn't present when that happened. He said MacIntyre purchased it after a trip to Washington, D.C., and "D.C. is scary enough at night."

"I did not like guns in houses full of children," Capano said.

He did say he saw Deborah MacIntyre the day she made the gun purchase. She wanted to have lunch in Wilmington, which Capano said was "inconsistent because I didn't want to do anything in public. I didn't want to hurt Kay's (his wife) feelings by going someplace in Wilmington." He testified he waited until she was asleep before he went over to his mistress's house. He had affairs with "numerous other women" he testified, but he was always "discreet about it."

He said he even admonished a member of his firm who was supposedly stepping out on his wife. The recalcitrant litigant was seen dining with a woman other than his wife in Wilmington, and Capano told him not to do that. Capano said he didn't care if the man had an affair but he warned the underling not to make his wife look bad. "She's the mother of your children. Don't embarrass her," Capano warned.

It remained for cross-examination as to whether or not Capano considered testifying in open court to a threesome with a mistress and a best friend—testimony that would make headlines all across the country—would or would not embarrass one's wife.

Capano said MacIntyre called him over to her Jeep at lunch the day she purchased the gun and showed it to him. He told her to take it back and she refused. He said he saw the gun again a second time in her home about two weeks after she purchased it. It was on the second floor, he said, in her bedroom. "I probably did touch it, but I don't remember," he offered.

He then saw the gun, he testified, for the last time on June 27.

"Did she ever give you the gun?" Oteri asked.

"No. She Did Not," Capano said, verbally capitalizing each word.

"Did you ever fire the gun?"

"Never, ever, ever . . . ," he said. He never got the gun and never fired the gun. He had access to many guns and could've bought them, but didn't, he explained. He could've gotten one from Gerry, but didn't.

Skipping ahead to his arrest and the fallout afterward, Capano said he promised MacIntyre he'd write to her every day and she promised the same thing to him. This arrangement became problematic as Capano was put into solitary confinement against his will, a move that Capano again took pains to point out was politically motivated, as he claimed other aspects of his prosecution were.

Capano said he struggled to stay close to MacIntyre because when he was arrested in 1997, he said his plan was to marry MacIntyre. "When I was arrested we were never closer," he said. "I thought it, our relationship, was wonderful."

But by the end of January 1998, a little less than three months after being tossed in jail, Capano said the relationship began to sour. "Her letters weren't as warm or loving, and the letters became accusatory," he said. He claimed it was because MacIntyre got a new "alleged" lawyer from Philadelphia: Tom Bergstrom.

Capano even insinuated that Bergstrom wrote some of the letters for MacIntyre because he said she started using lawyer terms like "hence" in her prose.

Capano said he thought the "sun will fall out of the sky before Debby will abandon me," but apparently, he got it wrong. After she signed up as a witness for the state, she began taping her conversations on the telephone with Capano. Those were the conversations Capano had sought to have barred from the trial. Since he had agreed to testify in his own defense, they now could be entered as evidence.

The dry transcripts provided to the media could not adequately represent the tortured emotions displayed on the audiotapes. Over and over again the prosecution had argued Capano verbally berated his mistress. In the very first call entered as evidence, dated February 28, 1998, Capano didn't even let MacIntyre get through her opening pleasantries. He sounded impatient, aggravated, and frustrated as he tried to find out exactly what she had told Colm Connolly.

Capano went on to deride MacIntyre for betraying him, even though at one point he admitted, or seemed to admit, she had told the truth. MacIntyre was flustered and near tears throughout most of the conversation. Capano accused her of deciding "a long time ago to do this" and also questioned her authorship of some of her recent letters: "It didn't sound like you," he said.

He demanded to know what she did with his previous letters. He was suspicious as to whether or not she'd let anyone know they were still communicating with one another. When she told him that her new attorney knew, he got upset that a "stranger" had entered their world.

That exchange led to another argument. MacIntyre said she was tired of living a lie, but Capano didn't want to hear it. He wanted her to "stop that bullshit. Let's talk about our, let's talk about our promises to each other." According to Capano, MacIntyre abandoned him when "I need you" the most, and "Now, more than abandoning me, you're destroying me." They argued a little more about the gun, its purchase, and MacIntyre's children before their fifteen minutes ran out and the prison disconnected the telephone call.

Oteri had the jury listen to this conversation via headphones that were supplied to them. They could read along with the conversation courtesy of the transcripts and they all paid rapt attention. Well-placed audio speakers in the courtroom allowed everyone else to listen along, as well.

In the stuffy, hot courtroom, the prickly conversation between Capano and MacIntyre sounded to many like nothing short of verbal torture. Far from showing Capano as a caring, nurturing partner to Debby MacIntyre, many of the jurors later said it showed him to be as manipulative and conniving as the prosecutors claimed. In court Capano even admitted to pushing, prodding, persuading, and manipulating MacIntyre: "You were trying to get her to do what you wanted," Oteri said to him as Capano sat on the witness chair.

"Yes. I mean, yeah," Capano admitted.

Capano told Oteri that the second conversation occurred shortly after the first. It was not recorded because MacIntyre said she did not know how to operate the machinery correctly. In it Capano told MacIntyre that he was protecting her. She had shot Annie and he reminded her that he was in jail simply protecting her.

Capano also told Oteri that MacIntyre had no local support. "She's mentally alone," he claimed—she had no family and few friends and he was throwing himself into virtual martyrdom because he cared so much for her. That's why, he said, he was crushed by her telling prosecutors the story about her purchasing the gun for Capano. It was not only a lie, he claimed, but it was "destroying me." By that, he told Oteri that her lies were destroying him emotionally.

MacIntyre appeared from the tapes to be the one most emotionally destroyed. She answered the phone on all occasions as if out of breath and made no attempt to hide how distraught the phone calls made her. Her high state of anxiety does not appear to be something she manufactured. The tapes show a very flustered and tense Deborah MacIntyre that the prosecution contended was being goaded into performing for Tom Capano.

On March 1, 1998, Capano again phoned MacIntyre and started out saying, "I'm awful. Now listen to me, okay? I have less than fifteen minutes because you're so fucking late getting home.

"Do you love me?" he asked and she responded that she did.

"Do you love me enough to fight for me?"

"Sure, I'll fight for you," MacIntyre replied.

"Do you love me enough to switch lawyers like I asked you to?"

"I don't know why I want to switch lawyers."

"Because I'm asking you to."

"I like my lawyer," she whined.

Capano kept beating away at this point, asking her to switch lawyers and telling her she already agreed to dump Tom Bergstrom. She wanted to know why Capano wanted her to switch lawyers. "Because he doesn't care about me," Capano said and quickly followed with, "He doesn't care about us."

For several minutes he continued to beat up on MacIntyre, telling her she'd made poor decisions and to let him do her thinking for her. How could a woman who claimed to love him do this to him, he demanded to know.

Then he started to stroke her and smooth her ruffled feathers. He was angry, he admitted, but he loved her immensely and would fire his own attorneys if it would please MacIntyre. Capano ended the call with begging her to fire Bergstrom, her new attorney, and hire the man he wanted.

In a conversation that was taped, dated March 2, 1998, MacIntyre told Capano she did not fire her attorney and she did not go see the handpicked attorney he wanted her to see. Capano sounded contrite and humble. He said he believed MacIntyre was kissing him off. He did have just one request: "Um, since you're not gonna change lawyers, uh, can I ask you that please don't talk to any fuckin' cops anymore or Colm Connolly anymore or anything like that? Promise me that?" She said she would try to honor his last request. Just one more thing, though. Capano repeatedly, although politely and humbly, asked MacIntyre to get rid of all the letters he'd sent her. Please, he said, don't give them to the "bad guys" (Connolly and Wharton). Please, he begged, don't let her new attorney talk her into that. If MacIntyre would do just this one last thing for him, he promised, "You're not gonna hear any more shit from me."

The last conversation entered into evidence that day was recorded on March 3. It began in an upbeat fashion as Capano and MacIntyre talked together about their future, his prison meals, and her thyroid condition. Capano explained to the love of his life how he connived himself a little extra time on the telephone and how this had caused him some trouble and how he was mistreated in prison by the guards. But that was all behind him now. Together they'd fight the oppression and the wicked investigation that threatened to tear their love asunder. If they could only stick together.

The phone calls, while reading like melodrama, played as that and worse. During the afternoon break Joe Oteri, showing his disgust with them and the testimony of his client in general, said he hoped he could finish up by the end of the day because he didn't want to see Capano during the weekend.

But it didn't look like Capano's testimony would draw to a close any time soon. He'd only barely touched upon his relationship with Anne Marie Fahey and hadn't talked about any of the specifics of June 27. For most of the day the courtroom audience had been held captive in the Capano/MacIntyre relationship.

It was sometime around this part of the trial that Juror #9, a white male who favored John Lennon-style glasses, began wishing he could run away from the trial. "I'd see the buses pulling in front of the courthouse every day and just wish I could get on one of them and get as far away from here as possible." But there was no escaping it. Not for anyone even remotely involved.

Late in the day Oteri finally got around to questioning Capano about Annie.

"She was the biggest flirt I ever met and I was a big flirt, too," Capano said.

He said Annie constantly bugged him to go out to lunch and, like Deborah before her, pursued him—not the other way around. Finally they went to lunch at the Hotel DuPont in March or April of 1993—apparently in violation of Capano's own rule about being seen with other women in Wilmington. The most expensive hotel in Wilmington and one of the nicest restaurants in town had to be impressive to Annie who'd aspired all her life to middle-class enjoyments. Capano also had to know it.

What he did admit was that his affair with Annie "started strangely." He said, "The whole thing was strange from start to finish."

Capano explained, "I was a little uncomfortable becoming romantically involved. She was a younger sister of people I liked and I thought liked me." He eventually got over those feelings because on January 27, 1994, he took Annie to an expensive restaurant in Philadelphia for Annie's twenty-eighth birthday. Then they made love.

"I was crazy about her. We talked every single day," he said.

He still had to maintain the rest of his life, though, which included his wife, Kay, Deborah MacIntyre, his daughters, and work—not necessarily in that order of importance—so he and Annie worked around the parts of his life of which she was aware. "One of my 'daddy elements' was taking my girls to school, and Anne Marie always called in the morning after I dropped the kids off," Capano explained to the packed courtroom.

During the next few months of 1994 Capano said he and Annie became very close. "We were best friends," he explained. She was down-to-earth, "had a very foul mouth," and "made me laugh," he said without a fleck of emotion in his voice. He could've been reading from the telephone book as he described his relationship with his dead mistress, saying she was "special" and at the same time saying she was a "very stubborn young lady." Her stubbornness and their age difference led Capano to try and break off the relationship sometime in 1994, he claimed. "I told her that I loved her dearly, but I'm an old fart. I tried tough love and wouldn't call her ... it caused her too much grief and eventually we got back together."

In fall 1995, Capano said, he found out Annie had begun dating Michael Scanlan. "I was a little surprised," he testified. "I thought she would tell me." He said he was mildly distressed and didn't like that Annie had hidden her relationship with Scanlan. "I don't like being lied to," he explained. "I said just let me know where you're going on this." Capano also said he was concerned about Annie in a platonic/big brother type of way, so he decided to have Scanlan "checked out." Despite the fact Scanlan knew the governor well and had been set up with Annie through Governor Carper, Capano decided to do his own investigation. Strictly as a friend, he told everyone. He wasn't jealous.

Capano eagerly testified that he'd kept a few secrets from Annie, too. Between September 1995 and June 1996, he told the court, he'd dated between eight and nine women on a regular basis. His statement was met with restless murmurs in the courtroom. "What a pig," one woman said from the back row. That prompted some laughter, and Judge Lee looked down from the bench with a withering stare and called for order.

According to Capano, he and Annie both had quick tempers. Both of them would blow up and then things would "blow over," he explained. Several times he said their tempers got the best of them. During the Christmas season in 1995 he testified he tried to give Annie a ticket to Spain. "She refused in a hurtful way," he said without elaboration. But in retrospect, he said, it was "almost funny in a way." That incident prompted a fight where he threatened to take back all the presents he'd ever given her, but he stopped short of doing that. "Nothing ever left that apartment," he said. This was contrary to earlier testimony where Annie's friends said Capano did take things back.

Another incident between the two occurred during Wilmington's "Grand Gala" in January 1996. Earlier testimony had Capano badgering Annie over the telephone for making a date with Scanlan instead of Capano for the gala. Others testified Capano threatened to show up and stalk Annie and ruin her evening. The "Grand Gala" was a formal event Annie always wanted to attend. Capano said he never harassed Annie and did not go to the gala to confront her.

Capano said by February 1996 he and Annie were closer than ever and talked about getting married at some point. He testified that they also began communicating by e-mail. But he said he also had his "largest confrontation" with Annie in February over her anorexia and bulimia. "She confided in me about everything," he told the court. "I know some extremely personal things about her." As he said this he looked directly at the Fahey family, who sat in the first and second rows on the right side of the courtroom along with their attorney, David Weiss. They shifted uncomfortably in their seats bracing for the trashing they thought was sure to come.

Weiss sat through most of this just smiling at Capano while Susan Schary, the courtroom sketch artist, sat in the front row glaring at Capano with daggers in her eyes. She could not keep her contempt from showing itself, and everyone in the courtroom noticed. A few minutes later when Capano asked his attorney Joe Oteri to move over so he wouldn't have to "see that," Joe turned around, as did many of the jury members, to find out what Capano was talking about. Schary thought it was her, as did most of the reporters and spectators. But it turned out to be David Weiss, who never did anything more than smile.

Capano said because of Annie's anorexia, he tried to get her to check into a clinic. That's why, he said, he got together the $25,000, which in part was made up of a loan from Gerry Capano. It had nothing to do with extortionists, Capano just wanted to help Annie.

Capano said he thought giving her $25,000 in cash would shock her into doing something about her situation. Just giving her a check would not have the same effect, he testified, so he gave her cash. He claimed she promptly threw it back in his face.

Chapter 21

"Debby did it."

Capano took the stand on December 21, 1998, as if ascending his throne. Joe Oteri began the morning questioning by approaching Capano and allowing him to apologize to the jury for statements he made the last time he'd been on the stand. Specifically, Capano apologized and explained his statement about "checking Scanlan out." Capano said he was just very protective of Annie so he just wanted to make sure Scanlan was the right type of guy for her. He also apologized for saying that Deborah MacIntyre, his longtime mistress, was the "least attractive member" of his inner circle of friends.

"I misspoke because of my medications," Capano explained with a straight face and puppy-dog eyes. "She was not my type. There were others in that group more my type," he said earnestly. Capano then explained his salutations to Susan Louth. The "Dear Slutty Little Girl" comment wasn't pejorative, he explained. It was a term of endearment.

"You weren't being nasty?" Joe Oteri asked, looking none too sure he wanted to hear the answer.

"No. Not at all," Capano explained. "Am I talking too fast? The pills are just kicking in."

Joe Oteri said Capano was doing fine, but he'd take things a little slower.

Capano proceeded to trash the Faheys. As Robert, Kevin, Kathy, and Brian looked on (Mark didn't show until after lunch), Capano talked about how Annie was abused as a child. Oteri asked if she was sexually abused and Capano said no. "All the deep, dark secrets about the Fahey family—I know them all," he said with a touch of venom in his voice. "But I keep confidences and I wouldn't talk about them then and I won't talk about them now."

What were these deep, dark secrets? Capano wouldn't say, but let the statement hang over the Faheys like a noose. David Weiss, their attorney, said he believed it was a threat meant to intimidate them in the civil suit they'd brought against Capano.

Capano hinted around about Annie's past, saying she had a "very wild period in her life when she was promiscuous" and she had to be tested for AIDS. She even had an interracial relationship, which Capano said didn't bother him because he was so open-minded and all about sex. Capano said Annie was "shocked" when it turned out the news didn't shock him. "I'm not prejudiced," Capano said as he turned and looked at the two black women on his jury.

It was indicative of several times during his testimony when Capano seemed to be speaking directly to individual jurors. Ferris Wharton noticed it and made note of it. "He talked about only buying American cars at one point," Wharton noted. "Or the comment he made about not being prejudiced. I think he studied the jury and tried to play to them."

On the morning of December 21, Tom Capano tried to convince the jury that he was Annie's one true friend. He described Jill Morrison, one of Annie's closest friends, as "not as close as she (Jill) would like to think." Kevin, Annie's oldest brother was "quiet." Mark, the next oldest, had a "horrible relationship'' with Annie. Capano claimed Mark was physically abusive, a perpetual drunk, and a loathsome sort that Annie didn't want to be around.

For Juror #11, a quiet, blonde, middle-aged woman, sitting through this testimony was the hardest for her. "He trashed everybody," she said of Capano. "His words hurt so many people and he didn't seem to care at all who he trashed or how bad he made them feel."

Luckily, Mark wasn't there to hear as Capano went about describing him in the basest terms. Robert Fahey fared a little better. Annie looked at him as a "surrogate father," but Capano said Robert was very judgmental and Annie feared her older brother, so wasn't always open with him.

The jury, the judge, and the audience were lulled into complacency as Capano systematically trashed the Fahey family. Judge Lee could be seen rolling his eyes, almost inviting an objection as he had openly invited one during Dr. Tavani's testimony, but it didn't come.

Brian Fahey was described by Capano as an "absentminded professor," whom Annie was constantly concerned about pleasing. He wasn't nearly as close to Annie, Capano claimed, as Brian liked to think he was. Kathy Fahey-Hosey, it turned out, was the member of the family Capano had known the longest. She'd dated a friend of his, and Capano said she was judgmental and controlling. "It's her way or no way," he said.

"If that ain't the pot calling the kettle black," the judge's sister-in-law said from the back of the court.

Capano described Annie's only sister as catty and petty, saying Kathy was angry because Annie wore a smaller dress size, and adding that Kathy told her not to buy a certain pantsuit because Annie didn't make enough money to buy it.

The Faheys never flinched. They never blinked. With the exception of a few squinted eyes, they stayed as calm as they had for the previous nine weeks of the trial. They were unflappable, and Colm Connolly often commented on how much character and class they brought into the courtroom. Money had bought the Capanos many of life's finest comforts, but as Connolly later pointed out, it could not buy them the class the Faheys showed throughout the trial.

Capano didn't rest with just trashing the Faheys, he also went after Bud Freel, his former close friend. Capano hated Freel more than "any human being in the world." Connolly finally objected to this line of questioning, saying, "We've had to sit and listen to him (Capano) trashing people . . . "

Capano responded as if he were shocked. "I'm trashing people?"

Oteri changed his line of questioning. He picked up with a Friday in June of 1995 when Capano said he found Annie curled up in a fetal position, a little incoherent, and saying, "I'll kill myself. I'll never get better."

"She scared me to death and I knew I had to stay with her," Capano said with big-hearted earnestness. Capano said he saw Annie later on that evening in a crowd and found how remarkably different she looked just an hour or two later. He said she had a big smile and looked happy, but she confided in Capano that "I'm a great actress. I've been doing it all my life to hide how I feel inside."

This revelation saddened Capano, who reiterated how much he cared for Annie. In Capano's world this led into a discussion about religion. He made sure to explain to the jury he was raised by the Jesuits and was morally superior to most men. Jesuits, according to Capano, can discern between a "good lie" and a "bad lie." For example, explained Capano, if he were hiding a Jew in Germany during World War II and was asked by the Nazis if he knew where any Jews were, well, then it was okay to lie. Capano would later go into greater depth about his moral superiority, but said as he discussed religion with Annie he discovered they were both "Cafeteria Catholics," meaning they picked what they liked about Catholicism and applied it to their own lives, rather than following all the rules and dogma of the religion.

"We got into a discussion about the death penalty," Capano volunteered.

"Objection!" shouted Colm Connolly.

There ensued another in a long line of sidebars while reporters speculated what the hell Capano would say about the death penalty. The sidebar broke up after a few moments and Joe Oteri found Colm Connolly's objection had been sustained.

"We talked about pro-life," Capano said.

"Objection!" shouted Connolly again. This, too, was sustained and Capano was very flustered.

"Can I talk about abortion?" Capano asked the judge.

Judge Lee shook his head as did most of the rest of the courtroom. Then the judge said what many were thinking. "The problem is these are not pertinent to this trial." This ended Capano's monologue on the death penalty and abortion, but it didn't stop him from talking about the sexual aspects of his relationship with Annie.

He said Annie hated her body. "She thought she had large, unattractive legs. She was sensitive about the size of her breasts, too. I told her she had a great figure, but she didn't think so. She wanted breast reduction and skinny, abnormal legs."

All Capano wanted to do, he said, was make Annie happy. He finally thought he found the right way to do that by taking her to an exclusive Virginia resort in August 1995 for an extended four-day vacation. He talked about golfing, massages, swimming, reading books in the shade, horseback riding, and dancing. At the end of it Capano and Annie made up a "Coke/Pepsi" list inspired by the two different soft drinks to show just how different each person was.

Annie wrote it up and Capano, for some reason unexplained, kept it and entered it into evidence as Defendant's Exhibit #91 and #113. Annie described herself as "Pepsi" to Capano's "Coke." She was a "Mick" and he was "Italian." She was a "Clothes Whore" and he wasn't. She liked old people. He did not. He was a "dumper"—meaning he was always going to the bathroom. She was not. She was nonjudgmental and he was judgmental. She didn't believe in a double standard, and he did. "I think there are things men should do and women shouldn't," Capano explained to the six-man, six-woman jury.

Annie said she was "clinically depressed" and he was "sane." He was "serious"; she was "goofy." She called Capano for the first time anywhere a "control freak."

Capano used the list to try and show how in-tune he and Annie were and how they could be honest and open about everything. To many outsiders it looked as if she were trying to tell him why they shouldn't be together.

While Capano thought the four nights in Virginia went well, Annie told Kim Horstmann it was a "complete disaster," Horstmann would later testify to this in court.

After this trip Capano and Annie would never be the same again. For the first time they had been able to spend a lot of time together, exclusively and romantically. It was a short time afterward that Annie broke up with him for the first time. What did Annie see in Capano that began to make her distance herself from him?

Jack O'Donnell, a friend for thirty years, later said he thought when he first saw Tom after his arrest that he was the same guy he'd known in college. Only when he got to spend an extended length of time with him did he figure out Capano *wasn't* the same. Did Annie's only extended sojourn with Capano show her the same thing O'Donnell saw many months later?

After the trip to Virginia, their relationship changed. At least according to Capano that's what gradually happened. By October 1995, Capano said, ten days went by where he didn't see Annie at all. Still, he said he and Annie "were happy and getting along extremely well," until "I tried to leave her again." Annie, who was in the middle of a growing relationship with Michael Scanlan, apparently couldn't handle the thought of Capano leaving *her*—despite knowing she couldn't marry Capano and at this point didn't want to. According to Capano, *he* wanted to leave and she became distraught.

He said by mid-March they had resumed their relationship, which sometimes included sex. He said they grew even closer in May and June 1996, but he wasn't sure where the relationship was going. "Do you want me to be your fifth big brother, your lover, what?" he asked her. He said she replied, "I don't know what I want. I'm so confused."

Oteri then decided to get to the heart of the matter and the reason for the trial.

"How would you describe your relationship with her on June 27, 1996?" he asked.

"It had never been better," Capano replied with a smile.

He also testified his relationship with MacIntyre was on about the same footing at the same time, so according to Capano, in June 1996, he was close to marrying two women and was dating a half a dozen others regularly.

Capano said on June 27 Annie got into his car to go to dinner at Panorama in Philadelphia in an unhappy mood. She was, Capano testified, upset with a doctor she said was gouging her. "I've tried not to trash people," Capano said, which sparked some laughs in the courtroom, "but Anne Marie didn't like this doctor."

Capano said he tried to cheer her up but they began talking about her anorexia, which didn't help matters. He said the mood at the restaurant was not "glum" as the waitress testified but more like "serious." He was just being polite when he ordered the food for her, he said he never told her what to eat. The waitress brought Annie the wrong appetizer (breaded calamari instead of sauteed). This, Capano said, made Annie "furious," but she didn't bring it up to the waitress. She just went along with the breaded calamari. After leaving the restaurant they drove to Annie's house, discussing the Atlanta Olympics, and while there Annie started to cheer up, Capano said. Then he said contrary to most of the testimony—including testimony outlined by his own defense attorneys—Annie did not change when she went home, but rather quickly ran upstairs and came back downstairs in the same floral-print dress she'd worn to the restaurant. The floral-print dress entered in evidence, while seemingly identical to the one she was seen in that night at the restaurant, was not the one she wore. According to Capano, Annie had two identical dresses.

Annie dropped the doggie bags of food from the restaurant at her apartment, then went with Capano to his house, where they relaxed and watched *ER*. Since it was warm in his house, he turned on the air conditioner and he said Annie took off her panty hose.

Capano said they ended up together on his "love seat," where Annie fell asleep in his arms while he watched the television show. He said at some point in time he remembered the phone ringing during the show, but didn't answer it. After the show ended, he got up, checked his caller ID button, and noticed that Deborah MacIntyre had called him. He called her back and said, "I have company. It'll have to be later." He hung up, he said, and went back with Annie on the love seat.

"The next thing I knew, Deborah MacIntyre was in the room. She was pretty ballistic," Capano said to a hushed courtroom. "We didn't even hear her come in because of the sound of the air conditioner."

When he did notice her, Capano said he saw her standing adjacent to the love seat and she began shouting. "She was very upset. 'Who's this? What's this all about? Is this why you can't see me?' She was snapping out, why was I with another woman. I told her to relax and calm down. She had on a T-shirt, shorts, and kind of a straw purse," Capano said.

He was in shock, Capano said, but he got up to face MacIntyre. "Oh, boy, is this a situation," he said to himself. Annie, hearing the commotion, got up and said, "Capano, what the hell is this?"

At that point in time, Capano said, Annie wanted to leave and MacIntyre began to cry. "Debby was all red from the neck up and not coherent. 'All these years I've waited for you . . . ,' " Capano said MacIntyre began sobbing, "Things that didn't need to be said."

At that point, Capano said Annie, a woman who didn't like her own legs, decided to hike up her dress and put on her panty hose in front of a sobbing Deborah MacIntyre. "The next thing I know, I see the gun in Debby's left hand," Capano said. Annie, he said, laughed and even he couldn't take it seriously. But MacIntyre, he said, had become suicidal and was saying things like "I have nothing to live for. I might as well kill myself," he said. "This is talk of someone who has lost it," he testified.

With the gun down at her side she began to raise it to her head. Capano said he reached out with his hand to stop her when the shot went off.

"I couldn't believe it. She couldn't believe it, either," Capano said calmly.

"Debby shot Anne Marie. I'm absolutely, positively certain it was accidental. She bought the gun in May and must have had it with her," in the straw purse Capano intimated.

Capano said he looked back at Annie who was motionless on the sofa. Capano checked her and found a head wound on the right side of her head near her ear. "I said, 'Oh, not this. This can't be possible.' "

Deborah became quiet from shock and Capano said he tried CPR with no results. He breathed in Annie's mouth and pumped her chest and checked her pulse. He found none and couldn't see any signs of breathing, either. Annie's eyes were open, so at some point he put a small pillow under Annie's head, Capano said. He testified he gave her CPR for as long as "we thought there was a chance." He did not, however, call 911. "That was the most cowardly, horrible thing I've ever done in my life," he said without fully explaining why he didn't call.

By now, he said, MacIntyre was crying and hysterical, and he was "being selfish and protecting myself," and of course MacIntyre. He knew Annie was dead. "I always thought I was a guy with some guts, and I guess I wasn't," he told the jury solemnly.

The next thing he knew MacIntyre dropped the gun, he retrieved it and took the clip from her car. Earlier he had testified there was no clip in the gun, just one round in the chamber—the fatal round.

He told MacIntyre it was "all my fault." After all, she had expected since summer 1995, when Kay Capano gave Tom Capano the boot, that she'd end up married to Capano.

Capano said he took about five minutes to calm down Mac-Intyre enough to get her home, promising her he'd take care of everything. After MacIntyre left, "I broke down. I cried, screamed, punched the wall," Capano testified. He knew, "I had to do something with Anne Marie's body."

What could he do? Call 911? Bury her in the backyard? Take her home and hope she'd wake up in the morning and forget the whole thing? While he considered many scenarios he wandered down into his basement and saw a fifty-five-gallon garbage can. "I couldn't bear the thought of that," he told a jury who stared back at him aghast that he'd ever consider stuffing her in a garbage can. No, he said, she deserved something more dignified. "So, I got the cooler."

The audience audibly groaned as Capano said he wrapped Annie in a cotton blanket and put her in the cooler. She went in real easy, Capano said, noting he did not have to break any bones or desecrate her in any way to get her into the tight cooler. The testimony was terrifying in its starkness and horrifying to the audience in its implications. But Capano had just started.

"For some insane reason," he said, he had the gun still in his possession, so he put it under the front seat of his car and drove like a "madman" over to Annie's apartment. There he went on "automatic pilot," he said, bringing over a gift he gave Annie and some perishables to the apartment to make it look like Annie had been there that night. He also touched *69 to see who had made the last phone call to Annie's house. He turned on the air conditioner and used the bathroom and then went back to his house.

That ended his day of testimony.

It was just four days before Christmas 1998 and Capano had finally told the Faheys and the world what had happened 2½ years earlier to Annie.

Not that anyone readily believed him. Even Jack O'Donnell said he was aghast at Capano's testimony. "He testified he didn't need to use the cooler because he had a big trash can. What? Like, I don't know what was on his mind, but whatever it was made no sense to me or Joe (Oteri) or Gene (Maurer) or Charlie (Oberly)," O'Donnell later said. He was also upset with Capano's insistence that Annie did not change her clothes when she stopped at her apartment that night. "He said the dress in evidence wasn't the dress. Everyone else said it was the dress. It would be better for him if it were her dress. That means she went home and changed her clothes before *voluntarily* going over to his house. He didn't get it. You know?"

Outside the courtroom the audience was stunned and numbed by the day's testimony. Susan Schary, one of the courtroom sketch artists, could not hide her disgust. "Come on, what woman in her right mind would stop and put her panty hose on while another woman is sobbing and screaming and threatening to kill herself. What a bunch of lies," she said, adding she was going to tell Colm Connolly and Ferris Wharton about her insights. Most men had missed that, but all the female reporters found that particular part of Capano's story exceptionally unbelievable.

Tom Capano resumed his testimony on Tuesday, December

22, 1998, by going over some of his previous day's testimony— explaining how upset MacIntyre was after she accidentally shot Annie in the back of the head while supposedly trying to kill herself. She evidently gave up all thoughts of suicide after killing Annie, but he still had to calm the suicidal woman down enough to get her to drive the few blocks home. "I did my very best to calm her down. I told her it was my fault," he explained. He got her off and then, again, he talked about how he had "my five minutes of trying to get it under control."

He testified that just minutes after watching one mistress try to kill herself and accidentally killing a second mistress in the process, he figured that rationally there "was nothing I could do for Anne Marie. So, I decided I had to protect myself and Debby."

He told the jury how he "compartmentalized" his feelings, "Which I've only done one other time in my life—when my dad died," he explained. With his feelings successfully tucked away he went and got some bleach and tried to clean the blood from Annie's head wound off the sofa. "Gerry didn't remember it correctly," Capano assured everyone. While Gerry had testified he saw a basketball-sized stain of something, which may have been blood, Tom said that was just Gerry's "Swiss-cheese-hole memory that Dr. Tavani talked about." There was a yellow stain from the bleach, not a bloodstain on the couch, Capano said.

He talked again about wrapping Annie in a blanket and putting her in the cooler and about his trip back over to Annie's home. "For some illogical reason I felt it necessary to go to Anne Marie's apartment," he explained. His illogical reason was for the rational concern, he said, of tainting evidence and planting a cover story. He said he made the *69 call on Annie's phone because he knew she had that feature on her Bell Atlantic telephone line and he wanted to find out if he had been the last person to call her.

He said he went back to his home and began to cry.

"You were emotional?" Joe Oteri asked.

"Yes."

"Why aren't you emotional today?"

"I'm drugged."

Capano said the drugs had made him null and void. "I'm not the man I used to be," he said, paraphrasing a Beatle's song. Capano said he was just "falling apart" because of the events of that night. He managed to recount how he wrapped Annie in a blanket before depositing her in a cooler. "I had several additional rugs to wrap Anne Marie in," Capano added as he nodded and said he had decided against that.

Capano talked about the call from Deborah MacIntyre that he couldn't get to and how he "69'd" her back. He said when he got her on the phone she was still quite upset, having killed Annie and all, and then driving home to leave Capano to clean up the mess.

"This is my fault," Capano said he reassured MacIntyre. "This is my fault because I love you. You didn't know there was a clip in the gun."

Capano said he tried to keep her calm and told her how he planned to dispose of the body. Capano said MacIntyre calmed herself down enough to come back to his home "no later than 1 A.M." and was composed enough to help him move Annie's body. Together, he said, he and MacIntyre carried the heavy cooler down the steps, then moved the furniture around and rolled up the rug. "It took two of us to roll it up and rearrange the room," he said with emphasis. Since Gerry found things already tidied up when he arrived, Capano wanted to make it clear to the jury that he had to have help getting the place tidy.

Afterward, Capano said, he took some time to console his faithful mistress, MacIntyre. He again reiterated how it was all his fault.

"Now, you keep saying that it was all your fault," his attorney Joe Oteri opined. "Tom, why is that? Did you fire the gun?"

"No. I did not fire the gun," he reassured the jury. It was all his fault because he hadn't paid enough attention to the emotionally fragile MacIntyre, who was having such a stressful time at her place of employment. Capano said after the accident he battled with his emotions and thought of what he should do next. "I decided I was going to keep it secret and bury the cooler with Anne Marie in it."

He knew some heat would come down on him. While Capano knew he had to keep everything secret, he said he really didn't have a plan to do so. He just thought the best way to dispose of the cooler was to dump it at sea and the best guy to help him do that was his own brother Gerry. After all, Gerry had a boat.

Early in the morning he made a call to Deborah MacIntyre. "I made it to create an alibi," he explained. Joe Oteri just shook his head. Nothing Capano was saying was helping his case much. Sounding more like the prosecution on cross-examination, Oteri lit into Capano.

"Were you thinking clearly enough to create an alibi?" he asked in disbelief.

"Yes, I was," Capano said evenly.

Capano continued from the witness stand telling the jury how the entire ordeal had made him feel "drained," and even though he'd been setting up an alibi, he didn't think he was thinking "clearly." He said he thought clearly enough, however, to drive to Gerry's, sit in his car and wait in the driveway for Gerry to leave for work while reading the newspaper—specifically, the sports page. While he was reading, Capano said, he noticed Gerry approach the car and ask him what he was doing there.

"I want the keys to the boat."

"Why?" Gerry responded.

"The less you know, the better. Just give me the keys to the goddamn boat," Tom Capano replied.

This led to a brief fight, Capano said, because he was adamant that he didn't want his little brother Gerry involved. But Gerry didn't trust his older brother to drive the boat, and Gerry told him he wanted to "take care of his baby," meaning the boat.

From there Capano's testimony varies little from the testimony of other witnesses. He went over to his ex-wife's house and got her car, he ran into MacIntyre while jogging, etc. But there was always his "spin" on the testimony. With MacIntyre, for example, they met at the track and discussed dumping the body, according to Capano. It wasn't as innocent as MacIntyre testified their meeting was.

After the break, Capano told the jury about *The Summer Wind* and the trip out to sea. Filling in gaps in Gerry's testimony, Capano corroborated most of his brother's testimony and said that he used the boat's anchor and chains on Annie after the cooler wouldn't sink. Gerry turned away from his brother while Tom went about his grisly work in broad daylight on the high seas, and Tom Capano said as he wrapped Annie in chains and dumped her over the side of the boat he couldn't look, either.

"I shut my eyes and glanced away. I couldn't look. This was someone I loved," he said flatly.

The jury looked on with equally flat expressions on their faces, but this was not the case in the audience. The Faheys were riveted and repulsed by Capano, and each of them let that show on his or her face.

After dumping Annie at sea, Capano said he went home and spent the early evening with his kids watching videos. Later, after the kids left, he said he surprised MacIntyre and showed up at her house. He used the key to get in and "I knew the alarm code," he said. So he surprised MacIntyre. They wrapped their arms around one another, and he stayed the night. He slept late on Saturday, June 29, made love with MacIntyre, and had breakfast. Later, back at his own home, he recalled the telephone call placed to him by Kim Horstmann.

He said he lied when he told her he didn't know where Annie

was, but when he suggested that Annie might have gone to the beach or the Jersey Shore, he said that wasn't a lie.

"Was that not an attempt to misdirect the investigation?" Oteri asked.

"No," Capano replied casually. "Because Anne Marie had told me that."

Capano neglected to say the only way Annie could've made it to the Jersey Shore that weekend was if she'd washed up on the beach. Since Annie had told him she might go to the Shore, then it was okay to tell Horstmann that. He wasn't trying to con anyone. He was just telling the truth.

The following morning when the state police first showed up on his doorstep, Capano said his "antenna went up" immediately. "I knew something wasn't right."

The cops were investigating Annie's disappearance. "I didn't like it," Capano testified. "They asked personal questions about me and Anne Marie, which was none of their business." Capano said the cops kept pushing him and he became "resentful."

When the cops showed up outside his kids' home the following day, they told him they "just happened to be there," he explained. That really got Capano pissed.

"I was extremely resentful of that because my children were involved," he explained.

Resentment aside, he allowed his home to be searched and meanwhile made plans with Louie to have the Dumpsters removed that held all the incriminating evidence. By then, Capano said he knew—even though it had yet to appear in any newspaper—that the federal government was going to get involved in the case and "Politics was going to be controlling this matter. It made me quite reticent to speak to law enforcement officials."

Capano explained there were huge leaks in the State Prosecutor's Office and that's how he knew the federal government was involved, even apparently before Connolly and his boss knew they were involved. Capano said he was also well aware of the government's strategy "Take Down His Inner Circle," which he said he saw on some notes during the discovery process. According to Capano, the feds were going to interrogate his ex-wife and other girlfriends and go after vulnerable members of his family.

In the end, Capano said, it was his fault for lying for so long to everyone.

Why, Oteri asked, did he do it? Meaning, why had he lied to everyone for so long?

Capano explained it was his "state of mind." He thought he'd be out of jail after the bail hearing and when that didn't happen he recovered and that's when he claimed Deborah MacIntyre started lying. Capano said he was crushed emotionally and mentally. He "went crazy," he testified. "I was selfish. I was hoping to keep myself from any harm and to protect Debby and Gerry," he said with a puppy-dog look of contrition on his face.

Okay, Oteri said, why didn't Capano come forward in February 1998, some ten months ago, when he found out MacIntyre had become a witness for the government?

"It would just sound like sour grapes, and to this day I can't believe Debby would lie like this," Capano said. "I was out of my mind."

He said he stayed that way for a couple of weeks as the doctors in prison "really jacked the drugs up," and maybe that accounted for his threatening to kill MacIntyre and Gerry, and having MacIntyre's house ransacked.

Capano said he struggled at all times to come clean with the government, but they wouldn't let him do it. He wanted to limit the discussion to the night Annie died, while he said the nosy investigators wanted to talk about everything else in Capano's and Annie's past, and he didn't want to talk about confidences. Capano said that's when the "White House" got involved and put pressure on the state to come after him. According to the Capano conspiracy theory, President Clinton himself called and asked that no expense be spared in going after Capano—who was also a Democrat. It was the combination of a conspiracy and the betrayal by MacIntyre, Capano said, which finally led to his arrest and trial.

"Late in February I learned the woman I loved and had been protecting had turned on me and stabbed me in the back," he testified. At that point he tore up and flushed all her letters down the toilet. He said the jail had copied those letters.

"It's blatantly against the law," Capano offered.

"Objection," Connolly blurted out.

"Sustained," said Judge Lee.

"Let me correct myself," Capano continued. "It is in violation of standard operating procedure." He smiled.

"Objection." Connolly bounced up.

"Sustained," Judge Lee said evenly.

Joe Oteri then decided to switch gears. Time was running out and court was about to adjourn for Christmas. There was little doubt that Oteri wouldn't get done before Christmas, but he was giving it a valiant effort. Prompted by Oteri's questioning, Capano outlined how he came to try and get Nick Perillo to terrorize Debby MacIntyre. Capano said he drew the diagrams and maps in about twenty minutes and got to Nick Perillo "I don't know how" after he found Perillo could probably do the job for him.

"In a moment of weakness," he said he used Perillo, but a few days after he made the diagrams he changed his mind and requested the information back from Perillo.

But "Slick" Nick outthought Capano and had already given the information to the prosecution, Capano explained—although Perillo had told Capano he'd torn up and flushed all the information down the toilet.

"Within a few days I recanted," Capano told the jury. He'd been a "fish" to "Slick" Nick Perillo.

With that said, the jury and the rest of the audience left for the Christmas break. Everyone had a family to go to and everyone involved said later they tried to put Tom Capano and the murder trial as far behind them as possible.

For Tom Capano, that was impossible. While Colm Connolly got to go home to see his wife and children, while Ferris Wharton, Bob Donovan, Joe Oteri, Jack O'Donnell, Eugene Maurer, Charlie Oberly, and the Faheys could all do the same thing, Tom Capano was stuck inside his one-man prison cell. A week alone. A week with nothing but prison rations and his own mind to keep him company.

It was Christmas 1998.

The eleventh week of the trial began on December 29, and by the court's planning there would only be one more day left for testimony in 1998. After December 30, 1998, the court would break again until January 4, 1999. More than one hundred people lined up to get in the general public section for that day's testimony, and began doing so before dawn. Those who got inside saw a scraggily-faced Tom Capano led into court. Apparently, there weren't any razors at Gander Hill because Capano said he was unable to shave.

Oteri, who would finish up the direct testimony around noon, talked with Capano about Annie, Deborah MacIntyre, Susan Louth, and another, unnamed mistress whom Capano helped out during the days after Annie's disappearance.

Louth and he didn't have "a thing in common," Capano said, "but we both had a lot of fun. She was great."

Capano also talked about the former housekeeper who testified she heard about a gun at MacIntyre's house. "She's as honest a woman you'll ever find," Capano said.

Oteri had Capano walk through some of his letters to MacIntyre and her letters to him that had already been entered as evidence. He talked about their "sexual banter" and how the letters showed that there was no way MacIntyre was under any kind of "spell" in regard to Tom Capano.

"Debby wasn't under my spell and never was, despite what she said in this courtroom," he told the jury in very exact terms. Capano and his attorney pointed out how she talked about going out for drinks and having a social life, which was emotional torture for Capano since he was behind bars and had vowed to protect her. He described MacIntyre as "pretty headstrong and pretty impulsive," and referred to a house she put a thousand dollars down on and then changed her mind about purchasing. He also said he took great pains to reassure her from prison, writing, "You didn't do anything wrong," and saying on the stand that he "meant it sincerely." Capano said he wanted to protect her. He had accepted responsibility and he would be the almighty protector.

"Did you ever in any letters mention the facts of what happened?" Oteri asked Capano.

"No. Absolutely not."

"Why not?"

"I wasn't sure of the privacy of the mail and I was trying to protect her," Capano explained. "Those you love, you don't allow to come into harm's way . . . ," he added.

Capano said he did what he did for love. He was love's fool, love's errand boy, love's play toy. He was overemotional and over the top as he described his deep love for MacIntyre. "I'm not guilty of murder. I was not guilty of murder," Capano explained. He was just guilty of loving someone too much. He admitted his love drove him to write to Deborah MacIntyre in the third person, calling her "an evil twin" and a "creature without conscience" for selling him out to the prosecutors.

Capano again talked about his fine Jesuit upbringing, the difference between good lies and bad lies, and how his superior Jesuit philosophy enabled him to lie for the sake of love. But, of MacIntyre's lies, those lies "were so horrible it had to be some creature that crept into her body," he wrote, and "Like the raptor you are ruthless."

As for MacIntyre's new attorney, "That scumbag lawyer, I

would hunt to the ends of the earth to make him pay for this,'' Capano wrote in one of his letters.

As Oteri ended up his direct questioning of Capano, he again went over the night of the murder and had Capano outline how he drove away ''at a high rate of speed'' like a Keystone cop and how he reassured MacIntyre everything would be all right.

''Did you kill Anne Marie Fahey?'' Oteri asked.

''No. A thousand times no,'' Capano said with conviction.

''No further questions, Your Honor,'' Oteri said.

He walked away from the podium and back to his defense table.

Connolly's cross-examination was still to come and that was not going to be anywhere near as friendly as Oteri's direct questioning.

Chapter 22

The "Squeaky" Factor

Colm Connolly began his cross-examination at eight minutes after noon on December 29, 1998. With a nod to the jury and the judge, and no audible nor visual recognition of the defendant, Connolly launched his first salvo right at Capano.

"Since June 28, 1996, how many crimes have you committed?" Connolly asked.

Capano outlined his attempts to suborn perjury, attempts to obstruct justice, perjury, and a host of other crimes.

"How many lies have you told?" Connolly wanted to know.

"I never told the truth."

"Too many to count?"

"Sure," Capano offered.

From the beginning the two had an adversarial relationship. Capano looked down on Connolly as a young upstart while he was the wily elder statesman. Connolly simply looked at Capano as a criminal, and not for one second did he show that he ever thought anything else about him. Connolly recounted how shortly after Annie's death, while Capano claimed he wasn't thinking clearly, he was thinking clearly enough to set up an alibi. Connolly noted that just seven hours after Annie's death Capano was calmly sitting in his brother's driveway reading the sports pages.

Capano, in the beginning, remained calm.

"You're capable of many things, Mr. Connolly," Capano said. "But you cannot read my mind . . ."

At another juncture Capano chided Connolly with the same volley of "No, no, no, no, no, no," that he often used on Debby MacIntyre. "I'll play your games, Mr. Connolly, but not that one. I deeply loved Anne Marie. You never knew her."

But Capano slipped easily, perhaps as easily as Connolly calculated, into arrogance and condescension. When Connolly asked Capano if he'd attended the bail hearing in the case, Capano just laughed.

"Is that a joke?" Connolly asked.

Again Connolly asked Capano if he had attended the bail hearing.

With what the jury later said was the arrogance of a snot-nosed schoolboy Capano pushed his glasses up on his nose and looked down upon Connolly. "You know the answer to that already," he commented. Judge Lee had to intercede and told Capano he had to answer the question. Capano did so, finally. Then Capano engaged in another tactic that would become familiar over the next few days: He began asking his own questions of the prosecution. Connolly routinely ignored them as he did most of Capano's histrionics, which only seemed to make Capano that much angrier.

Connolly calmly asked Capano if Capano thought the cooler would sink at sea. Capano answered, yes. That was a major point in the case. Had the cooler sunk and never been recovered, Gerry's testimony could not have been corroborated.

Connolly outlined how a few hours after Annie's death Capano was conducting business, and how less than six hours after dumping her body he was back home in Wilmington having pizza and watching videos with his children. Less than thirty-six hours after Annie's death, by his own testimony, Capano was in the arms of and making love to Deborah MacIntyre, his trusted mistress.

Capano grew agitated during the opening rounds of cross-examination, fidgeting with his microphone and raising his voice where he thought it was appropriate. When Connolly asked early on about Capano's daughters, Capano warned him, "Don't you go there."

Connolly dropped it for a while. Then he went over the events around Annie's death.

"I couldn't even take it seriously," Capano said of MacIntyre's alleged claim of public suicide. He said Annie's response was even wilder. " 'Who is this wacko? Just get me out of here, Capano,' " he claimed she said. "Debby was completely flipped out," Capano explained, and when the gun went off, she said, "What the hell was that?"

It was a small hole without a lot of blood coming out, Capano testified of Annie's head wound caused by the hysterical MacIntyre. Capano said he searched for the hole and found it through Annie's thick hair. "I can't believe this. Look what you've done," Capano claimed he told MacIntyre after finding the wound.

Connolly had Capano describe the wound, its size, its shape, its location in relationship to the rest of her body, the type of blood and the type of blood flow.

"I was surprised there was not a whole lot of blood," Capano said matter-of-factly.

Capano described how he got a flashlight from the kitchen and looked into Annie's eyes, which were still open. The flashlight did not cause the pupils to change size. He blew air into her lungs and her chest went up. Her lips were wet and her jaws were not clenched. He opened her mouth and depressed Annie's tongue.

Afterward he took the gun from MacIntyre's hand, he said.

Connolly pointed out that on December 21 Capano testified he picked the gun up after Deborah MacIntyre dropped it. Now he was claiming he took it from her hand. Which was it? Capano couldn't explain.

Connolly also pointed out that in Capano's current version of events he placed a pillow *and* a blanket under Annie's head. Facts he didn't mention on December 21. Was Capano having a hard time keeping track of all of his lies?

That was Connolly's blunt assessment as he continued to chip away at Capano. It was not just Capano's testimony that he worked on, either, but Capano's very fiber. Capano, the suave, intelligent, compassionate man who could charm as many ladies as he liked, had to be exposed as a conniving, villainous, evil manipulator who would stop at nothing to get his own way. Connolly, many said, effectively let the jury see that side of Tom Capano themselves. He had to do it subtly enough that the jury got the point and at the same time blamed Capano and not the prosecutor for the fireworks that would surely follow. Capano was smart enough to see if Connolly were setting him up and he would fight it the entire way.

Connolly managed to snare Capano with Capano's own words. Connolly would, for example, ask Capano if he had ever manipulated anyone. Capano would deny it, wholeheartedly, and then Connolly, using Capano's own words in a letter or e-mail he'd written, would point out where Capano described himself as manipulative, then he would ask again if Capano had ever manipulated anyone.

It was a tiresome tactic that worked beautifully in favor of the prosecution, but it was something Capano didn't seem to "get" until the very end. He fought every description, every phrase that Connolly threw at him. Connolly would say, "Okay ... then turn to tab ten, page twenty-seven (in the bound books of letters and e-mail that were supplied to the jury members during the trial)" and then quote the words written by Capano to rub Capano's nose in it.

Capano only gave up fighting these horrifying descriptions of himself on the last day he was on the stand, obviously too tired and worn down by Connolly's tactic to fight the inevitable anymore. But by then he was lost. Most of the jurors, many of whom said they were sitting on the fence, decided after Capano's testimony that Capano was guilty.

Capano lost a lot of sympathy with the jury because not only in his direct testimony, but most especially during the cross-examination, he seemed too far removed from the gruesome testimony he gave. For example, he had to ''force her (Annie's) feet in (the cooler)'' but he ''didn't break any bones.'' Capano testified to that horrible bit of business with all the care of ordering a spare part for a broken bicycle. He testified so dispassionately about putting a woman, that he claimed he cared for so deeply, in a cooler that it was a moment that seared itself in the jury's collective consciousness. They began and ended their deliberation with that cooler, emotionally as well as physically close to them.

''I was operating on nothing but panic,'' Capano told Connolly as he stuffed his lover into a cooler. ''It didn't take any time at all.''

The heat was nearly unbearable in the courtroom as Connolly shook his head in disgust at that comment and then listened as Capano said, ''There really was no reason to go to Anne Marie's apartment. It's just something I did.''

''Why did you want to know if you were the last person to call Anne Marie Fahey?'' Connolly asked.

''If I were, then it pointed directly to me,'' Capano replied.

''You were thinking clearly enough to know the police would want to know who the last person was who called Anne Marie Fahey?''

''Yes.''

''Thirteen minutes after her death you are trying to make a false alibi?'' Connolly made no effort to disguise his indignation.

"That is correct," said Capano.

Capano explained it away as something irrational, but Connolly took a great deal of time and effort to show that Capano's acts were very rational indeed. They were the rational effort of a man trying to hide his involvement in a murder. Capano again pointed out that if everything had been left in the hands of the Wilmington Police, everything would have gone differently. Capano trusted the Wilmington Police. "They play by the rules," he explained.

It was just the mean, old federal government who screwed things up, according to Capano. Well, if that were the case, Connolly pointed out, why did Capano take such great pains to destroy all the forensic evidence? The blood, the couch, the body, the rug? If he trusted the Wilmington Police Department, why did he do all of those things?

"My statement would be more important if the forensic evidence wasn't there," Capano said evenly.

The building's heat seemed to be in overdrive that day, and the jurors responded to some of the toughest questions of the day by fanning themselves, struggling to stay awake.

Then, Connolly dropped a nice, little surprise into the case that kept the jurors, defense, and everyone else glued to him. He mentioned Squeaky Saunders. The same Squeaky Saunders Capano had himself successfully prosecuted more than 20 years ago for a murder when Capano himself was a prosecutor. The same Squeaky Saunders whom Capano used as a character witness when he was in jail, and the same Squeaky Saunders whom Connolly accused Capano of trying to buy.

Squeaky Saunders had been convicted of shooting someone in the back of the head, getting rid of the gun and some forensic evidence, and then trying to dump his victim at sea. Connolly began asking Capano if that was the model for his own crime— the killing of Anne Marie Fahey.

At first Capano was so stunned, he denied much involvement in the Saunders murder case. "Perhaps I can end this nonsense by saying it (Annie's death) had nothing to do with this case (the Saunders case)," Capano said.

But that was a strategic error as Connolly had already pulled the transcripts of the Saunders case and held them up to show the court. "Did you look up the transcripts of all the cases I tried?" Capano asked with a sneer.

Connolly didn't answer him. Instead he quoted from Capano's closing arguments in the case. "The most important thing is to get rid of the gun. Mr. Saunders once again shows us how smart he is . . . ," Connolly said while quoting from Capano. There was no mistaking that Connolly rattled Capano, who became more argumentative as Connolly went on to other lines of questioning.

Capano got especially nasty during questioning about his family, at one point telling Connolly, "No, no. That wasn't your question." At another point he asked a question, and when chided by the judge, quickly said, "I withdraw the question," as if he were the lawyer trying the case instead of the defendant on trial.

But he got the jury's attention when he accused Connolly of being involved in something seedier and more dangerous. "There have been threatening letters against my kids and you've done nothing about it," he shouted from the witness stand.

Connolly dodged it and quietly said, "Now on the subject . . ."

"What have you done about it!" He bluntly accused Connolly of putting his children in harm's way. Judge Lee finally had enough. "You will limit your remarks to the appropriate response or I will take the appropriate action," he told Capano.

Now with the defendant a little more sedate, the prosecution walked Capano through his rehab/extortion scenario wherein he took money from his brother. Connolly pointed out that Capano got his dates wrong and proved it by the date on the back of one of the canceled checks entered as evidence and then pointed out that the Tom Capano who painted himself as a "blue-collar" man who got his fingernails dirty helping his father out in the construction business had, on average, in the beginning months of 1996 more than $155,000 in his personal checking account.

"Gee, I can't believe I did that. That was really stupid," Capano said of himself after Connolly confronted him with the facts. Capano took every opportunity to be combative, with even the most obscure and meaningless facts. Eventually it wore everyone down, including Capano.

By the end of the day on December 29 the judge felt he'd had enough to say that "I will not surrender control of this court to the defendant or anyone else."

It had been clear from day one that Judge William Swain Lee was in control of his court. He was going to be kind, gracious, and fair to everyone—and in the end all the attorneys praised him for that effort. But he wasn't taking any guff, either. At the end of the day Colm Connolly tried to slip some in.

Connolly had been questioning Capano about "leg breaking," to which Gerry had testified his brother was interested. Capano laughed, saying that finding a leg breaker for an alleged extortionist was all Gerry's idea.

"It's like a line out of a movie," Capano exclaimed. "I laughed."

"Ever heard of Linda Marandola?" Connolly asked.

The bottom dropped out. It seemed the whole defense team objected. The whole line of questioning was dropped and the case adjourned for the day. The next morning the judge sustained the objection and the jury didn't get to hear about Tom Capano's threats to Linda Marandola in the early 1980s. All of that was deemed irrelevant to the trial and charges at hand. If the jury was going to hear that information it couldn't come until the penalty phase.

The last day of testimony of the year started with yet another apology from Tom Capano.

He basically apologized for being an ass—except when it

came to his children. He wouldn't apologize for being the caring father he was.

Connolly spent much of the day using Capano's letters against him and getting Capano to admit to things that the prosecution hoped would destroy Capano's credibility. On cross-examination Capano said he basically got rid of the gun just to get rid of the gun and when pressed he admitted, "I knew without the gun it would make it a lot more difficult to prosecute me or Debby."

The mood was ugly in the hot courtroom as the year drew to a close. It was ugly with Capano's remarks about his former friends and colleagues. Connolly showed how Capano trashed people, how he wrote his e-mails, how he conducted himself in a pattern that indicated his manipulative nature.

When in February he e-mailed Annie and then had his daughter send Annie an e-mail, Connolly suggested Capano used his own daughters to try and manipulate Annie. Connolly also showed how Capano saved these e-mails and indicated they were saved, not out of love, but out of a coldhearted plan to commit murder and then use those letters as evidence.

Though there was not much made of the authenticity of the e-mail correspondence during the trial, the tenuous nature of electronic mail and the ease with which it can be duplicated or invented did cause at least one of the jurors some problems. The handwritten letters by Capano and Deborah MacIntyre's signed computer printout letters made a much deeper impression as did the recorded telephone conversations. Connolly went through them all, much to Capano's chagrin.

"You told her (Deborah MacIntyre) she was innocent," Connolly said at one point.

"I told her that innumerable times," Capano said after reading aloud from one of the letters.

Why Capano would do such a thing, if in fact MacIntyre had pulled the trigger was a question he never answered adequately, and it led to another revelation as Connolly marched through the letters and the telephone conversations.

" . . . Because she had a good heart she let people push her around," Capano said of MacIntyre. "She knew she was being manipulated but she was too kind."

"She was a doormat to people?" Connolly asked with his eyebrow slightly arched.

"Yes."

"Submissive?"

"Yeah. At times. That's your word, though, not mine."

"Oh, yeah?" Connolly had him. "Let's turn to the letter you wrote dated March 10, of 1996."

Connolly pointed out where Capano used the word "submissive" to describe MacIntyre at least a half a dozen times. He pointed out the letter Capano wrote to MacIntyre's son in which Capano said MacIntyre wasn't strong and let people walk all over her. Capano did it, too, he confessed, but that was okay since Capano loved MacIntyre. Then Connolly pointed out how Capano used his kids in some letters to MacIntyre as an attempt to get her to do something he wanted.

"Invoking your kids is the same thing you did to Anne Marie Fahey," Connolly accused.

"You're way out of line here," Capano boomed.

"When you wanted to manipulate Deborah MacIntyre, you used your kids," Connolly said with equal force.

"Don't go there," Capano warned.

It was an ominous sight. Capano's gray pallor combined with his bad prison haircut, his intense dark eyes, and a voice that reporter Robert Dvorchak said seemed to come straight from the depths of hell, painted a ghoulish and somewhat frightening picture for the jury. Capano, it seemed, was on the verge of losing it.

Connolly backed away from further probes, letting that wound fester, and Capano tried to apologize, saying he was an overprotective father. But there was little doubt about the revelation; if someone wanted an instant hot button with Capano it was through his children.

Connolly started asking Capano about the one-two punch he would employ with MacIntyre in his letters: at one point insulting her and then quickly following that up with a compliment. Capano didn't see it. He claimed he was still deeply in love with MacIntyre, and his letters were filled with exaltations of his deepest, most sincere love for a woman. Connolly remained unconvinced and saw the letters as mere manipulation.

"These letters are replete with these examples, aren't they?" Connolly asked in reference to the insults followed by compliments.

"This is an example of me pouring my heart out," Capano replied. "This is not the CIA technique you ascribe to me."

Capano denied he ever controlled Deborah MacIntyre, and as Connolly went to ask him another question, Capano blurted out another question of his own to the prosecutor. Connolly ignored it and went on, or tried to. But Judge Lee, who'd increasingly engaged in eye-rolling exercises during the bulk of the Capano testimony, calmly interjected.

"Mr. Capano knows the rules and Mr. Capano needs to abide by them," he said as if he were scolding a recalcitrant schoolboy. The case went on and Connolly questioned Capano about Tom Bergstrom.

"Tom Bergstrom you hate," Connolly said.

"Oh. Yes, I do," Capano said with a smiling, blunt sneer.

"He's a Philadelphia sleazeball . . . ," Connolly said.

"Yes. I hate him."

Capano went on to tell the jury how Bergstrom had transformed his loving and lovely Debby MacIntyre into a prudish librarian who wore collars up to her neck. This was a man, Capano said of Bergstrom, who made Tom du Pont look like "Jesus Christ before his trial."

Connolly pointed out that Capano once thought of hiring

Bergstrom himself. He also pointed out that Capano apparently unethically tried to make MacIntyre choose between himself and Bergstrom—something Capano knew was unethical since he, too, was a lawyer. But Capano didn't see it that way and referred to Bergstrom as "pond scum" and a "piece of filth." As Connolly read the descriptive phrase for the jury, Capano even blurted in with a smile, "I wish I could've thought of some more. . . ."

Juror #11 turned away. She was becoming increasingly sickened at the endless name-calling. Capano was hurting his chances and didn't even seem to know it. Meanwhile Connolly scored another point against Capano. He quoted from the telephone conversation when MacIntyre told Capano she'd just talked to prosecutors and told them the truth about the gun. Under Capano's scenario this meant she just confessed to accidentally shooting Annie or at least confessed that Capano had nothing to do with purchasing the gun. Capano, however, on the recorded conversation wasn't happy when he heard the news and Connolly pointed that out, wanting to know why?

"When she said that, I wanted to know what she meant by that," Capano replied.

"You don't say, 'Thanks, Debby'? She just basically exonerated you and you're not jumping for joy?" Connolly asked with a touch of sarcasm.

Capano got angry and claimed that a second conversation, unrecorded by MacIntyre because she did not know how to use the machinery correctly, was actually unrecorded on purpose. It was during this second conversation that Capano said he confronted MacIntyre about her actual involvement in Annie's death and that she was to blame and not him.

"Don't pretend that second phone call didn't happen," Capano shouted while pointing his finger at Connolly. "I was a sucker. She took advantage of me," Capano added in describing how MacIntyre used him during the phone conversations.

That was the last word from Capano for the year. Connolly

had spent the day accusing Capano of playing on MacIntyre's weaknesses and sympathies in a futile attempt to keep her from testifying against him. It had been shown Capano even used his own children in that attempt. Capano had responded with courtroom theatrics that strained Judge Lee's patience to the point of breaking. The year-end break, courthouse regulars said, couldn't have come at a better time.

Sex, lies, and audiotape were all essential to the Capano case, as was a videotaped pornography collection, but it all paled in comparison to what went on the first day court reconvened for the new year.

During the break Deborah MacIntyre settled into her new life of pseudo-media star. Through her attorney, she began negotiating to appear on *20/20* and *Good Morning America*, portraying herself as the injured, tortured, innocent bystander to all that went on.

"I couldn't have done everything Capano said I did," she told a reporter one day. "I didn't even have a key to his house."

MacIntyre also spent those days getting ready to move. Her phone number, address, layout of her home, and her private security code for her burglar alarm had been passed around Gander Hill like a communal copy of *Playboy*. It was in her best interest to move, and her home had too many memories of Tom Capano. Debby appeared to be faring well, despite the attacks on her credibility and character Capano made almost every minute he was on the witness stand.

The same could not be said of one of the true victims in all of this mess, Kay Ryan. Caught on the steps outside of court one day, she was in tears, bemoaning the fact that her life was in ruins "thanks to that bastard up there," pointing up the stairs and indicating her former husband. She wasn't exactly fond of having her children watch their father in court every day, but Capano wanted it, as did Joey Capano. Kay felt it was necessary to be there for her children. But listening to tales of peccadillos, mistresses, and the secret life her husband had led for so many years, was a painful thing for Kay. She could not and did not attend court as often as her daughters, and when there, it was obvious she wanted to be elsewhere.

"She never deserved any of that," Jack O'Donnell later said. "She's a smart, classy woman who's raised four exceptional daughters. The Faheys went through a terrible tragedy, no one is going to deny that, but if you look around, there were so many other horrible tragedies wrapped up in this and Kay's was one of the largest."

The pain caused by Annie's death was beginning to grind everyone down. When court reconvened, the defense team had the appearance of whipped dogs. Reporters would only find out later that behind the scenes they were still having monumental struggles with Capano. They could not, by law, talk about his testimony while he was still on the stand, but Capano never made it easy for any of them. It was sapping their strength.

On January 4 Connolly launched into Capano about some of the purple prose he'd written to Deborah MacIntyre and some of his outlandish testimony. Especially irksome to Connolly, was Capano's statement that "The sun would fall out of the sky," before Capano believed Deborah MacIntyre would betray him. Capano had written and testified how he took a note from MacIntyre, folded it, and placed it over his heart. A member of his defense team, Capano wrote, had said, "My God, you really love her." But, under cross-examination Capano admitted it may not have ever happened.

Connolly went after Capano's statements of enduring love for Deborah MacIntyre. In March 1998 Capano wrote to MacIntyre early in the day saying, "I love you with all my heart and beg you to give me another chance." Later the same day he wrote to Susan Louth, and mentioned how a relative of his had seen MacIntyre on television and said, "She looks like a shrew and a backstabber.'' Capano found that amusing and wrote to Louth saying how perceptive his relative was.

Connolly read this aloud in court and then turned to Capano and asked him if the information was correct. Capano explained away the disparity between the two letters with, ''It was later in the day.''

Connolly spent the day dancing around Capano, spending a few minutes here and a few minutes there, bobbing and weaving and scoring points the entire time, like a prizefighter just wearing out his opponent, waiting and looking for the blow that would bring about a knockout.

Connolly hit Capano with Perillo, saying he looked forward to having MacIntyre's home burglarized. Capano lashed out saying he just wanted to ''blow off steam'' and never had any real intention of seeing the burglary through.

Connolly hit Capano with racism charges. Capano had insisted to the jury, which consisted of two black women, that he was no racist. But Connolly produced an e-mail containing racial slurs about an Asian/Indian client of his law firm. ''Some dot-head,'' Capano had called the client.

Connolly pointed out Capano had his attorneys inform the FBI that someone resembling Anne Marie Fahey was seen at the Newark International Airport in August 1996—an obvious lie since Capano admitted he'd dumped Annie at sea on June 28.

Connolly used Capano's own psychiatrist against him. Dr. Joseph Bryer wrote that Capano said Fahey got a bloody nose the night of June 27 after she attacked him, but Capano eventually took her home unharmed. How many stories did that make about the blood in Capano's home? Capano also told Bryer he feared Fahey might be a victim of suicide or street violence.

Bryer wrote that Capano appeared ''authentic and genuine'' in telling those stories. By now everyone knew Capano had admitted that those stories were all lies. The implication from

Connolly's perspective was that Capano was a pathological liar.

Connolly hit him with his own words. Remembering how Capano had chastised a subordinate in his law firm about fooling around on his wife inside Wilmington city limits: "She's the mother of your kids," Capano had said.

Connolly showed how through Capano's own personal correspondence he admitted to having extramarital sex at the New Castle County Airport, in his office "numerous times with women," at a 1995 Christmas party, and one time with Deborah MacIntyre at her home just before her husband came home. They had quickly got up and pretended Capano was at the house fixing a VCR.

"You enjoyed the risk, didn't you?" Connolly asked.

When Capano denied it, Connolly just smiled, shrugged, and said, "Really?" He then urged Capano to turn to "tab seventeen."

Connolly next asked him about the time his wife, Kay, almost caught Capano and MacIntyre having sex, "standing up backward in a coat room."

"So you like risks," Connolly jabbed again.

"You are so wrong, Mr. Connolly," Capano said with little conviction.

Connolly brought up other letters Capano had written, prompting Capano to say, "I didn't think even you would sink that low (as to open mail)."

Connolly kept up his relentless pursuit, accusing Capano of only making up his latest story weeks, even mere days, before the trial was to begin. Connolly referred to the incident at the beginning of the trial where Capano referred to Anne Marie Fahey as an "alleged victim." The defense objected to this line of questioning and following a sidebar, Connolly went after Capano with a different combination: Dan Lyons.

Capano long maintained that his brother Gerry made up most of the important facets of his testimony to save himself after the feds raided his home. But Gerry had waived his attorney/ client privilege and allowed another attorney to take the stand in this case. Lyons's big bombshell was that Gerry Capano told him the exact story he told the feds more than a half a year before the raid on his home.

Connolly said it was Lyons's testimony that caused Capano to shift gears and go from arguing he had nothing to do with Fahey's death, to blaming MacIntyre. She was always his fall-back position was the insinuation. The accusation stung and hurt Capano.

Now Connolly went after loyal brother Joey Capano.

Tom Capano wouldn't admit to Joey's criminal past, which included a charge of unlawful imprisonment and unlawful sexual conduct with a woman Joey had been dating. Joey Capano, with Tom Capano's assistance, eventually pled guilty to a misdemeanor charge of criminal mischief and assault.

None of this would have been entered into the record, but a stubborn Capano wouldn't admit to his brother's past. Now Joey, many years removed and hopefully a changed man, had to have his past dragged out in the open much as Keith Brady had. Joey Capano's credibility was now possibly damaged.

Connolly proceeded to the conspiracy. Capano told Connolly how willing he was to come forward and tell the truth, from the very beginning. It had just been when Connolly and the FBI became involved that he changed his mind. He was particularly upset that the FBI claimed jurisdiction just because Anne Marie Fahey might have been the victim of an interstate kidnapping.

"You guys (the feds) obviously have no morals and ethics, and I couldn't even think about talking to you," Capano lashed out, adding it was a wise decision. "Look what happened. Look at what you've done."

Capano was yelling and accusing President Clinton of getting involved. "When the President of the United States gets involved, I'm diving as deeply as I can," Capano said about his unwillingness to talk.

Connolly said the Faheys had written him a letter begging him to come in, why didn't he?

"It was a farce, Mr. Connolly. You blasted your way in and took over. I would have nothing to do with you, your officers, or your investigation. Boom. End of story."

Capano said it was the worst thing that ever happened when the federal government got involved. "It was a political football. If the Wilmington Police had handled it, it never would have come to this. It never should have come to this." But it had, and Connolly knew he had his man.

With Capano on the edge, and angry at Connolly, the prosecutor decided now was the time to pick up the hot button issue he'd left behind before. Capano admitted to using and misleading almost everyone in his life to cover up his activities on June 27 and 28, 1996.

"You used your daughters," Connolly said evenly.

Capano was enraged. "Do you really want to get into that? You tormented my daughters. You tormented my mother." Capano was almost standing up in the witness chair. Behind him, the tall bailiff was cautiously eyeing Capano with a look fathers often use on wayward children.

"Let's talk about your daughters," Connolly replied without equivocation.

"No, you're not," Capano shouted.

Connolly calmly reminded Capano he could have kept his children out of harm's way by simply reaching a deal before his arrest. Speak to Bob Donovan about Annie's disappearance, and Connolly would agree not to contact his girls, provided Capano gave his word the blood in his apartment wasn't his children's. Capano did not agree to such measures.

Capano went wild. Gene Maurer objected before Capano could find enough composure to speak, and the attorneys approached the bench for another sidebar.

As they approached, Capano took a swing at the microphone in front of him. "This is bullshit," he seethed.

Mel, the bailiff, kept a close watch on him.

After a few minutes Maurer's objection was overruled, but Maurer hoped at least Capano had composed himself enough with the delay to answer the question. It did not work.

As soon as Connolly could, he simply and calmly asked Capano about using his own daughters yet again. The suave, debonair Capano was gone. The demon had arrived.

"You're a heartless, gutless, soulless disgrace of a human being!" He belted out each word, slowly, deeply, and with the resonance of a bass drum.

"Why don't you explain what you've done to my mother!?"

Capano was shouting so loudly now, Connolly couldn't get in his objection.

He needn't worry. Judge Lee had had more than enough. "Would the bailiff please take Mr. Capano out of the courtroom," Judge Lee said evenly.

The bailiff took one step forward as Capano began pointing at Connolly shouting, "He's a liar!" But when Capano saw the former basketball-star bailiff moving forward, he calmed down immediately. Mel took him in hand like an unwanted flea and led Capano away without further incident. The jury sat openmouthed as the scene erupted into bedlam.

Shaking off the histrionics, Judge Lee produced a smile for the jury. "I know everyone has complained about the heat in the courtroom," he said. "It just got a little hotter."

With that, he dismissed the jury and adjourned court for the day.

Outside the courtroom the Capanos were not happy. Nor were Capano's attorneys. Maurer shrugged, Oberly quietly shuffled away, and O'Donnell and Oteri seemed to be disheartened. There seemed to be little hope for their case now. A thirty-four-year-old assistant U.S. attorney, trying his first major murder case, had tripped up the suave, worldly Tom Capano so easily as to make it look like child's play.

As the sun went down on Wilmington that day, there was

an odd flurry of activity near Deborah MacIntyre's house. Around 6:30 P.M. a smartly dressed young man, unseen at the trial previously, showed up at MacIntyre's home with a manila folder filled with papers. Shortly thereafter, Bob Donovan and other investigators arrived. There was additional activity near MacIntyre's garage and someone began taking pictures.

Chapter 23

"An independent, credible witness . . ."

Judge William Swain Lee does not suffer fools gladly and he wasn't glad to have Capano back in the courtroom on January 5. It was the eighth day of Capano's testimony, his fourth day of cross-examination, the thirty-third day of testimony in the trial, and the judge was quite through.

Before he brought the jury in, he turned to Capano and let him have it.

"There will be no apologies to the court or to the jury. You are to simply answer the questions," Judge Lee told him. "Failure to do so will bring the appropriate admonishment in front of the jury and other measures I deem appropriate. There are more severe, Draconian sanctions which will be considered, sanctions which will take place," if Capano didn't clean up his behavior. Further, the judge warned, "You will quit manipulating the questions Mr. Connolly asks to the ends you want." Judge Lee rubbed his eyes and seemed quite enraged.

"I have attempted to afford you every consideration, but I will do my job. Do we understand each other?"

The judge looked directly at Capano as the defendant sat in the witness chair.

"Does that mean you want an answer from me?" Capano sneered.

The judge, obviously annoyed, dismissed Capano without even a look. To Mel he simply said, "Bailiff, please bring in the jury."

Connolly again avoided any salutations to Capano and quickly launched in at the point where the trial had stopped the day before: Capano's daughters. This time Capano kept himself in control, barely. He said he and his wife, Kay, tried to keep his daughters from giving blood samples in the case, not as a delaying tactic, nor as a way to protect Tom Capano, but to protect his daughters. "I would not allow you to act as evilly as you could," Capano told Connolly with no trace of subtlety in his voice. Later he said he wouldn't allow his children to suffer "any more degradation" at the hands of Connolly and the rest of the prosecutors and hoped they would influence Gerry and Louie into protecting Capano. Capano said he even told his mother that she had to choose between Gerry and himself. He wanted his mother to testify on Gerry's many "character defects."

Capano blamed Robert Fahey for part of the problem and said Robert invoked "political conditions" in coming forward and Capano said he didn't want it to end up that way. Capano did, however, consider writing his own book and putting together his own movie deal and in one letter said he would "focus on the book and movie stuff after the hearing is over next week."

By the time Connolly finished the cross-examination that morning there was little doubt, mainly because Capano admitted it, that he'd openly used everyone in his family, including his children in an effort to keep himself out of prison.

Oteri tried valiantly during redirect to show how Capano had been loyal to Debby MacIntyre and to replant the idea that it was MacIntyre, and not Capano, who ultimately pulled the trigger. There just wasn't much the defense could do at this point to pull a rabbit out of the hat. Capano had already cut up the hat and killed the rabbit. Particularly annoying for the defense team, and what really got to the jury was Capano's continuing insults aimed at the Faheys, and even his own family. He said his younger brother Gerry had committed more crimes in a year than Joey had in a lifetime—which left at least one juror wondering who was being insulted on purpose and convinced both brothers were, whether intentional or not.

As Capano discussed how Robert Fahey was one of the causes behind the mess everyone was in that day, Oteri didn't seem to have much patience anymore for his own client.

"I was gonna tell Robert to call off the politics and do this the right way," Capano told the court and his attorney as he explained that he wanted to try and sit down and discuss things with Robert Fahey after Annie's disappearance. But Capano admitted he wasn't going to tell Robert that Annie was dead. There was still some question as to what political influence Robert Fahey could have over Tom Capano. Robert wasn't wired into the Wilmington political structure like Capano. He didn't have Capano's money nor influence anywhere in the system.

Oteri bypassed that and seemed to cross-examine his own client on another mound of lies. "We've got to get this thing depoliticized," Capano said, but when questioned by his own attorney, Capano admitted he wasn't going to tell the truth.

"So you were gonna lie to him?" Oteri asked in a great moment of role reversal. He now sounded more like Connolly than Connolly.

"No, no," Capano assured him.

"Well, how can you square this, sir, with your plan to protect Debby and explain this to Robert Fahey?" Oteri asked. Capano didn't have a decent answer. During the midmorning break the Capano camp was again glum.

After the break Capano was back in charge on the stand, telling Joe Oteri to slow down as he asked his questions. Capano was seemingly orchestrating his own defense again, and felt it necessary to explain his Jesuit upbringing some more. "There is no such thing as a dumb Jesuit," Capano assured the jury.

Capano once again explained it was okay to lie sometimes and that a lie was only evil if it had evil intent. He admitted he had lied in the past, but what he did wasn't wrong, for he was lying to protect the woman he loved. As the jury tried to swallow that, he then confessed he could kill in the heat of passion and his personal philosophy—grounded in his strong Jesuit studies—allowed him to kill "justly." There was no mistaking the shaking heads in the jury, nor on the defense team as Capano explained his highly moral upbringing, which allowed him sex with whomever he pleased, whenever he pleased; the ability to lie about his friends and family and drag everyone he ever knew into the dirt with him; and to kill if necessary.

Capano continued to address Anne Marie on occasion in the present tense, as if she were still alive. Finally, shortly after 3 P.M. that day, Tom Capano left the witness stand.

Oteri wanted people to completely forget Capano and the many mistakes the defendant had made on the witness stand. The only way to do that was with a miracle.

Kim Johnson was intended to be that miracle. Johnson, with a master's degree in criminal justice, worked as a substitute schoolteacher and lived across the street from Deborah MacIntyre. She described herself as a "casual" neighbor to MacIntyre and they occasionally said hello when they saw each other. Johnson did not know Capano nor any of the other principals in the case. She harbored no grudges against MacIntyre, and neither she, nor her husband knew MacIntyre intimately. When she was called to the stand after Capano, no one in the jury nor the audience knew why she was there, but Oteri and the prosecution did.

Sometime in the late spring or early summer of 1996 Johnson said she remembered going upstairs to the second floor of her house to close a bedroom window. She remembered it being after the evening news, sometime around 11:40 and 11:45 P.M.

As she approached the bedroom window she heard the sound of a "very loud" vehicle coming up the street. Then she saw what she assumed was MacIntyre's black Jeep Grand Cherokee pulling into MacIntyre's driveway. At that point Johnson said the trees in the driveway briefly obscured her view, but she heard the brakes applied so hard on the car that the tires squealed as the Jeep came to an abrupt stop.

Johnson said MacIntyre stumbled out of the car very quickly, and no one else was inside the car but her. Johnson saw in the light cast down by two twin spotlights on MacIntyre's garage a flash of MacIntyre's hair and face. Johnson said she was sure it was MacIntyre.

When MacIntyre got out of the car, "she issued an anguished sob," Johnson said, and then ran to the side of the house. It was, Johnson said, a "loud, gut-wrenching sob."

Johnson could not be sure of the exact date, but said she knew it was in June 1996, after June 14 and before July 4. She gave those dates by placing the event between two things she remembered occurring that year, but she couldn't say exactly when she saw MacIntyre in such distress. But she remembered it because "I never saw anything like this before or after," she said earnestly.

Capano, back at the defense table furiously scrawling additional notes, nearly beamed with pride as he heard the petite, brown-haired substitute teacher testify.

Johnson testified she had *never* been questioned by the government, even though she lived right across the street from MacIntyre. To Capano, that was proof the government never had any intention of going after anyone but him. After all, Connolly and Donovan had gone out of their way to secure bank photographs outside of a money machine to corroborate part of Gerry's testimony, yet no one had ever bothered to walk across the street from MacIntyre's house and talk to the neighbor of a key prosecution witness.

If the cops on television could canvas a neighborhood, members of the Capano family wondered out loud, why hadn't Donovan and Connolly done the same thing?

Johnson said the government investigators finally got around to talking with her just last night at her home, four men to be exact, who asked her the details of her story.

On cross-examination the roles seemed to be reversed. Joe Oteri, Gene Maurer, Jack O'Donnell and Charlie Oberly had spent most of the trial trying to tear apart witnesses. Now, the prosecution was forced into taking a similar posture with Kim Johnson. But, try as they did, Johnson's story struck a resonant chord with the jury.

Ferris Wharton, the state prosecutor, handled the cross-examination and painstakingly went through all of Johnson's testimony: the position of the trees, the window Johnson said she looked through, the type of clothes MacIntyre wore, the sound she made, and how the garage-door lights looked.

One thing Johnson did admit on cross-examination was she wouldn't allow the prosecutors into the second-floor bedroom to take a look and see what Johnson claimed she saw. It was curious, as was the fact that the ornamental trees that partially obscured Johnson's view had been fuller and much larger in June 1996. The question remained, what could she really see 200 feet away from an action hidden behind some trees?

Oteri said Wharton made one key mistake in the cross-examination. "I would have asked one question: 'Can you say for certain this happened on June 27? No? No further questions.' Then I'd sit down," he volunteered to reporters.

Gene Maurer said Kim Johnson could well be the most important witness in the entire trial. "She is an independent, credible witness who had nothing to gain by coming forward," Maurer told the afternoon assembly of reporters. "I think it's very obvious she saw something," and hopefully, the defense attorneys said, it would be enough to cast reasonable doubt on the prosecution's entire case.

Wednesday, January 6, 1999, broke bright and clear but cold in Wilmington. As the case against Capano reconvened in the Daniel L. Hermann Courthouse, the defense was winding down, and Oteri was hoping to rest his case soon. Since Capano was still in charge, there would be more witnesses to follow.

First was Capano's brother-in-law Lee Ramunno. He was convinced it was Capano's brother Louis who had turned the federal government on to Gerry Capano and was the reason why the federal investigators were able to get a warrant to raid Gerry's home. From the stand Ramunno leaned back in the witness chair, crossed his legs, played with the microphone like he was onstage, and generally seemed to enjoy himself. He had thinning gray hair pulled back in a ponytail, was stout and small of stature, gesticulated his answers to questions, and grinned whenever he saw he had scored a point.

Ramunno's testimony concerned a conversation he had with Tom Capano during the Fourth of July weekend following Annie's disappearance. While the family was huddled together at Stone Harbor, New Jersey, Ramunno asked Capano why he hadn't gone forward and spoken to the police. Ramunno said Capano told him he was protecting someone. He couldn't speak to police Capano said, "without involving somebody else."

It would be logical to assume that the "somebody else" was Capano's own brother Gerry. But Ramunno said outside the courtroom that wasn't likely. Gerry, Ramunno said on the stand, "is basically the big boy who never grew up." You could never rely on what Gerry said, Ramunno offered, "from one day to the next."

"Gerry simply doesn't tell you the same thing from minute to minute even," Ramunno told the jury. How that related to

Tom Capano's inability to protect his younger brother Gerry wasn't exactly explained in the courtroom. But under direct questioning, Ramunno felt it necessary to fill in other areas of the case he didn't think were adequately explained.

"It's an incredible thing. I haven't seen anything like it in thirty-five years," Ramunno testified regarding the prosecution's desire to question Marguerite Capano, Tom Capano's mother. "As far as I'm concerned, it was harassment."

Ramunno didn't say how it was harassment or what exactly was harassing about wanting to question Capano's mother, but his testimony wasn't necessarily for the benefit of the jury. It certainly was for the benefit of the Capano family, who solemnly clucked their approval as Ramunno painted the prosecution as a group of overzealous Boy Scouts abusing their authority.

Marian, the diminutive, soft-spoken, and sweet-natured sister to Tom Capano sat among the reporters during her husband's testimony. "He is a sweet man," she said of her husband. Of Tom Capano she said, "My brother could never do what they say he did."

Ramunno obviously agreed with his wife about Tom Capano. But there was apparently no love lost between Ramunno and Louis Capano. "Louis is a pathological liar with no morals," Ramunno gleefully told the jury. Convinced Louis had set up Gerry for the feds, Ramunno referred to sealed court documents the prosecutors had filed, which were the basis for the warrant to raid Gerry's home.

Ramunno was convinced it was a "secret agreement" between Louis and the feds. When asked what he believed was involved in that agreement, Ramunno waved his hands and gesticulated widely. "It's a secret agreement. How would I know? It's a secret. I've seen the written deal (a deal Louis had signed with the prosecution in return for his testimony). It's the written deal. I'm not gonna see the secret deal. It's a secret!"

The courtroom erupted in laughter.

Ramunno next went after Gerry Capano, again saying when Gerry got drunk that "three plus three doesn't equal six. It equals nine. He doesn't add. He multiplies."

When Ramunno left the stand, he almost took a bow. The seriousness of the murder trial had for a moment been side-tracked by family squabbles and an attorney who didn't mind airing the most mundane family laundry in an open court.

Marian followed her husband on the witness stand. She started out by saying, "I love all my brothers very much."

Hers was a strange appearance, jurors later said, for a Capano and almost anyone else on the stand throughout the course of the trial. She trashed no one—not her brothers (of Gerry, she said she knew of his drinking but not of any drug addiction), not Debby MacIntyre, not the Faheys—no one. She left the witness stand, untarnished.

The defense called Detective Bob Donovan back to the stand following Marian Ramunno. Donovan went over the tactic of "taking down the inner circle," which had defined the prosecution's aims—at least according to the defense.

At 2:35 P.M. the defense rested. Rebuttal began immediately with Robert Gallagher. He was the man who had been seen outside Debby MacIntyre's house the night before Kim Johnson's testimony delivering papers to MacIntyre. He was a handyman and testified he installed a two-bulb socket above MacIntyre's garage six months after Annie died.

Gallagher told the prosecution the socket he installed was a floodlight system, which flooded the ground surrounding the garage with light. The old socket contained a regular lightbulb that did little for illuminating the grounds.

Kim Johnson had told the jury she distinctly remembered seeing Deborah MacIntyre run out of her car sobbing. One of the reasons she could positively identify MacIntyre from a distance of more than 200 feet through thick trees from a second-floor window in her house was because she distinctly remembered two floodlights bathing the area around the garage with light.

According to Gallagher's testimony, the new lighting system Johnson said she saw in the late spring or early summer of 1996 hadn't been installed at MacIntyre's home until six months later.

Gallagher, a tall, thin man, sat on the stand dispassionately pointing out how and when he replaced the socket. He remembered because the old socket was so hard to replace. He produced a twin to that socket he found in MacIntyre's garage along with the receipt.

The handyman's testimony was damaging to the defense's star witness from the day before, and Gene Maurer, who handled the cross-examination, knew it. With a fury he hadn't even used on Deborah MacIntyre, Maurer went after Gallagher.

Was he licensed? Why was he producing the twin of the socket he replaced and not the original? What good did it do to have the twin?

Dressed in his blue suit, white shirt, and red tie, the handyman sat through a barrage of questions not flinching, trying to be as polite as possible. He changed lightbulbs for a living, but Maurer bore into him as if he were accused of murder.

Kim Horstmann reappeared on the stand and called Capano a liar. She testified Annie saw him as a father figure not as a best friend. She said Capano told her his daughter Katie had a brain tumor that had to be treated.

Several members of the Wilmington Country Club also testified. Capano had said he bought the chain and lock he had used to dispose of Annie's body because of break-ins at the country club and because the president of the country club had sent members a letter requesting the locks. The president of the club and the locker-room maintenance people, as well as a club secretary, testified they had no information regarding break-ins and never requested members put locks on their lockers.

By the end of the day Tom Bergstrom had also testified, refuting Capano's allegation that Bergstrom had written some of MacIntyre's letters. Also testifying was a man Robert "Squeaky" Saunders had written to from prison, as well as an IRS agent and other members of the community whose collective sole purpose for testifying was in one way or another to call Capano a liar.

Testimony in the case concluded on Monday, January 11, 1999. A member of the Board of Bell Atlantic came on the stand to discuss Louis Capano and his relationship with the federal government.

That day, Joey Capano made another appearance on the stand, as well, changing his earlier story and now saying that he never heard his brother Tom talk about someone trying to extort money from him.

Some of the most damaging testimony came from Andrew Ursin that day. He was a representative of Beretta U.S.A. and testified about the pistol that MacIntyre bought. The prosecution had Ursin, a tech advisor, go through the operation of the handgun.

Before they could do so, Judge Lee interrupted the proceedings. "I would assume there is no impending tragedy about to occur," he said in reference to making sure the gun was unloaded as the lawyers began handling the gun.

Ursin said that there could be no "flinch shot," as Capano testified had occurred. "You must make a conscious effort to pull the trigger," he advised.

Charles "Bud" Freel got on the stand that day, too. He went over the events that occurred when he traveled to Stone Harbor, New Jersey, and tried to get Capano to talk to authorities.

Freel's testimony was poignant and painful. Capano had been a friend of his for years. So had the Faheys. He found himself in an unenviable position between the two and crushed by the knowledge that Capano had fooled everyone in town so thoroughly for so many years. Freel was able to see how his former friend's actions had destroyed another group of friends and brought tragedy to an entire town.

The testimony in the trial concluded with Robert Fahey. Robert got up and read from the letter he and his brothers and sister had sent to Capano begging for information regarding Annie's disappearance. At least three jury members openly wept as he read from the letter.

On cross-examination Oteri asked Robert Fahey about attorneys and legal advice. At one point, he asked Fahey if he would hire an attorney and ignore the advice the attorney gave him?

Fahey looked right at Capano and then back at Oteri. "I believe I've heard that sometimes happens," he said with a straight face.

The courtroom erupted in laughter. Even the judge smiled and grinned before grabbing his gavel and pounding it several times, demanding order in his courtroom. One of the bailiffs in court that day said it was the first gavel she'd heard in almost twenty years.

At 3:20 P.M. the case finally came to a close. Closing arguments were set for the next day.

Chapter 24
The Devil of Deceit

The courtroom was again packed for closing arguments on Wednesday, January 13. Judge Lee, making provisions for what he thought would be a lengthy day, decided to start court early. The attorneys began arriving shortly after eight in the morning and Joe Oteri looked especially chipper as he strode up to the courthouse wearing a dark suit and black cowboy boots.

"These are my lucky boots," Oteri told reporters, adding that Capano kept him from wearing them during the course of the trial because Capano said it wouldn't play well to a conservative Wilmington jury.

Inside the courtroom Colm Connolly was nervously adjusting several displays he would use for the jury. There were television monitors, audio monitors, earphones, binders filled with letters and e-mails, and a huge white easel that Connolly took special care to position appropriately. On the floor was the cooler.

Court began at 9:20 A.M. and Connolly began his closing arguments five minutes later with what was *not* in dispute: Annie's death and burial at sea. As recently as the jury selection when Capano called Annie an "alleged" victim, those facts had been disputed and Connolly made that point bluntly. Connolly pointed out how Capano, just nineteen days before the trial began, wouldn't concede Annie's death and how Capano had his attorney Charles Oberly call the U.S. attorney and alert him to a possible sighting of Annie at the Newark, New Jersey, airport, when Capano knew she was dead. Connolly detailed how Capano's own psychiatrist talked about how Capano spoke of Annie in the present tense a year after he conceded he dumped her lifeless corpse in the fishing lanes of the Atlantic Ocean, and how convincing Capano sounded as he did so. Connolly went over Capano's resentment of the investigation, and a multitude of other pieces of evidence he said pointed directly to Capano's guilt.

For close to four hours Connolly painstakingly went through every shred of evidence pointing out that Capano's many different stories were "ludicrous," and how things that he said defied common sense. "It is not credible Deborah MacIntyre would come over. It is not credible Anne Marie wouldn't take Deborah MacIntyre seriously. It is not believable she put on her panty hose . . . ," Connolly recited.

More importantly, Connolly pointed out it wasn't credible, if in fact what had happened was an accident, that Capano wouldn't call 911. He was good friends with the second highest-ranking law enforcement officer in the state, Keith Brady. He knew everyone of importance in Wilmington and had dealt with many of these important people on a personal level.

"If anybody had the leg up, if anybody would be given the benefit of the doubt, it would be the defendant," Connolly said.

Connolly said time and again the only thing the defendant wanted to do was get away with murder and "he contorted his defense, and tailored it to fit the facts." The prosecutor's contention throughout the trial, and one he made during closing, was that Capano planned to kill Annie. "We do not know how

Anne Marie Fahey physically died. What we have proved is the defendant took steps to kill Anne Marie.''

Connolly urged the jury to review the three months of evidence, which he said would prove Capano's guilt. He divided the evidence for the jury into five categories:

1. *Gerry's testimony.* Connolly termed it the ''most important piece of evidence.'' It was painstakingly corroborated, down to photos from the money machine showing Tom Capano withdrawing money the morning after Annie died.

2. *The cooler, the lock, and the chain.* The cooler, Connolly told the jury, sounded like pure fantasy to investigators when they first heard it from Gerry Capano. But when it was found, it was the most damning and most important piece of evidence to corroborate Gerry's testimony.

3. *Deborah MacIntyre and the gun purchase.*

4. *The defendant's demeanor on June 28, 1996.* It was very calm, Connolly said, on the day after the murder. This was not indicative of an accident.

5. *The defendant's own testimony.* Connolly said it wasn't credible, but was consistent with the deeds of a manipulative control freak.

Connolly spent some time talking about Annie and how she was vulnerable and susceptible to control. She was immature, had a bad childhood, was involved in an adulterous affair, and wanted to live beyond her means. When she finally grew out of those childish desires and found Michael Scanlan, Tom Capano couldn't handle it. He would show up places where Annie went with Scanlan, like the ''Grand Gala,'' and dumped gifts on her while criticizing her and calling her constantly.

Connolly also tackled the money Capano had told Gerry was for an extortionist, and Capano said was for Annie to enter rehab. ''He didn't need to give her cash. He didn't make sense by taking back the cash. The only thing that makes sense is that Gerry now believes he's (Tom Capano) being extorted. Now Gerry understands why Tom Capano would come to him and ask for a gun and ask if Gerry knew someone who could break legs,'' Connolly explained.

Connolly went through the e-mails and the letters and Annie's doctor's notes. He outlined every aspect of the relationship and Capano's obsession with controlling Annie's life. He covered Deborah MacIntyre and talked about how Tom Capano took Deborah MacIntyre to Washington, D.C., for a professional conclave, while he took Annie to the "ritziest resort." Annie got the Hotel DuPont and Ristorante di Panorama, while Deborah MacIntyre got the Motel 6 under the Delaware Memorial Bridge and Arners, a local Wilmington low-priced restaurant. Capano, Connolly said, always used MacIntyre: "Deborah MacIntyre is his doormat."

Connolly went over the last months of Annie's life—her growing infatuation with Mike Scanlan and Capano's growing obsession to control her. Finally, on June 27, 1996, Annie apparently had enough. She and Capano had dinner, and Connolly said, "We do not know exactly what happened at that dinner, and never will," but he did not hesitate to add, "At that dinner Anne Marie Fahey set a limit. And that is why she was murdered and stuffed in a cooler."

Connolly spent a lot of time telling the jury why they should believe both Gerry Capano and Deborah MacIntyre. Gerry's testimony was so well corroborated, and he told the same story from the very beginning; no matter how many drugs he liked to use in his spare time, Gerry was credible, believable, and factual, Connolly said. As for MacIntyre, Connolly urged the jury to consider MacIntyre's demeanor in court. That coupled with her demeanor on the day of the murder and the day after, he argued, spoke to her credibility.

Those who worked with her at Tatnall had said she appeared perfectly normal the day after the murder. Could Deborah Mac-

Intyre have pulled off such an act if she'd accidentally killed someone, and her rich, influential boyfriend had dumped the body at sea? Who could believe such nonsense, Connolly wanted to know.

Further, who could believe she had tried to commit suicide? No one at the swim meet saw her despondent, there was no history of it, and wouldn't she even be more suicidal if she'd accidentally killed an innocent, young woman? Wasn't she instead an honest, decent woman who had been ensnared in Capano's tangled and twisted life? Connolly pointed out that even Capano wanted to call her as a witness because of her believability in a courtroom, and if MacIntyre had an agenda, Connolly argued, couldn't she have made up a better story?

Connolly also referred to Capano's letters in which he wrote to MacIntyre in the third person and referred to her as the "Evil Debby." Who was evil? Connolly seemed to ask, inferring it was Capano. He furthered that point by showing how Capano told MacIntyre how to act, what to drink, who to see, etc.

Connolly's tour de force in the courtroom brought praise from Oteri during the break.

"These prosecutors have to build a foundation and a house," Oteri said. "They can't be like the defense, as flamboyant. But he's doing a very good job. He's like other federal prosecutors I've met. He's bright, he's got a lot of tools at his disposal, and he knows how to use them. He's also very honest. A real straight arrow."

Inside the courtroom, meanwhile, Capano was playing with his lips while Connolly continued his close. Connolly covered "Slick" Nick Perillo, and how Capano said the map and detailed directions he drew for Perillo were throwaways he'd completed in a hurry. Connolly practically laughed as he urged the jury to look at the exquisite detail of the maps. If the jury did so, Connolly argued, then they would see there was no way they were drawn in haste.

Every activity Capano engaged in, Connolly said, his entire demeanor "belies anything but guilt."

Connolly not only seemed upset that Capano was guilty, but insulted that he concocted such an unbelievable story to explain away Annie's death. After spearheading the drive to arrest, try, and convict Capano, Connolly seemed upset that Capano was such a "poor liar." Capano's story, Connolly said, "just doesn't make any kind of sense."

Connolly covered the panty hose angle. Annie was "a woman who hated her own legs. She's going to expose them to a woman she never met who was holding a gun on her?"

Connolly brought up Capano's contention he needed MacIntyre's help to move the cooler, which Connolly called a lie. He hammered Capano about disposing of a body. "He knew an autopsy would confirm an accident and that's why he got rid of the body, because it was no accident."

Connolly went after Capano's grand conspiracy theory. "Why would the President of the United States know, let alone care, about Tom Capano?" Connolly said. Capano didn't even look up. He was busy taking notes again. For what, even his attorneys said they didn't know.

"That just speaks to his (Capano's) arrogance," Connolly said of the alleged presidential involvement.

Connolly was also unmoved by Capano's stated concern for his daughters. "This is a man who doesn't care about his daughters," Connolly said. As for the surprise witness, Connolly dismissed Kim Johnson with a simple "she got the dates wrong . . . Even if she saw what she thinks she saw, it happened much later," he said. As for Lee Ramunno, Connolly said Ramunno was probably telling the truth when he said Capano told him he was protecting someone. But since he referred to this person in the singular rather than the plural, Connolly said it was logical to assume Capano was speaking about his brother Gerry.

At the bottom, Connolly said for perhaps the sixth or seventh time during his closing arguments, Capano's story defied all common sense and logic. "If you believe it you have to believe an enormous number of other people have to be lying."

The way it boiled down to Connolly—either Capano was lying or everyone else was.

Capano, Connolly said, was in a war with Anne Marie Fahey over who the ultimate master of her fate was—she or Capano. "Here is a man who plays by his own rules and that's why he's resentful, because this time he couldn't," Connolly said. "There are rules we all have to play by. Now is the time for justice . . . the only verdict consistent with all the evidence is a verdict of guilty."

With that, Connolly sat down and prepared for Joe Oteri to give his closing arguments.

Capano, who seemed to have gone through spasms during portions of Connolly's closing, sat muted and with a look of frustration as Connolly ended.

Joe Oteri started with a smile and a thanks to the jury. He took no break after Connolly's closing, but instead launched into an explanation to the jury of what constituted burden of proof and reasonable doubt. He knew, he said, most of what laymen knew about the law they got from *Perry Mason* or *Matlock,* but he wanted to clear a few things up for them.

He began with a history lesson of how the United States was formed centuries ago by disaffected white men and then took up the issue of reasonable doubt. "Tom Capano sits here wrapped in a cloak of reasonable doubt," he told the jury.

It was the entire United States government with all its vast resources against Capano. "It gives them a hell of an advantage," Oteri said. He urged the jury to weigh all the evidence carefully. "Six months from now when you look back, you might say, 'Oh, my, I was wrong.' But there is no appeal for Mr. Capano," Oteri said.

Capano was a "bright kid," who had a pretty good life, who did a "number of things you might find offensive," Oteri said, turning to his client. "I know I do," he added. "Those things may offend you and well they should, but Tom Capano is not on trial for those things," Oteri said. When you cut to the chase, he said, there were two questions that had to be answered: Who caused Anne Marie Fahey's death? And, was it the result of an intentional plan?

Oteri reiterated what Connolly had said: No one would ever know for sure what happened in Capano's house that night. But he said the bulk of the evidence was circumstantial. He dismissed the cooler as a gift, after all Joey had said it was. He dismissed much of what the prosecution had said was evidence of planning. The government, Oteri said, wanted to paint his client as "some kind of evil genius," but if all that the government said were true, "this was the gang who couldn't shoot straight."

He dismissed Gerry as a spoiled, rich kid "who's had everything handed to him." According to Oteri, Gerry was "a walking pharmacopeia who's tried every drug known to man."

"Gerry has no respect for anything . . . that's what Gerry's like." Capano sat smiling while his attorney destroyed his younger brother's reputation. Oteri dismissed Gerry's story about extortion as the "ravings of a drug-addled mind," and said Gerry was a "wise guy wanna-be," who only came forward to the government after he had a gun put to his head. Oteri also dismissed Dr. Kaye as "Dr. Wooden Hat," while he praised Dr. Tavani as a "feisty, little lady with great qualifications."

The jury sat impassively. It was closing in on 5 P.M. and the judge during the break had said there would be no waiting. The closing arguments would be finished this day, no exceptions and no matter how late.

After Connolly's marathon closing of three hours and forty-seven minutes, it appeared Oteri was going to try to equal if not best it. Oteri brought up Gerry's alleged phone call to his own mother, where he supposedly said, "Call me back or you can go fuck yourself," as an indication that Gerry was a cretin with little moral fiber. The day seemed to drag on as Oteri continued. He took off his jacket and continued by going through Annie's diary, the e-mails, and the letters.

During the course of the trial Oteri and Connolly often used similar if not the same passages from the diary, e-mails, and letters to highlight completely different values and actions. What was evidence of controlling and domination when presented by Connolly was evidence of a mutual relationship when Oteri spoke. What was worse was both sides seemed to make sense.

Oteri told the jury that if Capano had planned the crime he was a "village idiot," but Oteri was convinced no one planned any crime. He added, "If Tom Capano planned to kill her, what kind of a moron plans to kill her in his own home."

Juror #11 broke in at this point as the judge reassured them they would finish with the closing arguments before they broke for the day. The juror wanted to know if she could get some coffee. The mind-numbing summations of the lawyers were getting to her.

Oteri continued after a short break pointing out that Deborah MacIntyre and Tom Capano had a quick phone call the morning after Annie's death. The pair talked for one reason, Oteri said. "And one reason only. She wanted to know what are you doing with the body?"

Oteri praised the prosecution and said it was led by "two very bright guys," but said they were reaching for absurdities to convict Capano. "They have no case," he said. "Your government spent money to get the transcripts of a twenty-two-year-old murder case," he said in reference to the Squeaky Saunders case. Then Oteri launched into Deborah MacIntyre.

"Who is Debby MacIntyre?" he asked. "The kind of woman who allows Tom Capano to grope her," he answered himself.

"The kind of woman who abandons her friend Kay Capano. The kind of woman who perjures herself in front of the grand jury (referring to her earlier admissions). The kind of woman who allows the poor stiff from high school to be seen by her lover while she has sex with him.

"She's a woman who's lied repeatedly at least sixty or seventy times," Oteri said. "If you believe it, she's got a bridge she'll sell you. It's all hogwash . . . she discusses penis size and the loss of virginity with her kids . . . she has no shame."

Oteri spit it all out: "She's a devil of deceit, this woman is." He claimed MacIntyre lied to everyone "she comes into contact with."

Her two children never came in and testified she was at home the night of the murder, Oteri pointed out. Why? As for Capano, sure he was controlling, but what powerful, rich man wasn't? As for Kim Johnson and Mattie Coleman (the housekeeper who heard someone say they heard someone had seen a gun at MacIntyre's home), Oteri said their testimony offered reasonable doubt in the case. "What happens in this court is forever," Oteri warned. "In that jury room you walk in the valley of decision. The agony of decision is upon you."

As for Louis and Gerard Capano, they were simply "false witnesses" against their neighbor and brother Tom Capano. After nearly three hours and forty-seven minutes, almost the exact length of time Connolly took, Oteri concluded.

Ferris Wharton approached the jurors just before eight o'clock that night in a packed, feverishly hot courtroom. He wasn't going to be as bombastic or as loud as Oteri, he promised, because "You get distortion when you get loud. It doesn't make it more true and it doesn't make it more believable."

Wharton, with his disarming charm, seemed to be more comfortable with his closing than either Connolly or Oteri. The first person Wharton wanted to talk about was Kim Johnson. "It's very hard to believe what she said," Wharton said softly.

He said Johnson's testimony seemed to be "crammed" into

the necessary time line, but that didn't mean whatever she saw actually occurred when she said it did. Mattie Coleman was dismissed as being a faithful employee of the Capanos'.

As for the cooler, which Oteri had said was a gift and no one intent on murder would ever buy it with their own credit card, Wharton said the cooler wasn't ever supposed to be found, so it didn't matter if it was bought with a credit card. As for brother Gerry, "He can't be all that bad, can he?" Wharton asked. If in fact his brother Tom was buying a gift to thank Gerry for taking care of the people Capano loved most, i.e. his children, then Gerry can't be just a confabulating liar and drug addict.

The fact was, Wharton asserted, that Capano could trash his little brother all he wanted, but Gerry had told the truth. "You can't escape the facts," Wharton warned. And, Wharton said the facts showed that Dr. Kaye deserved better than being called "Dr. Wooden Hat." Wharton praised his psychiatric witness and dumped on the defense's expert witness, Dr. Tavani. "Dr. Tavani purports to know so much about drugs," Wharton said, "But doesn't know the price of an eight ball."

According to Wharton, the defense went out of its way to trash Gerry because when Gerry came forward, "Gerry solves the case." Wharton wouldn't give Oteri the fact that Gerry called his mother and threatened her, either. He attributed that to retribution for Gerry testifying. "Where are the tapes" of the phone call, Wharton asked.

He casually went through other aspects of the evidence, promising not to go over the e-mails and letters again. "I'm not going to read the e-mails because you might come out of the jury box and strangle me," Wharton said, which earned him an exhausted laugh from a grateful jury. Capano, meanwhile, shook his head at Wharton as the dedicated prosecutor plowed through the evidence. Capano had at one point said everyone in life "gives to get," but Wharton found that disgusting and said "sometimes you kiss your kids because you love them," you don't necessarily expect to get something when you give something.

Court broke for about ten minutes around 9:15 P.M. Capano's daughters, who had come to watch, said they were going to stay and watch the sordid end. When assembled back in the courtroom, Wharton went after the central theme of Capano's defense: the senseless accident. If it were a tragic accident, think of all the consequences, Wharton said. "Careers are shattered, reputations are shattered, he's incarcerated, his wife is labeled the wife of a philanderer. His secret life is exposed and his children are labeled the children of a murderer. This case has come between them all. And ask yourself for what? An accident? That doesn't make sense," Wharton added. "You lie for one reason. You lie because you're guilty."

If the murder had occurred as Capano said, Wharton urged all of the jurors to pick up the gun and put it to their head in the manner Capano said it happened, and see if another juror standing reasonably close could stop it from happening. "You can't stop it, even if you know it's coming," he told the jury as he raised his hand repeatedly to his head from his side.

No, Tom Capano was no "village idiot," Wharton said. He was a very smart man who "almost got away with it. For seventeen months this investigation dragged on, and if it weren't for Gerry he'd have gotten away with it."

Around 9:30 P.M. the judge began charging the jury. It had been a marathon legal session, a marathon trial filled with strange twists. The six-man, six-woman jury now had to take it all into a conference room at a local hotel and decide Tom Capano's fate.

Chapter 25

Guilty

No one thought the jury would deliberate too long. Members of the press began a pool to see when the jury would come back, and what the verdict would be.

The jurors took their job a little more seriously. Juror #2, not a religious man by nature, said he and the others prayed they would find the correct answer. It was a heavy burden for them to carry and they wanted to do it right.

"I remember when we all got together, when we'd been taken to deliberate," Juror #8, a tawny-haired, young lady with a passing resemblance to Annie, remarked. "We all just stared at each other and I can't remember who, but somebody said, 'Okay, anybody read the paper?' No one had. No one looked at the television, either. We took into the deliberations exactly what the judge told us to."

They began by poring over every letter, every piece of e-mail, and every shred of evidence—trying to piece the story together. "A lot of what we heard in the courtroom was taken out of context," Juror #9, a bespectacled, quiet man, said. "We decided to go through everything in the order it happened and see how it all really happened.''

This procedure would mean there would be no quick verdict, but that was okay with the jurors. They'd listened to Joe Oteri and all of them took his warning to heart. No one wanted to look in the mirror six months down the road and think they'd made a wrong decision.

Juror #11, the quiet, blonde female with deep religious convictions, said she was put on the jury because of God. She took her time each night to say her prayers. ''I know some of them (the attorneys and the press) thought we were stupid, but we're just normal people.''

While those twelve normal people were locked up in a hotel conference room trying to figure out Capano's guilt or innocence, the town was wild with speculation.

Joe Oteri and Jack O'Donnell were treated as local celebrities in some circles, dining with members of the local and out-of-town press and offering their views on the case.

''I'll tell you this, Colm Connolly is the most honest prosecutor I've met in my life,'' Oteri said over drinks one night during jury deliberations. Oteri was impressed with Connolly's closing arguments, as was O'Donnell. The only thing they'd have done differently—''I'd have gotten in the cooler,'' Oteri and O'Donnell both said. They also discussed their own closing arguments. Jack O'Donnell thought Oteri should have recounted the night Annie was murdered in a little more detail and from Deborah MacIntyre's perspective.

The anger Capano had sown in his hometown had split it right down the middle, and many expected the attorneys in the case to openly advocate guilt or innocence. That Oteri and O'Donnell did not, caused confusion and pain among some of the Faheys and their friends.

* * *

Every member of the jury tried Ferris Wharton's challenge of putting the gun to their head and having someone stop them. "Ferris was right," a black female juror said. "We all tried that and none of us could stop the other."

Confusion and arguments were also part of the deliberation. Part of that was caused by the "circuslike atmosphere" at the trial, said Juror #11. Juror #8 agreed. "Every time you thought you knew what was going on, you'd get surprised."

The arguments, although spirited, were not mean-spirited. Juror #2 was convinced early on that Capano was guilty and as he and other jurors began discussing the evidence, he made his opinion known. Part of his opinion, he said, was derived from Capano's attitude from the defense table. "In the beginning of the trial he would stare us down until we looked away. Well, I started staring back and he'd finally turn his head. Then toward the end of the trial he wouldn't even look at me," Juror #2 said. Other jurors noted Capano's theatrics, histrionics, and the way he would "trash anyone and everyone" he knew. They wanted to vote guilty. But some wanted to wade through the evidence and try and take the emotion out of it.

All of the jurors say it was Juror #1, the foreman, who kept the deliberations in line and forced everyone to confront their prejudices and the evidence before casting a vote.

"We only took one vote," Juror #2 said. "We waited until we had discussed everything and then we voted."

It took three days and an emotional toll on everyone. Juror #8 was especially touched. "I kept hearing evidence, and everything about her (Annie) reminded me of me. It was very hard to take sometimes."

The most difficult time came when the jurors decided someone had to get inside the cooler. It was Juror #8. She was the logical choice, but to this day she has a hard time talking about it.

"I'm five foot eight, and she (Annie) was two inches taller

than me,'' she said through tears. ''I just can't imagine what that was like. I had a hard time getting in that cooler.''

Juror #2 flashed on Annie's memory as he saw his co-juror get in the cooler. ''Sitting there, I imagined I saw Anne Marie in the cooler. I'm not a religious man, but it affected me deeply.''

By January 16, 1999, the jury had come to a decision. After casting the one ballot they all gathered around the cooler and put personal items of Annie's into it. It was a memorial service for a woman they'd never met, an acknowledgment of a life tragically cut short as Annie had finally learned how to live.

Tears nor words could express the feelings of the jury members. They, like many others, had been deeply affected by the trial, both emotionally and personally. One jury member who wished to remain anonymous broke up with his wife during the course of the trial. ''I can't say it was the total reason we broke up, but it got to us,'' he said. Others experienced financial hardship as they sacrificed their incomes to sit on a jury and earn $10 a day.

They all had sacrificed. They all had suffered. And now it was time to put it behind them and issue their verdict. About 8 P.M. that night the world found out the jury had a verdict. It came after a three-month trial, thirty-seven days of testimony, which included eight days of Tom Capano testifying on the stand, more than one hundred witnesses and four hundred pieces of evidence. Twenty-one hours of deliberating during three full days had brought the jury to a decision.

Now the world would have to wait slightly more than thirteen hours before court would be called into session and the decision announced. Notification of all the major parties was to be swift. Judge Lee had helped coordinate a plan so the lawyers, the media, Annie's family, and the Capano family were notified, but it didn't work. No one bothered to notify Kathi Carlozzi, the ''door warden,'' who was supposed to begin the notification process.

Consequently, even Capano's attorneys found out later than

some of the general public. Many picked up the news from Dave Madden and KYW radio in Philadelphia. Madden had staked out the courthouse, refusing to leave until there was a verdict. He'd heard it from Todd Spangler, the AP reporter, who had heard a rumor of a verdict and had taken the time to call the judge at home, who confirmed it for him.

It was even later for the defense attorneys.

"We were the last to find out," Jack O'Donnell said. "Nobody told us. We had reporters telling us, that's how I found out."

The following day looked like a riot. Local citizens began arriving at the courthouse at 5:20 A.M.—more than four hours before the verdict was to be read. By 7 A.M. it was bedlam outside. People had crammed their way into the entrance hall, and unable to get past the closed inside doors, they pushed and shoved as if in a crowded subway terminal.

Once Capano's mother showed up, the crowd inside quieted significantly. A man shouted that it would be nice if everyone let Capano's mother enter first. No one seconded that offer. Meanwhile, Marguerite Capano was telling anyone who would listen that Deborah MacIntyre "is a drunk and my son didn't do anything wrong."

Cheers greeted Colm Connolly and the judge as they entered.

By 9:30 A.M. the regular reporters, family, and most of the public were seated, having for the last time passed through the second metal detector.

The judge entered shortly thereafter and admonished the court there would be no emotional outbursts whatever the outcome of the case. He ordered the courtroom locked and sealed. Eight extremely large Wilmington policemen stood directly behind Tom Capano. The message was clear. He wouldn't react and in turn the whole audience wouldn't react.

The jury entered. None of them looked at Capano. One, Juror

11, the small, blonde woman who had cried days before when Robert Fahey read out loud his letter to Tom Capano, again showed a hint of a tear. She turned and smiled at the Faheys.

Capano's fate was sealed.

It seemed anticlimactic as the jury foreman read the verdict. "We find the defendant guilty as charged," he said as he stared directly at Tom Capano. Capano never budged, never flinched, and never moved. Kathy Fahey quietly wept and her older brother Kevin let a thin smile momentarily cross his face before he returned to the quiet, dignified stoicism that ruled his countenance during the twelve weeks of the trial.

The Capano daughters openly hugged and wept while their mother did the same and tried to comfort them. Tom's mother also silently wept. Then Marguerite Capano tapped Kay Capano with her cane. "Now are you happy?" she hissed.

Outside the crowd that couldn't get into court burst into spontaneous and tumultuous cheers as Kathi Carlozzi told them the verdict. The cheers could clearly be heard by everyone, including Tom Capano, inside the courtroom. The judge thanked the jury and instructed them as to the short penalty phase that would begin on Wednesday, January 20.

He then dismissed Capano with no ceremony. "The bailiffs will remove the defendant," he said. Capano rose, had the cuffs once again slapped on his wrists, and walked out the courtroom's side door escorted by the cops.

He never once looked back at his mother, ex-wife, nor even the children he professed in court to love so much. He just walked away, defeated and ready to rejoin his friends at Gander Hill with a new moniker: Convicted Murderer. As he was taken away, one of the guards approached him in the hall outside of the courtroom, pulled up Capano's sleeve, and started to tap his wrists with two fingers.

Capano was momentarily stunned. "What are you doing?" Capano asked.

"Checking for a vein." The guard smiled as they took him away.

Outside the courthouse bedlam reigned again. Hundreds had gathered to hear the verdict. As the police struggled to keep them at bay, the reporters struggled to get outside and assemble near a makeshift podium of microphones.

First the judge left the building to a tumultuous round of applause. The prosecution then exited to similar applause.

Breaking a three-month silence on the case, lead prosecutor Colm Connolly thanked everyone in law enforcement who ever had even the most remote connection to the case. To many in the press corps it sounded like a verbal recitation of a movie's screen credits. He noted that no one should forget Anne Marie Fahey. He ended by thanking his partner in the prosecution, Ferris Wharton. Wharton added his own list of thank-you's and complimented Connolly. Attorney General Jane Brady spoke next.

The Faheys and attorney David Weiss followed and before the cameras reminded people the whole ordeal was about Anne Marie.

"I challenge the media to refer to her as someone other than Tom Capano's mistress," Weiss urged the assemblage of reporters. The Faheys nodded in silent agreement.

The defense attorneys finally arrived and were greeted by hecklers—a first for them, and a first for many of the reporters.

"This is a feeding frenzy," said lead attorney Joe Oteri as he surveyed the dozens of cameras and reporters swarming around him. The Wilmington Police kept reporters at a distance until the participants assembled and then they escorted all of them to the end of the block.

Putting in an encore appearance after the verdict, was the long-elusive Deborah MacIntyre. The much maligned mistress showed up on the courthouse steps to answer questions, brought there by her attorney, Tom Bergstrom. "I told her she could either do no media or everyone at once," Bergstrom said. "It wouldn't be fair to do some and not others."

Nearing tears, MacIntyre expressed relief and said she was looking forward to going on with her life. She said she was sorry at Anne Marie's passing and optimistic about her own future without Tom Capano. "The man I thought I knew, never existed," she said, echoing her earlier pronouncements.

Moments later the Faheys had a news conference at a nearby bank building. Dozens of cameras crowded into a closed cafeteria setting as Kevin, Mark, Robert, Kathy, and Brian thanked everyone for their support and declared that the prosecutors were "a gift from God."

Robert said Annie's last fight was nearly over, and the family could soon rest. But, he added, the "dark hole" would never close in their lives.

Even as they seemed festive and upbeat, Annie's spirit hung over them—a spirit that would have loved the fun and the festivity more than anyone.

Chapter 26

The Jury Recommends Death

The biggest hurdle was behind the jury and the town now. Thomas J. Capano was guilty, and nothing in the future could erase that mark. At O'Friels, there was a host of celebrants assembled to toast the verdict. The Faheys smiled and embraced each other as they met, first in the media conference across the street from the courthouse and later at O'Friel's. A *People* magazine photographer snapped photos of them there. Several television crews showed up, sometimes more than one from the same station. The local newspaper put out a special edition, the Philadelphia stations broke into programming. Television reporters were almost as thick as attorneys in Wilmington that afternoon. People driving stopped others on the street asking what the commotion was all about. There was joy in Wilmington as people *celebrated* the verdict that for many was vindication for everything the town of Wilmington had gone through since Annie's death in 1996.

The people of Wilmington knew of Capano's wealth and power and feared that no matter how strong the evidence against him, no one would convict Capano. He had been found guilty, but now the jury had to recommend a sentence, and there were but two choices: life in prison without parole, or death by lethal injection. Judge Lee would ultimately decide Capano's fate, but the jury in Delaware can recommend a sentence and the judge is expected to put "great weight" into what the jury decides.

It was a far cry from where Capano found himself upon his arrest. Early on, Colm Connolly confirmed, Capano had been offered a plea deal. It would have resulted in a maximum ten-year sentence. Though it was never formalized, it also never had a chance. Capano was convinced, Joe Oteri told reporters, that he would be acquitted of any charges. Hence, Capano wouldn't even consider any plea agreements.

Now Capano was pleading for his life and was convicted of murder. In Delaware there are close to two dozen different aggravating circumstances that can serve as a basis for asking for the death penalty in a murder case. Only one of those applied to Capano—a planned, premeditated murder. That's what Connolly had argued all along Capano did when he killed Annie. Connolly had his work cut out for him. That aggravating factor of a planned murder had to outweigh any mitigating circumstances, which would save Capano's life. Among those were the facts that Capano had never been arrested before, had a record of community activities, and was involved in political and public functions, as well as various religious and school associations that helped out many in Wilmington, most especially the poor.

On January 20, 1999, the jury began hearing the state's case to give Tom Capano the death penalty. They began by hearing about Linda Marandola. Her name had been uttered by Connolly during one of the days when he cross-examined Tom Capano, but her story had never been told to the jury before.

When they heard that as long as twenty years ago Capano had been involved in an abusive situation with a woman, it made many of those who felt slightly uncomfortable at finding him guilty rest a little easier. "Certainly it made us all feel much better," Juror #9 said. "It really showed us who he was and what he was capable of."

"This was his town and I couldn't stay in it," Marandola said Capano told her after their relationship went south. It was shocking testimony for the jury, but nothing like the gut-wrenching experience everyone in the courtroom felt when the Fahey family got back on the stand and told how their lives had been changed forever by Tom Capano. Robert Fahey got to the heart of the matter. He used to love walking on the beach with his children. He no longer could.

"My sister is out there somewhere and it hurts," he said. Thinking about her demise brought him close to tears. She's likely "in a million pieces," he said on the witness stand. "It is a black hole without boundaries. It is as black as it gets. There is no light. You never know how deep it is or when, if ever, you will get out of it."

Kathy Fahey-Hosey told about how her two young sons feared that "the bad man" who killed Annie will kill them and stuff them in a cooler, too. Brian Fahey said he was haunted just thinking about Annie's last moments. She was a brave woman, he said, but would drop the bravado when scared. "People say that she would have fought back, that she was a big, strong girl," Brian said. "But when Anne Marie was frightened, she would become like a child."

Brian was tormented thinking that in her final moments Annie was scared. "My fear is that she knew she was going to die. She didn't deserve that."

He said he had nightmares from persistent rumors after Annie disappeared that her corpse was shredded by a wood chipper or entombed in a store's foundation, and thoughts of the ocean haunted him. Brian kept seeing visions of Annie's decapitated head bobbing in the ocean.

The emotional testimony brought everyone to tears in the

courtroom—reporters, lawyers, members of the jury, and members of the public. Even the defense team seemed choked up by the raw feelings Annie's death stirred up.

Certainly, Jack O'Donnell understood. "What can I say to the Faheys. I understand? I do, but it's no comfort to them. I think they acted with a lot of class and I hope I would act the same if I were ever in that position, God forbid."

Marian Ramunno, Capano's sister, said she understood, as well. "He (Tom) was callous, cruel to the Faheys, and arrogant," she said. "But he's my brother and I love him." Marian's pain was obvious in her red-rimmed eyes and her quiet composure. Occasionally pulling out a tissue, she tried hard not to let people know her pain, making it all that more noticeable.

The pain of the Fahey family weighed heavily on everyone in the courtroom—everyone except Tom Capano it seemed. He barely took notice of the Faheys as they got on the stand and laid bare their torment.

From the stand the Faheys also filled in some of the blanks in Annie's life, making her a more well-rounded person than had been portrayed in the trial. David Weiss, the Faheys' attorney, had expressed to the public his fear that Annie would only be known as one of the multitude of Capano mistresses.

But Brian did much, as did Kathy and Robert, in showing her tender and kind nature. Annie had been close to her nieces and nephews and visited the hospital daily when one of Kathy's sons required medical care after his birth. Kathy talked about how she and her only sister were best friends, not the battling, catty duo Capano described. Brian talked about how he and Annie could communicate without words in a crowded room, and Robert detailed how her disappearance shook the family. For two months they kept a vigil at Annie's apartment until they were convinced she'd never return. The empathy the jury felt for the Faheys' torture and anguish was apparent on many jurors' faces.

Robert talked about visiting Capano's home after Capano

moved out and how his brothers and sisters said a prayer for their sister in the room where she died. "That was the only way we could say goodbye," he said. Deprived of even a burial for his sister, Robert Fahey seemed angry as he talked about Annie being "thrown into a section of water known as 'Mako Alley.' It isn't her mother she is with, but sharks. That is the image I carry."

On Thursday, January 21, 1999, details of Capano's battles with the Gander Hill prison management came to the fore again. He'd already refused to shave, shower, or wear his suit on at least two occasions; now the public got to see the details of his struggles inside the walls of a prison. Entered into evidence were dozens of citations for violating prison rules. Most of these were for minor infractions like smuggling cigarettes and food into prison when he returned from court. For his actions Capano was punished by losing visitation rights, recreation, and phone privileges for up to fifteen days. Prosecutor Colm Connolly and Ferris Wharton gave those prison records to jurors to support their contention that Capano believed he was above the law and therefore deserved to die.

The records also showed how Capano successfully fought against the rules he thought were unfair—getting matches classified as nondangerous contraband rather than dangerous contraband, and successfully arguing that giving the finger to a video camera was not the same as giving one to a guard even if a guard was watching the video camera's monitor.

But Capano failed in one other attempt to fight the prison establishment. He complained that solitary-confinement prisoners are not allowed to keep prison-issued disposable razors in their cells like other prisoners. His appeal was rejected and Capano complained of bias. He said during his hearing a prison official looked at him and said, "This is not Tommy Capano's country club. This is Gander Hill prison."

Connolly and Wharton used the prison reprimands and other evidence from the trial to also show that not only had Capano planned to kill Annie, but by reaching out to try and terrorize MacIntyre and his brother Gerard, Capano was to be feared even behind bars. He would never stop trying to avenge those he'd seen as wronging him. He had to be put to death.

The defense was having a problem getting Capano's cooperation in pleading for his life. Gerry Capano, who once had hired Jack O'Donnell as his attorney on an unrelated matter, called O'Donnell through his current attorney (Dan Lyons) and told O'Donnell he wanted to testify on behalf of his older brother. Louis wanted to do the same thing. They'd helped convict him, but neither one of them wanted to see their brother die.

When Capano found out, he was furious and again threatened to fire his attorneys if they called either of his two brothers to the stand.

"You're fired," he said.

"What is that, about the eighth time you've fired us now, Tom," Gene Maurer said.

"You haven't got the balls to fire us," Oteri remarked.

"Okay. You're fired," Capano repeated.

"That's nine," Maurer replied.

Oteri urged Capano to bring it up in court if he had any problems. O'Donnell and Oberly just rolled their eyes. Nothing more ever came from it. The following week the defense got its chance to save Capano's life.

Kay Ryan took the stand and in an emotional display, she extended her sympathy to the Fahey family. "I'm not here to stand by my man," Ryan said with distaste as she looked at Tom Capano from the witness stand. "I'm here to stand by my daughters. I am as repulsed by his vile actions and behavior as most of you here in this courtroom. But I will say that for everything that he's done, he's been a loving father."

Capano barely acknowledged his ex-wife's existence. After twenty-six years of marriage he couldn't bring himself to look her in the eyes.

Kay made a good impression on the jurors, some of whom

afterward saw her as yet another victim in Capano's long string of victims. "If she hadn't had his kids he probably could've killed her, too," one female alternate juror later said. "It took a lot of guts to get up there like she did after all that man put her through."

"I'm so sorry for your loss," Kay told the Faheys through a veil of tears. "I can't imagine what it's like to lose a sibling. I'm so sorry. I'm so sorry Tom is somehow involved in that."

Kay left the stand after begging the jury to spare her philandering ex-husband's life. She was replaced by her youngest daughter, Alex, who said her father was "still there for me."

The dark-haired seventh-grade student/athlete at Ursuline told the jury that even though she has limited contact with her father, she "can still talk to him," even when she can't go to her mother or other sisters. It was riveting testimony.

On the afternoon of January 26 Jack O'Donnell brought Lee Ramunno back to the stand. The jury collectively smiled at his encore performance, but he was much more somber on this occasion. He had a succinct and brilliant point to make before the jury: "If you give Tom life, then you punish him. If you give him death, then you punish everyone who loves him." It rang true.

Late that afternoon O'Donnell called Christy Capano, the college honor student, to the stand. A dark-haired, attractive girl with an acerbic and cynical wit, she noted that her father was "not only my father, but my friend. He inspires me and challenges me. I love him very much."

Louis who was present in the courtroom, sitting among the reporters because his brother-in-law Lee Ramunno wouldn't let him sit with the Capano family, was in tears as he watched Christy testify. Kay was solemn and Marguerite watched with little expression on her face. Christy told the jury how the trial had scarred her to some extent. She told about hearing comments in public and listening as people ignorantly joked about her father.

Tom Capano greeted this news with his head in his hands and stooped over at the defense table. For the first time in the trial his pain appeared genuine as he heard how his actions had harmed those he loved the most. Christy then talked about her interaction with her father and how he had taught her to drive. She wanted to continue with him in her life, even if it were only in a limited way. "Please let that continue," she begged the jury. "We all need him." The jurors seemed touched by Christy, and Juror #11 wiped a tear from her eye.

Jenny Capano, a fifteen-year-old dark-haired girl, then got on the stand and through her tears told the jury how her father helped her learn to ride a bicycle. "He's so important in my life," she cried. "There's glass between us, but I can still see him. Please don't take him away."

Though Jack O'Donnell knew the girls and handled them carefully, Jenny then broke down completely, and most of the jury did so also. Colm Connolly and Ferris Wharton decided against doing much cross-examination of the girls.

Louis Capano was called to the stand. He told the jury Tom had been a "perfect brother" throughout most of his life. He was Louis's role model "ever since I can remember." When he was in trouble with his parents, it was Tom, Louis said, who would help out. He'd tell his own parents to "lighten up on me."

Louis never saw a mean side to Tom, and while he knew one of his nieces, Katie, thought he'd been disloyal to his brother, Louis knew he'd misled the grand jury and had committed crimes himself. He had been put in an uneasy position of being loyal to his brother when it became apparent Tom had done something illegal. "I tried to balance family loyalty with the right thing to do and I made some mistakes. I know that and I have to live with it," Louis told the jury. But killing his older brother was not the price Louis had in mind.

Louis told the jury through tears that his younger brother Gerry was now living at his home and was close to a nervous breakdown. Louis stopped and started several times during his testimony as he told the jury both he and Gerry were tortured by the case, which seemed not to make any impression on Tom Capano. He sat passively as Louis poured out his heart and begged the jury to spare Tom's life.

Marian tried to plead for life, too, and told everyone Tom Capano "was the golden boy."

Gerry Capano took the stand. He was nervous and quiet and looked at his older brother, but Tom didn't even seem to care. It apparently made no impression on Capano that the younger brother he had his attorneys vilify as an addlebrained drug addict and a hopeless liar, a man Capano even threatened to kill while he was in prison, would appear on his behalf.

The jury was certainly moved, though, and sat numb as Gerry pled for Tom's life. He spoke to the jurors for close to ten minutes about how Tom had been such a positive force in his life, virtually taking over as a surrogate father once his own father had died. Tom was the person, Gerry said, he always went to for advice. Gerry went to him for advice on raising kids. "Tom is a great father," he said. "This whole thing is horrible. Horrible for the Faheys. Horrible for us, horrible for the kids," Gerry added.

His own young children "talk about giving Uncle Tommy a needle and making him go to sleep," Gerry said through sobs. "He's not the Tom I know. I don't know what happened. Something happened. This is not the Tom I knew growing up."

Again the jurors responded with tears as Gerry recounted the pain. "The Tom I knew was smart. He was *the man*. I just don't understand what happened." In his suit and close-cropped hair, Gerry Capano gave the impression of a loving brother tormented by pain. He had, like his sister, Marian, and former sister-in-law, Kay, acknowledged the Faheys' pain and begged for his brother's life. "Taking his life isn't the right thing to do. He needs to be there for the kids and for my mom. I'm the one who testified against him. Please don't do this."

Because of a procedural problem the prosecution had not yet called its last witness. Connolly and Wharton did so now.

Harry Fusco, a pasty-faced, long-haired inhabitant of Gander Hill, sported a ratty, pencil-thin mustache and an unkempt appearance as he approached the witness stand in his prison whites. He had been in prison on four counts of indecent exposure and two counts of unlawful sexual contact with children under sixteen years old. He was a convicted pedophile.

What was the loving, caring Tom Capano, the father who worried so much about his four daughters, connection to Harry Fusco? He had given Fusco his home phone number, pictures of his daughters, and encouraged the pedophile to write to his children.

As Fusco was called to the stand Joey Capano urged Kay to remove her children from the courtroom. "No. They need to see this," Kay replied in open court in a voice loud enough to capture the attention of several reporters. She wanted her daughters to see the man who had been calling and writing them for several weeks.

"It got to be too much. I was having inmates call the house and write all the time," she said. "Some of them promised to look up my daughters when they got out of jail. I have my ex-husband to thank for that."

Correspondence between Fusco and the daughters had surfaced after Ferris Wharton decided to uncharacteristically cross-examine Katie Capano. Katie, another student/athlete and attractive young lady, had just told the jury how much her father meant to her and how she needed him when Wharton stood up to ask a couple of simple questions. Katie said she exchanged letters and accepted phone calls from Fusco, but gave no indication if she knew why he was in prison.

The forty-year-old Fusco, the day's last witness, said he met Capano while in prison and became friendly with him. Capano, he said, asked him to call his daughters periodically to check on their well-being. It was another way Capano dodged the phone rules in prison.

Fusco and Capano also exchanged letters by using his daughters as middlemen since Gander Hill rules prevent inmates from corresponding with each other. Fusco would write to Capano, send it to his daughters, and they would, in turn, send the letter back to their father.

Fusco also wrote the girls with Capano's knowledge, which extended to knowing what Fusco was serving time for. "I told him I was innocent," of sex offenses against children, Fusco told the jury. Wharton then entered several of the letters Fusco had written into evidence. Most were innocuous, if not a little creepy, jury members later said. Fusco even claimed to other inmates that a group shot of Capano's daughters was his own.

It was a wake-up call to Tom Capano's daughters. Afterward, O'Donnell spoke with them at length about their father's possible sentence.

"You know your father is not the same man," O'Donnell told the girls. "Would the father you love so much and loved you, would that man ever let you in a million years talk or write to someone like Harry Fusco?" After all, Capano had urged his oldest daughter, Christy, not to even take the subway in New York City, but to always take a cab. Yet, it was the youngest, Alex, who spoke up. "He wouldn't even let us talk to kids who go to public school," she said.

The Fusco revelation led the defense team to ask for a day to have a battery of psychiatric tests conducted on Capano. That also meant that the following day, January 27, 1999, the court would remain adjourned on what would have been Annie's thirty-third birthday.

On January 28, 1999, court reconvened and Joe Oteri brought in an octogenarian priest who'd been a member of the priesthood for sixty-three years. He testified how much Tom gave to the church. He was "extremely impressed" by Capano and thought "a man like that should live."

At 11 A.M. Marguerite Capano, looking frail and tired, got to the witness stand to talk about her son Tom. She outlined her upbringing, her husband's, and how she tried to teach her boys right from wrong. "Their father was strict, I was strict sometimes," she said. She had talked to Gerry the day before, she told the jury, and despite what had happened she said she loved him deeply. "Certainly I love him. He's my son," she said through tears.

As for Tom, "My son's not a murderer. He's not guilty of killing Anne Marie Fahey. I love him. I need him. He's my right hand," she explained through more tears. "Please don't kill my son. I need him. Don't take my son from me."

Juror #3 seemed profoundly disturbed by Marguerite's testimony. Juror #8 openly wept.

Even Tom expressed some emotion, looking like he would cry during a sidebar break as he exchanged looks with his mother. Capano now wanted another chance. He wanted to take the stand and plead for his life.

The judge allowed it, but not before going over some ground rules. Capano had to limit himself to expressions of remorse, pleas for leniency, hopes and plans for the future, and evidence of his own good character. Judge Lee said he would not tolerate any attacks on the prosecution or the evidence, or else "I will terminate the allocution." Capano was not under oath, there would be no cross-examination, and he couldn't dispute the facts of the case.

Capano walked to the stand and sat down. The bailiff poured him some water. Capano then began with, "Your Honor and ladies and gentlemen of the jury. . . ." He told them he had prepared some remarks and hoped to stick to the judge's guidelines, "but it's hard to speak to people who've already rejected me."

Not a minute into pleading for his life and Capano had already proved the prosecution's contention that he couldn't handle rejection very well. "This is a tragedy for a great many people. I wish I could take it all back. If I could trade places with Anne Marie I would,'' he said. It was true he was unfaithful to his ex-wife. ''That's between me and my wife and God and I won't talk about that,'' he said. But perhaps the jury was blinded in their verdict, he suggested, because of his philandering.

Quoting a Beatles song, Capano said, ''I'm not half the man I used to be.'' He continued, ''I don't know me anymore. I don't know the man you've characterized here.'' The Tom Capano who used to exist, he said, speaking of himself in the third person, was a man people trusted—with their lives. People liked him, he said, and his cousin said he was as ''loyal as a dog.'' But, Capano said, maintaining the idea that Annie died in a tragic accident, he had momentarily ''lost his moral compass'' when he failed to call 911 after Annie was shot.

To Brian Fahey he tried to offer consolation. ''She did not die in fear,'' he told Fahey from the stand. ''She never knew what happened to her.'' The courtroom sighed and several jury members just shook their heads. Nothing Capano said anymore should have surprised them, but that statement certainly did.

Capano went on, saying Annie ''gave as good as she got,'' and that she didn't cower from anyone. Still, Capano maintained, he was accepting responsibility for his part of the tragedy. However, ''If I were a 100-watt lightbulb in 1995, what am I now, a 25-watt, no probably a 7½-watt night-light now,'' he said.

He blamed the ''duplicity of friends'' for his demise and said he gave his friendship too easily and trusted too much. He was loyal to a fault, although he didn't doubt he was somewhat controlling. ''I had a chance to make my life mean something,'' he said, but had failed a moral test.

He quoted Hubert Humphrey, saying the moral test of government is how it treats those in the dawn of life, how it treats those in the sunset of life, and those in the shadows of life. He wanted to be that moral man. "I'm not saying I did that, but I tried to do that."

Then he broke into tears and lashed out at the prosecution. "My kids were harassed . . ."

He never finished. The judge, staring straight at the back doors of the courtroom, interrupted Capano. "You're done," he said evenly. "Bailiff, please remove Mr. Capano."

It shook Capano to his foundation. He tried to ward off Mel coming over and removing him from the courtroom.

"Can I take it back?" he asked the judge.

The judge gave it to him. "I'll allow you to finish," Judge Lee said as calmly as he had interrupted Capano. "The next time you blatantly disregard the rules you will be removed for the rest of the trial," he warned. Capano acknowledged that and then said he had simply "rationalized" his actions by protecting Deborah MacIntyre. Capano should have remained loyal to Annie, he said. "We had a special relationship," he explained. "Annie and I made our peace a long time ago. I kept her confidences."

If he trashed anyone, he did it inadvertently, he explained. He told the jury he wasn't going to beg for his life. "I don't beg. I'm not going to beg for my life. I ask you not for me, but I ask you to consider my daughters and my mother and allow me to live. They should not be punished for my sins." He continued for a few more minutes, then finished, leaving the stand by turning to the judge and saying, "Sorry if I broke the rules."

His rambling rhetoric left the jury stupefied. He had quoted Seneca the philosopher, Arab proverbs, the Beatles, and Hubert Humphrey, but had never actually admitted he killed Annie and had made a point of saying he wouldn't beg for his life. His speech had little to do with the guidelines the judge had set forth.

When the jury eventually left to take a vote on their penalty recommendation, Juror #2 told the other jurors, "Do we have to even talk about this?'' This juror was particularly disgusted by seeing Harry Fusco. ''That pedophile did it for me,'' said the father of three.

Capano had angered them all. Juror #11 was particularly incensed by his constant moralizing. ''Referring to the Jesuits didn't score any points with me,'' she said.

Jack O'Donnell, who was slated to deliver the closing statement for the defense, knew Capano had once again angered the jury. He had a plan to counteract Capano's damage, but he wasn't sure it would work.

Colm Connolly began the closing arguments thanking the jury for its ''extraordinary service,'' and noting that Annie's murder was ''the result of substantial planning.''

''You represent the conscience of the community,'' he told the jurors, reminding them that the only person who could testify as to what happened to Annie was Tom Capano, and as of yet he had still not offered a rational explanation for the murder and the cooler, lock, and chain.

''Think of how close he came to getting away with murder. The cooler, the blood. If we hadn't found that, we wouldn't be here today.'' Capano thought of no one but himself, Connolly said. He calmly read the newspaper in the driveway of his brother's home while Annie was stuffed in the cooler. ''Think of the callousness to stuff Anne Marie in the cooler,'' Connolly told the jury. ''What kind of person do you have to be to do that?''

Capano was a ''vacuum of evil who sucked in everyone,'' Connolly explained. Here was a man who used his talents ''and connections for illegal and evil purposes. He respects no one but himself. He cares for no one but himself. . . . He can use anybody and his character shows he obeys no rules.'' Connolly also said the Linda Marandola affair proved Capano had a long track record of violent and abusive behavior.

Connolly said Capano had ''extreme arrogance'' and boldly contemplated a book and movie deal while in prison. He was actually going to profit from killing Annie. He forced his family to choose sides, and with his wealth he proved he'll reach out to harm those who he thinks have wronged him—even from prison. "Only one man is responsible for all the depravity you've heard about. That man is Tom Capano," Connolly concluded.

After lunch Jack O'Donnell ambled up to the podium to try and spare Capano's life. "I'm here to ask you to spare Tom's life. For his mother, for his daughters, and most especially for Gerry," O'Donnell said. O'Donnell did not excuse Capano's actions. Rather, he suggested that Anne Marie stood up to Tom Capano and paid with her life, but "the evidence is substantial that whatever happened on June 27, 1996, it was a rash and impulsive act. It is not our intention to condone anything Tom Capano did . . . ," O'Donnell said.

Slowly and deliberately he first looked at the Faheys and then back at the jury. "There is not much I could say or could offer the Faheys. Their loss is devastating and their testimony was powerful, compassionate, and understandable," O'Donnell said. It was the first public showing of any kind by the defense team to the Faheys. It was no accident it came from O'Donnell. He'd spent time on two occasions talking with Mark Fahey at local pubs, expressing his sympathy for Annie. He was an Irishman who'd defended an Italian against killing a woman of Irish descent. The one bar in town where O'Donnell, the outgoing and happy Irishman, would have loved to visit, O'Friel's, he felt he could not enter because it was the base for the Fahey family. He was a friend of Capano's and had been for years, and all the complexities of that and the case manifested itself in O'Donnell's closing arguments.

O'Donnell did not dismiss Capano's actions. Instead he said if Tom Capano were a pack of playing cards he was missing his face cards. "He's not playing with a full deck." While the results of the psychiatric tests were not made public, O'Donnell noted that he had known Capano for some thirty years and he wasn't the same person O'Donnell thought he knew.

Capano sat with his head in his hand, numbed as his friend and attorney pled for his life—something Capano himself had refused to do. "There was evil in him and substantial evil and perhaps it was there all along," O'Donnell said. But in deciding whether or not to take Capano's life, O'Donnell urged the jury to consider a few things. What would be the greater penalty for Capano?

"This is a man who had it all, and I mean had it all. He could eat at the finest restaurants and will now eat bologna and cheese the rest of his life. He could travel the world and he's now confined to a six-by-nine cell. He'll never hug his daughters again. They will lead full and interesting lives and he'll be lucky to talk to them once a month or write. They'll graduate and lead lives and he'll never be around."

The gravity of the situation was sinking in on Capano, who listened and watched with a deepening gloom spreading across his thin, sallow face. "If you can't do it for Tom, for his mother and for his daughters, or for Kay who testified with grace and dignity, please find it in your heart to do it for Louis and most especially Gerry."

With that, O'Donnell sat down.

There was a pall, an uneasy quietness, over the courtroom. Later, the judge and the other attorneys said O'Donnell's closing arguments were the finest they'd heard. But for now, all was quiet. The jury stared at Capano as they came to grips with the weight of their decision.

Ferris Wharton then got up and accused the defense of using Gerry Capano yet again by pleading for Capano's life. In his short and succinct closing, Wharton said Capano was not "a rash man and impulsive man. He is a premeditator, a plodder and planner."

There was no evidence of a rash or impulsive act. It was an evil act.

"That type of evil must be ended."

With that, Wharton was done, and by the midafternoon break the judge had charged the jury. They had to decide on two questions. Was there without a reasonable doubt an aggravating circumstance which led to Annie's death (such as planning). And secondly, considering the preponderance of evidence, does the aggravating circumstances outweigh the mitigating circumstances. In other words, if Capano planned the crime, did he therefore deserve to die even if he'd led such a great life and could still contribute in some form or fashion to the greater good and to his family. Neither of these questions, under Delaware law, had to have a unanimous vote. It was merely a poll that would guide the judge when he imposed sentence.

In no time at all, it seemed the jury was back. By 11-1 they said it appeared Capano did plan the crime, and by a vote of 10-2 they recommended he die. Juror #8 was in tears as the decision was given to the judge. The courtroom was silent, and as Capano was led away, he looked at his sobbing mother and told her everything would be all right. Then he was quietly led away.

"God bless you all," the judge said as he brought the jury's involvement to a close.

Outside the courthouse was another round of bedlam, complete with cheers for the prosecution and jeers for the defense team. Hundreds packed the area, thousands more watched on live television from at least a half a dozen different cameras and live trucks, which had surrounded the courthouse.

Joe Oteri said he was devastated. It was the first time in his long career he'd ever had a client sentenced to death. Gene Maurer was more reflective. He felt the jury had rejected Capano, not his work product since he'd never been able to run the case as he wanted.

* * *

Everyone reassembled for the official sentencing on March 16, 1999. Joe Hurley, who'd long ago abandoned Capano as a defense attorney, showed up with him in the packed courtroom that day as did most of Capano's family—including Joey, who was much thinner and healthier-looking following a bypass surgery.

Tom Capano himself looked healthier that day. His usual gray prison pallor was replaced with a rosier, healthier glow on his cheeks, and he had a better haircut than he'd sported during most of his trial. It had been some six weeks since the principals involved had been gathered in the courtroom, and now it was time for the endgame.

Judge Lee prepared a twenty-one page opinion for Capano's sentencing. It included an outline of the crime, of Capano's life and his many good deeds for the community, and ultimately his desire to keep Annie for his own.

"Fahey had been trying to end the relationship with defendant," Lee wrote in the opinion, because she'd begun a new, potentially meaningful relationship with Mike Scanlan. "About the time Fahey was working on her new relationship, defendant had separated from his wife. When Fahey began pulling away from defendant, defendant became extremely angry at Fahey and he expressed his rage at her during several violent episodes."

And while Capano said he could not show emotions because of his heavy medications, Lee noted that he had shown "a plethora of emotions" during the trial, including anger, defiance, contempt, and concern for some of the members of his family. "He just has not shown the appropriate emotions: remorse, sadness, guilt, horror at his actions." Judge Lee felt his formal sentencing opinion lacked something and he provided a five-page supplement, which he read in open court.

"After completing the process," Lee said, "I was left with a feeling that the legal and intellectual exercise required by our law was inadequate to describe what occurred in this trial. For that reason, I have chosen not to read from my opinion but to supplement it with my remarks today. I believe that it is important for any reviewing court to understand what occurred in the courtroom that cannot be reflected in a transcript. The gradual revelation of the personality and character of the defendant clearly was a factor in both the verdict of the jury and its recommendation concerning appropriate sentence. It is a significant factor in my sentencing today.

"Thomas J. Capano entered this courtroom on trial for his life, a man presumed innocent and, almost immediately, he embarked on a course of conduct which rebutted that presumption."

Capano looked up to eye the judge at the mention of his name and then looked back down at the table. He barely acknowledged the judge's words and ignored him completely as Judge Lee described Capano as "an angry, sinister, controlling and malignant force which dominated the courtroom for months." Judge Lee scolded Capano for his "withering stares" at witnesses, and his contempt for the prosecutors. "Thomas Capano needed to show everyone that he was in charge and that he held all those he viewed as adversaries with contempt," the judge said.

This he observed even extended to his own attorneys, and the judge said ultimately led to his conviction. ". . . The possibility remained he would be acquitted until he insisted . . . on testifying and solidifying the remaining area of weakness in the State's case by presenting a story of Anne Marie Fahey's death which the jury found incredible. Having sealed his fate on the question of guilt or innocence, he displayed the malevolence of his nature, which became crucial in determining sentence."

Judge Lee chastised Capano for his "chain saw" approach to his defense and reprimanded Capano for his allocution. "The defendant fully expected to get away with murder and, were it not for his own arrogance and controlling nature, may well have succeeded," Lee said tersely. "If the virtuous Tom Capano had ever existed, he no longer did," Lee added.

The judge found Capano's manipulation of his own brothers, daughters, and other members of his family completely distasteful, and chided Capano for telling Gerry to "be a man" when Capano had never done so himself. "The selfishness, arrogance and manipulativeness of Thomas Capano destroyed his own family as well as the Fahey family," Lee said.

The only mitigating factors Lee added did not even involve the defendant. Rather, it is the "impact on his remarkable daughters" and brother Gerry that bothered the court the most and gave Lee pause in considering what sentence to hand down. Lee noted that Capano planned Annie's murder, but it was a contingency he hoped he would never have to deal with, but did.

In passing sentence the judge said, "Tom Capano does not face judgment today because friends and family failed him. He faces judgment because he is a ruthless murderer who feels compassion for no one and remorse only for the circumstances in which he finds himself. He is a malignant force from whom no one he deems disloyal or adversarial can be secure, even if he is incarcerated for the rest of his life."

Judge Lee then sentenced Thomas J. Capano to die by lethal injection on June 28, 1999—exactly three years to the day after he unceremoniously dumped Anne Marie Fahey into the ocean.

Author's Note

Thomas J. Capano burst onto the national scene in a strange case of perversion, lust, betrayal and murder that at least one local Wilmington reporter said hadn't been seen since the Kennedys decided to vacation in the Hamptons.

By conventional standards, however, the story of one of the most powerful and rich men in Wilmington, Delaware, killing his mistress, who was the governor's scheduling secretary, and dumping her at sea was bizarre and sad. The subsequent tales of multiple mistresses, sexual threesomes, attempted fratricide, and tales of prescription and illicit drug abuse by some of the principals had all the trappings of a Jerry Springer special. One local radio reporter said the Capano case discussed sexual perversions like "dish soap," and when he overheard it being discussed on the radio, he joked that it was heaven-sent for the Howard Stern show. Others couldn't help but note that Capano was a high-powered Delaware Democrat going on trial for murdering his mistress at the exact same time high-powered Democrat President Bill Clinton was being impeached for lying about a mistress. This made Capano the living embodiment of everything G. Gordon Liddy feared about the Democrats: loose with their morals and "horrible liars." Certainly, the Capano trial and all of its associated bedlam was great fodder for national magazines and talk shows.

But in all of the heat generated, there seemed to be very little light. In Wilmington the division was deep, often overly emotional and sometimes got to be very physical. You were either for Capano or against him. If you were for him, then you despised Anne Marie Fahey as a harlot and her family as sponges. If you were for the Faheys, then Capano was described as an animal and all of those associated with him were Neanderthals.

Things were not that black and white. In fact, after all the months spent researching this project, I can tell you there were plenty of victims on both sides of the case. I came to find empathy with the Fahey family, all of whom struggled hard to keep stiff upper lips and a measure of civility on their tongues as they watched the sordid tale unfold in the courtroom. The harder they struggled to maintain their dignity the more their pain became apparent to me. "Watch the eyes" my father always taught me to take the measure of a man. The Faheys could not hide the pain in their eyes.

But I also came to know Kay Ryan, Capano's former wife, her children, Capano's mother, sister, and all of the attorneys in the case. By the end of the trial against Tom Capano, there wasn't one pair of eyes among the aforementioned group that didn't have a certain degree of pain.

How would you feel if your husband were described in court as a Lothario, a philanderer and a cold-blooded murderer? What if it were your loving and kind father who was so protective of your well-being he wouldn't let you take the subway when you visited New York City but insisted on taxicab rides? What if that same father were exposed in court giving your name, photograph, and telephone number to a convicted pedophile?

What if this were your son, the man you'd come to depend on in your old age to provide you with comfort and security? What if this were your brother you counted on to mediate family squabbles? What if it were one of your dear friends whom you'd known, along with his wife, for nearly thirty years? What if you had to defend him in court? What if you were the attorney for a man who wouldn't allow you to wear your choice of footwear into court? What if you were the brother of such a man and helped dump a corpse at sea and couldn't get the brother to voluntarily come in and talk to police?

All of those questions and many more bubbled under the surface and occasionally exploded in the courtroom during the trial of Thomas J. Capano. Never had I seen so many people in one room caused so much pain because of the action of one man.

One reporter described Capano as "among the more vile human beings" he'd had the misfortune of doing time with on the planet. "He acted as if the Ten Commandments were written just so he could break them all," a court spectator said one morning during a break in the testimony.

Capano preached of his Jesuit upbringing and then used those teachings to defend actions the prosecution described as depraved and diabolic. Capano spoke of morality, others said, as if it were something to be bought and traded like so many pork-belly futures on the open market. His admitted "liberal" or cavalier attitude toward sex included guttural descriptions of the act of love and of bodily functions that made many a veteran prosecutor, reporter, and cop blush in embarrassment. After such admissions in court, Capano's conviction and sentence surprised no one.

As I write this, the machinery of appeals is already in motion. Joe Oteri thinks the judge should have included lesser charges in the choices the jury had in finding Capano guilty. There are other procedural events that also captured his attention, but that will be for the appeals lawyers. In short, it will be many years before Capano dies by lethal injection, if he ever does. Gene Maurer thinks his frail health will mean Capano will probably die in prison, and at least one of his daughters thinks that is likely, as well.

I wrote to Capano for comments on this book. He wrote me back a letter that deserves some mention here. Capano told me he had to have the "absolute last word" if he were to cooperate in a venture with me.

"I always get the last word," he said.

I had to shake my head. Did he learn nothing from his trial?

Of course the *nice* side of Capano was in evidence, too. As he often did in his letters to MacIntyre he came on strong and then followed it up with a compliment. He found the James Carville interview I had done for *Playboy* magazine to be "very interesting." He wanted to read the interview because he found Carville to be his "very favorite lunatic."

Capano's sense of humor showed itself elsewhere, as well. The day after he was officially sentenced by Judge Lee, Capano agreed to meet with several television reporters in intimate interviews at Gander Hill. Early that morning dozens of reporters, cameras, lights, videotapes along with miles of cable showed up. Rick Kramer from *Inside Edition,* along with producers from *Good Morning America* and *20/20,* were going to get their chances to talk to Tom Capano. All of the equipment and reporters were ushered into the prison, searched, and then waited for the appointed hour for Capano to begin talking.

Instead, he changed his mind. "For the first time in his life he took my advice," Joe Oteri said outside the prison walls to the throng of reporters. There were no interviews.

When the judge pronounced his sentence, four of the jurors were in attendance. Later they met with the Faheys at a local restaurant and heaped praise on the judge and the prosecutors.

"If Colm Connolly or Ferris Wharton wants to run for President, he has my vote," one female juror said. Connolly heaped more praise on the judge, saying that Judge Lee had said in ten minutes during the sentencing what Connolly struggled to say in more than three hours of a closing statement.

All of the jurors said they were profoundly moved by the trial and couldn't stop thinking about Annie.

I find myself thinking of Annie now and then. I never met her. Never knew her, but everything I've been told about her reminds me a lot of my own sisters. I can't imagine losing someone so vital. I can't imagine the pain of finding out how it happened and the frustration knowing that her killer apparently thought of her as little more than a broken play toy to be tossed away when no longer useful.

Therefore, watching Jack O'Donnell, friend and attorney to Tom Capano, and Mark Fahey, brother of the deceased, reach an understanding in a bar one night during the jury deliberations was a moment of revelation for me. Mark had been trashed by Capano more thoroughly than his brothers or his sisters, he not only listened to O'Donnell but did so with an open mind, and Jack, the outgoing attorney who liked to call himself "an asshole," showed he had deep feelings for those who had suffered.

Susan Louth was a surprise, too. She testified for Capano during the sentencing phase of the trial, but did so reluctantly. She thought Capano just wanted to call her back to get "one last look at my ass," and gauging from the looks she got when she entered the courtroom, she was probably right.

Louth said she, too, was touched by Annie. Louth saw Capano before he left for the Ristorante di Panorama in Philadelphia the night Annie died. "There but for the grace of God, go I," she said once she heard about the facts in the Capano murder trial.

I was most impressed, surprised, and saddened by the Capano family. Kay never ceased to amaze me. Her head was on straight and her only concern during the process was for her daughters. She did not venture into self-pity.

I got to talk with Tom Capano's mother and sister one night outside of court and afterward could not help but feel empathy for them, as well, despite some of the things Marguerite said and did to the media and despite Marian's belief that her brother is not guilty.

As for Capano's daughters, they impressed me as intelligent and well adjusted beyond their years. Judge Lee felt impressed enough about them that he was compelled to specifically mention them in his sentencing report. After speaking with them at length there is no doubt they understand fully what happened on June 27, 1996, and yet they still love and cherish their father and the memories of all the things he did for them.

Many of my colleagues during the trial said this was a horrible story that spoke volumes about morality, or the lack of it, at the end of the millennium. Some of those who say this are my friends. I respectfully disagree with all of them.

Annie's death is a story told time and again throughout the history of man. Jealousy, control, and vengeance are as old as man. Perhaps it is just that such activities have no place to hide in a world that has so much instant media available.

By the end of the trial that so many watched and commented on, dozens of new friendships had been established, and people who probably never would have met, got the opportunity to do so. It was a unique experience, and Kevin Freel said one night he was happy that he'd met so many good people, but ultimately and tragically sad about the way he had done so. Annie had brought people together her entire life, he told me. I'd like to think that she did one last time. Robert Fahey said he and his brothers and sisters viewed the trial as Annie's last fight.

It's nice to know Annie won it.